The Story of An
Entrepreneur
Who
"Is Not College Material"

A Disciple of Ayn Rand's Howard Roark and the Jeffersonian Republic

Note for Librarians: a cataloguing record for this book that
includes Dewey Decimal Classification and US Library of
Congress numbers is available from the National Library of
Canada. The complete cataloguing record can be obtained
from the National Library's online database at:
www.nlc-bnc.ca/amicus/index-e.html
ISBN 1-4120-3243-1
Printed in Victoria, BC, Canada

TRAFFORD

Offices in Canada, USA, Ireland, UK and Spain
This book was published on-demand in cooperation with
Trafford Publishing. On-demand publishing is a unique
process and service of making a book available for retail sale
to the public taking advantage of on-demand manufacturing
and Internet marketing. On-demand publishing includes
promotions, retail sales, manufacturing, order fulfilment,
accounting and collecting
royalties on behalf of the author.
Books sales in Europe:
Trafford Publishing (UK) Ltd., Enterprise House, Wistaston
Road Business Centre, Wistaston Road, Crewe CW2 7RP
UNITED KINGDOM
phone 01270 251 396 (local rate 0845 230 9601)
facsimile 01270 254 983; info.uk@trafford.com
Book sales for North America and international:
Trafford Publishing, 6E–2333 Government St.,
Victoria, BC V8T 4P4 CANADA
phone 250 383 6864 (toll-free 1 888 232 4444)
fax 250 383 6804; email to bookstore@trafford.com

www.trafford.com/robots/04-1070.html

10 9 8 7 6 5 4 3 2

Part I

The Story of An Entrepreneur Who "Is Not College Material"

Chapter I
Early Life on Bear Creek Ranch and Stinnett, Texas

I, Harvey L. Ratliff, Jr., was born in St. Anthony's Hospital, Amarillo, Texas, April 11, 1931, and lived on Bear Creek Ranch in Hutchinson County, Texas, until I

A sketch made by the author of J.A. Whittenburg from a photograph in April 10, 1948, when the author was 16 years of age.

was 3 years of age. This was the headquarters of the some 35,000-acre ranch owned by my great grandfather, James Andrew Whittenburg.

My father, Harvey Lee Ratliff, worked for J.A. as he was often called. He oversaw this and other ranches in New Mexico and Oklahoma for J.A. I have many memories about this ranch. I remember spending hours in the blacksmith shop watching the blacksmith work. I watched him make complete wagons and paint them what to me was a pretty red. I watched him make horseshoes and other things that were very impressive to me. This was from 1931, when I was born, until 1934, and although I knew nothing about depressions at the time, we were in the "Great Depression"; so, my dad had the luxury of employing a blacksmith who was one of the reasons the ranch then looked immaculate. Nearly everybody else was broke, but oil had just been discovered under J.A.'s land; so, these luxuries could take place. It was always a great disappointment for me to go back, because the ranch was always, comparatively, run down in later years. I remember the story about a man named Bill William's, who was one of my childhood heroes or idols. My dad told the story that he just walked onto the ranch and went to work. He worked harder than any other hand for about a month or two with no pay. My dad was so impressed with his work that he asked Jay Harvey, the ranch foreman, what he thought of him and they both decided to hire Bill, who became my dad's favorite hand.

Above is a picture purchased by the author's father from a hand on Bear Creek Ranch.

2

The above is a picture of the author's mother and father, Harvey and Lillie Ratliff.

From there I was moved with my mother, Lillie Frances Whittenburg Ratliff, father, and sister, Frances Virginia Ratliff, to Stinnett, Texas, in order that my sister, who was 6, could go to the school there. My memories of life in Stinnett include becoming acquainted with Violet Anderton, who helped my mother take care of Virginia, my sister, and I. She was with us when we went through the "Black Blizzard" of 1935, which was an unforgettably bad experience resulting from past incorrect farming practices that damaged the land and made terrible dust storms possible. Another memory of Stinnett was the daughter, Emily Jane Bledsoe, of my parents' friends, Robert and Elma Bledsoe, in a special way. My mother always told me she was against giving spankings although she broke down and gave me three or four. I was at Emily Jane's house one day when she was spanked, and I must have made the mistake of saying my mother doesn't give spankings. Emily Jane could not get this out of her head and possibly that same day we were at my home and she caused me to get spanked by teasing me until I grabbed her hair and she jumped out into plain sight of my mother with me pulling her hair. This caused

3

me to receive my most unforgettable spanking by my mother and quenched Emily Jane's efforts. We remained in Stinnett until I was 5 years of age.

The above is a picture of the author and his sister, Virginia, about the time they lived on Bear Creek Ranch.

Above is a picture of Virginia on Socks and Harvey on Billy about the time they resided at Bear Creek Ranch.

Above is a picture of, from left, Harvey Ratliff, Sr., Harvey Ratliff, Jr. and Virginia Ratliff on Bear Creek Ranch.

One of the stories my mother told me about how the J.A. Whittenburg land was accumulated has always stuck with me. My mother's father, George A. Whittenburg, paid for a significant part of that accumulation of some 35,000 acres by being a governmental subcontractor. He submitted the lowest bid to be the mailman of that day and delivered the mail by horseback. The mail carriers of that day were not bureaucratic employees; they were subcontractors. Honest subcontracting saved Americans an enormous amount of taxes. I wish we had such honesty today. One of my mother's favorite points was that J.A. and Tennessee Whittenburg went one entire year spending only $30 in order to accumulate that spread of land.

When it was found out by the bankers that there was oil under J.A.'s land, the bankers foreclosed all loans to J.A. and George, who had been careful to never borrow money on their land and only put up cattle as security. The bankers tried with this foreclosure to obtain a foreclosable lean on the land. No banker in the entire Panhandle would loan them money enabling them to pay off the perpetrators of the foreclosure. They were trying hard to take this land away from J.A. and George, who had to go clear down to south Texas to get the money to pay off the perpetrators of the foreclosure effort. This was one of my mother's most impressive stories to me that I have never forgotten.

Chapter II
Life in Canyon, Texas

At this time my family moved my sister and me to 2304 6th Avenue, Canyon, Texas. I suppose this was because they considered the schools better there and the location more centralized with relation to the three ranch areas my dad was overseeing.

The Panhandle Plains Historical Museum was located some two blocks north at about 2401 4th Avenue and the home of my grandparents, George Allen and Lillie Frances Archer Whittenburg, who was known as "Fannie," was located about four blocks west at about 1813 6th Avenue. We referred to this home as the "family home." The Buffalo Drug Store was located on the south side of 4th Avenue at about 2304 4th Avenue. I have pleasant memories of this Drug Store and Tom Knighton, the man who owned it.

The above picture is a sketch of Tom Knighton made by the author in 1943 when the author was 12 years of age.

My mother gave me an allowance. At first it was $0.20 per week. The first week I took my friend, Glynn Dowlen with me and rather than getting a dime changed into ten pennies I spent one dime for him a one-cent ball of gum and the other dime for me a one-cent ball of gum. My mother told me I had to wait until the week had completely passed before I could get two more dimes. That taught me a lesson, which I never forgot and in the end resulted in Tom Knighton telling my mother that Virginia and I handled our money better than most college kids. Tom Knighton then told Virginia and I that he wanted to meet my dad. Every year after that, my dad and Tom Knighton had a standing agreement to go Deep Sea fishing together every year. As I remember, it turned out to virtually always be in Tampico, Mexico.

The West Texas State Teachers College Training Grade School was located about a block or a half block north of the museum. This is the place I spent my first two years of schooling. There was a part of it termed the "Training School," I think. Mostly the college teachers would show observing college students how to teach. While I was in attendance there, it appeared to me that the college teachers did nearly all of the teaching and the college students just observed   Things happened in this school that had a huge influence on my later life, which I will go into further later.

I always considered living in Canyon the happiest time of my childhood. I spent many hours in the Museum two blocks north looking at everything there, but I was particularly fascinated by the dioramas there. These highly impressed me and ultimately had a very big influence and ultimately lead to most of my 28-patented inventions in my later life. Either while looking at them or in later thinking about them, I thought, "Wouldn't it be wonderful to create pictures in three-dimension better than those dioramas" and often found myself thinking about how to do it.

Our house in Canyon was in the west half of the block. We also owned the east half of the block, which was fenced in. We had the luxury of owning and keeping two horses brought from Bear Creek Ranch, one for my sister and one for me in the fenced in east half. My sister and I had many pleasurable moments riding these horses. My horse, "Billy," was a full blood, solid black Shetland pony and my sister's horse "Socks" was a half Shetland, sorrel in color with white stocking feet. My horse was much smarter and did more aggravating things. We had a bridle that was split in a way to fit over the horse's ear not generally needing a throatlatch. Billy could rub this type bridle off at will. Billy had a way of holding his breath when he was saddled and after a person would ride him for a short distance, he would let out his breath, step sideways and the person would find themselves on the ground in an instant. I remember this very thing happening to John Robert Archer, whom I will describe in more detail later. At times Billy would just decide to lie down, and I had a terrible time getting him up. Whenever we, Virginia and I, would run, or race, Billy would not let Socks get in front of him, even though Socks was actually a faster runner. Billy would notice when I was bare footed, at which time, he would ease his foot on top of mine, and it was miserable. I remember being in the "family home" one time when I was about 4 years of age and somehow tripping and rolling down the steep stairs. This was an unforgettable experience, but apparently I was not hurt. Another unforgettable experience while being 4 was the death of my dad's father. What I remember about that was my mother or somebody putting me on the train and before my mother could get on, the train started. I was a scared little 4-year-old. I don't remember how, but she got on later and everything was fine. Another memory was a beautiful full-length picture of my mother's father. I spent many unsuccessful years looking for that picture. I have since concluded that it was my view of him in his casket.

I don't remember if the following was true in the same time period, but to the west of our home on 6th Avenue lived my mother's uncle. He was the youngest brother

7

The above is a picture of the author when he was 5 to 6 years old.

The above is a photo taken when the author lived in Canyon, Texas. From left are Deanie Windsor, Virginia Ratliff, Claire Windsor, Tie Mills, Leona Mills, Harvey Ratliff and Basil Walker.

of John McQuetty Archer's second group of children and my mother's mother was the oldest of that group. John McQuetty had 21 children. Ten were with one wife and 11 were with her sister. My mother's uncle's name was Branch T. Archer. His wife's name was Luta Bob Archer. They had five children, Branch T., Jr., John Robert, Mary Elizabeth, Luta Bob II and Richard Keys. Luta Bob II was my age. These children, my sister and I spent many hours playing in our yard.

The above is a sketch made by the author of Luta Bob Archer II
In about 1948 when they were both either 16 or 17 years of age.

We also had a lot of fun flying kites. I believe my Uncle S.B., whom I will describe in more detail later, taught me how to fly a kite. Also living west of this home of ours, lived my future first-grade teacher. Virtually everybody I heard talk about her, including my mother, said she was the best teacher in the world. She expressed great anger toward me, and I never understood why. I surmised that she detested the way my mother raised me. Maybe it was Ayn Rand's *Ellsworth Toohey* showing up in her, as I was a very imaginative boy, which seemed to make me very popular at that time with my peers. One time I remember her running over my tricycle and wagon. She said she was "very sorry," but I always believed she did it to teach me to keep them out of her way. I also remember her getting me out of sight of any adult or anybody else one time and telling me she was going to give me the hardest spanking of my life, she was going to "wear me out." I never knew why or understood what for. Also somebody poisoned our dogs several times. We never knew who did it, but I always thought she did it.

While walking with the Archer children several times, I remember us encountering a friendly boy named Tony Rusk, who somehow attracted me. As I remember it, the Archers said he was a very bad boy and to stay away from him. The first telephone of my life happened about this time in our home in Canyon. Our number was just two digits, such as 19, although I don't remember the number. Richard Archer and I spent about an hour calling each other back and forth. I also remember being out with my sister one time and noticing a boy, I don't remember who it was, across the street. We looked at each other a while and the boy picked up a rock and threw it at us.

9

My sister picked up the rock and threw it back at the boy. This went on for a while and finally the rock hit my sister on the head, and my sister and I ran home crying.

Along about this time, I was 5 years of age and went to kindergarten. I don't remember much about my teachers except they scolded me when I hummed a western or country song from my record player at home. They just seemed to be baby sitters and nothing else. I remember a boy known as "BB," whom I never encountered in later life. He would hit me very hard in the stomach. This made an unforgettable impression on me. One day Violet asked me what we did at kindergarten. I told her I blew a huge bubble, and we all got in it and flew over China. I could not understand why nobody believed me. Along about this time, my sister took me with her to a store to get me a model airplane kit. I think it was her idea. She had decided it would be neat to have a model airplane, and I could build one. The store salesman said I was too young to make model airplanes, and my sister told him her brother could do anything. In following years, I made dozens of model airplanes from the structural plan using balsa wood, glue and a special paper that we would shrink with water and paint with model airplane "dope" to make it look good and fly better. I had a lot of fun flying these models, and for a while I dreamed of being a pilot, but somehow I lost interest in that. About that time, however, my Uncle Jack Liston, Aunt Bonne's husband then, did take me up in an airplane; I believe it was a "Piper Cub." I remember Basil, my first cousin, was with us, setting behind me laughing at me all the time and Uncle Jack did some maneuver, I don't know what, and I became very sick.

It was getting close to time for me to start school. I remember dreaming about how nice it would be to be able to read. I wanted to know everything, and now I could learn about it by reading. My mother told me she was specifically told, I think it was my first grade teacher, that nobody should teach me anything about reading before I started school. My mother told me I used to lie on the floor and look at pictures, cut pictures out and draw for hours and hours. She told me I could cut things out with exactness from the time I was 2 years of age. Everybody told me how lucky I was. I was going to have the best first grade teacher in the world..

Finally the day came. We finally started school. This was one of, if not the, greatest of disappointments of my entire life. I remember sitting in the class. This wonderful teacher divided the class into two groups, but I was left out of both of the groups. She would take one group into another room and teach them reading. Then she would take the other group into the other room and teach them reading. She never taught me one thing about reading. Much later in my life my now brother-in-law Dr. Allen Early told me that she told him the reason she didn't teach me to read was "that Harvey Lee was just not ready to learn to read." This had a terrible effect on me in every way imaginable. Being a child of that period of history, I thought it was a foregone conclusion that adults are always right. After it was all said and done, my mother hired a private tutor to teach me to read, but I was, from then on, a poor reader and ashamed to admit it. This first grade teacher humiliated me in another way also. For some reason, unknown to me, she decided I went to the bathroom too much, and she would not let me go to the bathroom. This forced me to wet my pants in front of the entire class. This was a terrible experience that I remember until this day. My mother told me that whenever she tried to talk to her about my school problems, she said, "don't you worry about Harvey Lee, he is the most popular child in my class."

Another thing happened in that class that had a huge impact on my life. There was a boy, who became my very good friend, in my first-grade class. His name was Peter Nichols, or Nickels. His mother was the head of the art department of the college and had come down to Texas from New York. Since her son was in the class, she taught art in my class. She was very impressed with my art talent, telling my mother I had more talent than any child she had known, and advised my mother in many ways how to cultivate and develop my art talent. Peter loved the American Indians and inspired a love for them in me as a child. We had a lot of fun pretending we were American Indians.

Luta Bob II started first grade the same year I did, but she had a much different experience. My first grade teacher was also hers and was so impressed with Luta Bob II's reading ability; she "double" promoted her into the third grade. I met a very small, short and rather slender boy named Fay Hand. He always wanted me to buy him some candy. What blew my mind about this boy was that he could throw me down about as fast as I could get up, but in general I faired well in physical prowess. But, my best friend, I thought, was Tony Rusk. We were inseparably together just about all the time from the time school was out until bedtime. We mostly played games and acted out fantasies that I would dream up. We would also go to the movie, which then cost 10 cents or 5 cents. Tony would not let me pay. We had to walk all over town until he found his "Mr. Johnsie" and get his dime from him. Tony's father had lost his leg and evidently made a very poor living if he made one at all. One day the teacher asked us to write down whom we wanted to sit by. I wrote down Tony Rusk and Glynn Dowlen. My mother told me that my first grade teacher told her that everybody in the class wrote down my name, and she did place me between Tony and Glynn. Mitchell Jones and Mac Morris were also my very good friends.

My mother was the oldest of 13 children. She had seven sisters and five brothers. After her were Annie, Jim (J.A., Jr.), Nannie May, John Jake, Georgia, Roy (Roy Robert), S.B. (Samuel Benjamin), Pattie (Mattie Pearl), Joe D, Bonne, Helen and Tennessee. My Aunt Georgia and her husband, Uncle Art, had a farm northeast of Canyon. Virginia and I used to walk there often either by ourselves or with each other or someone else. It was a wonderful place to us. They had peacocks and other exotic animals that were very fascinating. My mother and her siblings along with their children, my first cousins, would celebrate Christmas and other special occasions at the family home four blocks west of our home in Canyon. I remember great times there celebrating Christmas. Before Aunt Georgia moved to the farm, she and Uncle Art lived in the family home. Virginia and I would walk over to visit them there too.

It was along in this period of time or maybe a couple of years earlier my Uncle S.B. brought Virginia and me each a kite. He taught us how to fly a kite. We had many hours of fun kite flying along with the Archer children during the years after that. He taught us how to make a kite bridle, put the tail on and all the tricks of flying a kite.

It was along about in this time period that Branch T., Jr. had a car known as the "Polka Dot." The Polka Dot was an open topped car. I don't know whether it was a convertible or not, but I never saw the top up. It was painted white with different colored Polka Dots painted on it. I heard a lot of people say what a neat car that was. He would take us, Virginia and me, riding in it sometimes. This was fun. One day while riding in the Polka Dot, Branch T. said I have a bunch of newspapers S.B. gave me to give out to people. We were or he was about to go some place. I don't remember where. Branch T.

said I've got to go dump these papers off before we leave, and we went with him to dump them. Virginia and I looked at each other with big shocked eyes. We "ratted on" Branch T. and told our Uncle S.B., who was trying to get the Amarillo Times, a newspaper, started. The Amarillo Times would play a very heavy role in my mother's and our lives later.

My second-grade teacher was Mrs. Schliger. I got along much better with her. My mother said she told her she just had to do the best she could with me. The first grade teacher just sent some children like me up about every year. I never had one bad experience under Mrs. Schliger, but I remained a poor reader.

It was along about this time in my life that my great grandfather, J.A. Whittenburg was killed when his nurse and driver, Mrs. Cantrell, drove into a train. It was then that my dad went to work for my mother's Aunt Mattie Hedgecoke. My dad later told me that he had watched my mother's brothers grow up. As a result of him seeing them grow up, my dad was determined to never work for any of my mother's brothers. For whatever reason it was a big "no no" among a large portion of my mother's brothers and sisters for my dad to work for Mattie Hedgecoke. I never really knew why this was but later surmised that there was a secret agenda explaining it, and it was likely my Uncle Roy's secret agenda. He was for a long time the family leader. Anyway, for some reason the family didn't want my dad working for Aunt Mattie. My mother was until the very last years of her life a loyal family member and follower of my Uncle Roy. She strongly encouraged me to idolize my Uncle Roy, which I did for many years.

As a result of this big "no no," my mother highly encouraged my dad to go into business for himself. As it turned out, my dad and mother decided dad would be a Phillips Petroleum Company "Jobber" or wholesaler in Breckenridge, Texas. Breckenridge was about 285 miles mostly east and a little south of Amarillo. It was about 100 miles due west of Ft. Worth, Texas.

It was along about this time my family took the only real family vacation in my memory. My memory of the family vacation is quite limited. I remember going west on a highway that I am sure was U.S. Highway 66. I remember going through the Hoover Dam and riding in a big Yacht like boat all over the Hoover Lake. I remember going through Yellowstone Park and seeing Old Faithful. I remember spending a quite long period of time at a southern California beach. A lady, I don't know who she was, spent hours holding my hands while we jumped waves. I could not swim at that time. I remember going to see huge Redwood trees. I think we were at a tree we could drive our car through. I remember meeting my dad's sister Lillian and her two sons, Franky and Winifred. I also remember meeting my dad's brother they called "Barney" after Barney Oglesby, the car racer in the funny paper of that day. His real name was Willis.

Chapter III
Early Life While Residing in Breckenridge, Texas

Then came what seemed to me a very sad day. We had to leave Canyon and move to Breckenridge, Texas. I remember hating to leave my friends in Canyon, especially Tony Rusk. My early memories of Breckenridge include sitting in our car waiting as instructed by my dad. A little boy about my age rode up to the car on his tricycle and taunted me saying things like "Hey, Pickle Puss what are you doing? Huh?

Why don't you come out and play with us Pickle Puss." I later found out his name was Soxy Vincent and he was a year older and a school grade higher than me.

We wound up living at 1101 East Walker Street, Breckenridge, Texas. I was to start my third (or fourth) grade at East Ward Elementary School, which was about three blocks east and a block north of our house there. Breckenridge had a 12-year system whereas Canyon had an 11-year system; so, my sister, who had been three grades ahead of me, was advanced to the seventh grade to put her in junior high school. She was a very good reader and student. I was tried in the fourth grade for a short while, but they quickly put me back in the third grade. I spent a large amount of time alone in Breckenridge. I spent hours acting out fantasies and drawing pictures and making model airplanes. I loved to pretend to be twins who were named Jack and Mack.

The above is a picture of the author while living in Breckenridge, Texas.

One day while I was at a school recess, I saw this little black-haired, brown-eyed boy who was about my size and in my class. We spent a long time staring at each other. I wanted very badly to make friends with him. His name was Ray Graves and we did become very good friends. He had a twin brother named Kay Graves. They were not identical twins and looked quite different. Kay was smaller, having blond or light brown hair and hazel eyes. It may have been that same day or a day or two later I had been pretending I was a cowboy wearing cowboy attire and my cap gun strapped to my side and was riding my bicycle around the block and around the house one block north of my house and across the street I saw Ray, Kay along with Bobby and Eddy Huffman playing cowboy and Indian. Ray came up to me, said hello, admired my cowboy outfit and we started playing cowboy and Indian. I was soon in their gang, which included Bobby and Eddy Huffman, Dickey Atkins and others whose name I can't remember. I soon learned that Ray and Kay lived in a house, which was in the northwest corner lot of the block just north of Walker Street and west of the street running north and south just west of my house.

After I was well acquainted with Ray, I had another experience. One time while walking down the stairs for recess, a boy named Tommy Smith walked a step or two behind me and would give me a kick in the rear each time I took a step down. I acted like nothing was happening until we got to the bottom of the stairs, and I whirled around and hit him right in the nose. He cried like a baby and never bothered me again. Ray later told me I was lucky he didn't beat me up. He was one of the toughest boys in the class.

There were family stories such as the one my mother used to tell. When she was growing up her parents would leave her in charge of Annie, Jim and Nannie Mae. Annie and Jim would team. up against her. One day they said we don't have to do what you say. We can bull dog you just like a calf. They did, they bull dogged her and ran roughshod over her. When her father found out about it he taught my mother how to hit in the nose. The next time my mother was left in charge of Annie and Jim, they got smacked in the nose and could not defy my mother. Jim used to tell the story of how cruel their dad was. He would just watch Lillie hit him in the nose and just laugh and laugh.

I don't remember exactly when it happened but for about a two-to three-week period while I was in Ray and Kay's gang, we had a running rock fight, which entailed throwing rocks at and dodging rocks from another gang of boys in the alley north of Dale Hitchcock's filling station and south of the Grave's home. I don't remember who the boys were in the other gang. Every afternoon after school and until suppertime we would continue that rock fight. I don't remember how the rock fight got started. I think it was already going on one day when I came over to Ray's house to play. I think Ray's parents finally put a stop to the fight.

It was along about this time I went to see Ray and Kay, who were unsuccessfully trying to fly a kite. They didn't know anything about it. I showed them how to install a bridle and put on a tail and lo and behold the kite flew. One time a while later, I was flying a kite with Ray and Kay watching and a big boy named Bobby Decker who was a year or two older than we were came up and tricked me into letting him attach a fairly large paper sack on the string up to the kite. It went up to the kite and the kite fell to the ground. Ray said you better run over to your kite. He is going to steal your string. I ran over there and protected my string. I don't know how Ray knew what Bobby Decker was up to, he must have done this to Ray before, but he was dead right about it. Bobby Decker never liked me after that and later would run into my bike with his car while I was riding my bicycle to school up in junior high, I think.

My third-grade teacher's name was Mrs. Greene, as I remember. I have few memories about Mrs. Greene, except as I recall she kept encouraging me to have my eyes checked. When I did get glasses, she said "See I told you so; you did need glasses, now you will do better in school." As it worked out, I didn't do better in school. Also, as it turned, out I hated to wear glasses because I hated the peer pressure exerted on me when I wore glasses. I stopped wearing glasses until much later in life. I also recall that in Mrs. Greene's class and in other Breckenridge classes, we were seated by intelligence, as sort of a reward or punishment for the grades on our report card. Only two class members were behind me in intelligence, Howard Henderson and a beautiful little blond-haired blue-eyed girl whose name I can't remember. Mr. Abernathy, whom I will describe more later, really liked this little blond-haired blue-eyed girl. Ray, Kay, Bobby Huffman and a beautiful blond-haired blue-eyed girl named Wanda Lane were always in the seats for the most intelligent. Also, on the first row but not the first seat was a girl named Beth Knight whose father had been in the oil business but was now dead. Through all of these type of depressing experiences, my mother always told me I was very brilliant and smart and my Uncle Roy thought so too.

We owned the west half of the block our house in Breckenridge was on. There was a north-south stream of water running right down the middle of the block. It ran through a culvert under Walker Street. Our land was west of that stream and Dr. Cartwright owned the land east of the stream in that block. About half way between Walker Street and the street south, the name of which I can't remember, was a huge, wonderful oak tree. It had to be very old. Ray and Kay Graves, Bobby and Eddie Huffman, Jimmy Pate, a boy named Rex Eubanks, other boys and I kept adding on to a tree house that had been started in that oak tree. We had a rope tied to a strong branch up in the tree. With the help of that rope, we were little tree apes climbing up and down that tree working on the tree house. We had a tremendous amount of fun up in that tree house, which was some 20-30 feet above the ground. We also had a wonderful hideout in a woodpile slightly southwest of this oak tree.

A sketch by the author in about 1943 of Jimmy Pate when they were both about 12 years of age.

Martha Mae Cartwright, the unbelievably beautiful daughter of Dr. Cartwright later became good friends with my sister. She told my sister that she could not believe the way we climbed that oak tree just like monkeys. One time I was with my sister and Martha and we took her to Alexander's, the Breckenridge ice cream place, where we both ordered chocolate malt. In the process we found out that Martha Mae had never had a chocolate malt. It never occurred to us that there was anything wrong with having a chocolate malt.

My mother, subsequent to Mrs. Nichols' advice, was always on the lookout for an art teacher for me. There was a nice lady who lived right across the street from us at about 1102 east Walker. Her name was Mrs. Clark. She had a nice husband named John. They were members of the very small Christian Science Church in Breckenridge. It seemed to me that my mother was the "first reader" and Mrs. Clark was the "second reader" of that church the entire time we lived in Breckenridge. Anyway Mrs. Clark gave me art lessons; it seems like, just about every afternoon for some period of time while living at Breckenridge. I was carried away by the movie, "The Wizard of Oz" and dreaming about that movie inspired a tremendous amount of my pictures drawn. Her house had the first air conditioner I had ever seen. Her husband made them a swamp cooler, which is an air conditioner that uses evaporation of water with a fan pulling air through the water as the cooling mechanism. That house was the nicest place to be on a hot day. Breckenridge had a lot of extremely hot days. My mother also had me taking piano lessons and violin lessons, which I hated although I always had a very good ear for music. I gained a lot of respect for violin players. I believe it is the hardest of all instruments to play. It seems to me you have to have perfect pitch discrimination to play the violin. From aptitude tests created by Johnson O'Connor that I've taken, this is about the only music aptitude I didn't have. I also had a problem of very low finger dexterity, which hurt me on playing the piano and other instruments requiring high finger dexterity.

We always had dogs and nearly always had cats. Walker Street was murder for dogs and cats. Cars ran over too many of them, but I always loved animals. One day a great big yellow striped tomcat meowed at our door. My mother let me take this cat in. My room was upstairs on the west side of the house, and my bed was right beside an upstairs west window. Many mornings for the rest of my life while being in Breckenridge, that cat would come to my window and meow, and I would let him in. We would greet each other and the cat would purr. I had taught him to do that when he first came to adopt us.

When it came time for the summer vacation, I was 9 years of age. My dad had decided I should work through the summer vacation period. He put me to work sweeping out floorboards of cars coming into Dale Hitchcock's filling station while others filled the car up, cleaned the windows and checked the oil and tires. Dale's station was located on the north side of East Walker Street and one block west of our house, which was on the south side of the same street. My mother, who was a frustrated architect, drew up the plans for a number of filling stations, which she and my dad built, with her money. Dale's station was the first one built of this type and the only one built in Breckenridge itself. Others were built in surrounding towns. I don't know how it worked, but eventually Dale Hitchcock owned the station himself. There is a story I heard about my cousin Jimmie Whittenburg, J.A. Whittenburg III, who is the son of my Uncle Jim. The story goes that when he heard about my working at a service station, he went down to a station near by and told them, "I want to work at your station, and I'm going to work here." I believe they let him work there a while.

I remember Charlie Hitchcock, who worked for his brother Dale at the station. He was a very likable man and later drove gasoline delivery trucks for my dad. At times I would ride with him and other men making gasoline deliveries to stations in towns throughout the area within about a hundred miles from Breckenridge. Dad had a gasoline and accessories warehouse in Breckenridge from which we filled the trucks with gasoline for deliveries. Either that year or the following year Bill Williams showed up and went right to work for my dad. He stayed quite awhile with us at our home in Breckenridge. I always thought Bill was the greatest.

I don't know all the details, but Bill Williams had a wreck in one of dad's trucks and was very badly burned over such a large percentage of his body that doctors said there was virtually no chance for him to live. My mother, the Christian Scientist, stayed at the hospital where he was. She prayed for him just about all day every day. She said she would read to him from the Christian Science Book termed "Science and Health" and the nurse would say, "Mrs. Ratliff he can't hear a word you are saying." Bill would say "Oh yes I can, Mrs. Ratliff, keep right on reading to me." He totally recovered, but never drove transport trucks again as I recall.

Before learning about Christian Science my mother had a great deal of trouble with religion. When she would go to churches in the Panhandle area, preachers would highly upset her with sermons about how evil my granddad and especially my great granddad were. My dad told me that my great granddad was known as the infidel of the high plains. My mother told me preachers would cross the street to avoid coming face to face with him. He knew the Bible better than most preachers.

I had two very similar experiences while working on delivery trucks that were being filled and while making model airplanes. I noticed at different times that it was very pleasurable to sniff model airplane glue or gasoline. Nobody had told me there was anything wrong with doing either. I believe it was gasoline first. I was sniffing it, and I just about passed out. I decided right then and there without talking to anybody, I better stop doing that and never did it again. Virtually the same thing happened with the glue. I never heard from others that it was dangerous or bad until many years afterward. Because of this, I have always felt that peer pressure is the main thing that causes undesirable addictions.

It was becoming time to start my fourth-grade year in school. My fourth-grade teacher's name was Mrs. Keys. I found out later that her husband was a barber named Haskell Keys who was a good friend of my dad. I also found out her maiden name was Sansing and she was kin to the optometrist of Amarillo of the same last name whom my wife and some of my children have been the patient of. The main thing I remember about Mrs. Keys was that she read to us about Franklin Roosevelt and talked about what a wonderful man he was. She also read about his opponent. I believe it was Wendell Wilkie. I remember her talking about how much more handsome Franklin Roosevelt was than his opponent. My mother hated Franklin Roosevelt, as did all her brothers and sisters. I don't know how I became friends with a boy named Jimmy Pate, but we became very good friends also. Jimmy Pate made the mistake of telling somebody at school that he was a Republican. The class went totally crazy. They carried him outside, put a rope around his neck and over the swing frame and were going to hang him. I don't remember what stopped them, but I thought they were going to hang Jimmy Pate. This made an unforgettable impression on me for the rest of my life.

My dad's mother lived in Graham, Texas, which was about 30 or so miles from Breckenridge. My mother supported and took care of her. Her name was Laura Lee Jones Ratliff. That is where the Lee came from. My dad seemed to harbor a great deal of anger toward his mother. I never understood why. The "Harvey" came from my dad's Uncle whose name was Harvey Stewart Ratliff. They called him "Bud" Ratliff. Ratliff Stadium in Odessa, Texas, is named after him. He was a very successful rancher in the Odessa-Midland area. He married a Sally Whittenburg, who descended from Jake Whittenburg. He was an older brother of my great grandfather, J.A. Whittenburg. I remember Aunt Sally and thought she was a very nice elderly lady. She lived to the age of 112 years, but she was kept alive in a vegetative state for the last 12 years of her life. Laura Lee was a staunch Democrat and idolized Franklin Roosevelt. She and my mother would argue for hours over the subject.

Another thing I remember about Mrs. Keys was that we put on a class play under her tutelage. When asked who wanted to play the main character, only I put up my hand. I believe she tried to get others to take it, but finally and reluctantly she let me have the part. To her amazement she was very happy with my performance, and I received a lot of praise over my performance. I remember the play going over really well. The play was about a group of mice that decided to put a bell around the neck of the cat of the house they lived in. I played the mouse that did ninety percent of the talking.

My mother loved to tell the story that at some school event that involved both the 4th grade class and their parents there was a conflict among the boys. Mrs. Keys said in front of all the parents, about me, "see there is my little peace maker, just watch him."

It was about this time that the father of Ray and Kay, who matriculated from Texas A&M and was the principle of Breckenridge High School, and his wife met and had a long talk with my mother. I believe the Graves were Baptist. Shortly after this I would be at events, I don't remember what events, and hear Ray's mother talking to somebody about Christian Science. When I got close, they would get real quiet. Also, Mr. Grave's attitude while I was around him showed substantial change toward me. I have since surmised that along about then these parents began plotting to get their sons out of my sphere of evil influence. Soon after that they moved to the North Ward part of town, which was also much closer to Breckenridge High and Junior High for the fifth and sixth grades, or possibly only the sixth grade.

Another interesting parental event happened about this time. As stated earlier my mother gave me an allowance and by this time I was to buy my own clothes. Once I noticed a pair of pants I loved. They were Levis. At that time few children wore Levis. I bought a pair and loved them from then on. The reason I remember this is that I found out later that this upset a lot of parents. Apparently many my age told their parents they wanted Levis like I wore, and their parents didn't like it. Along about this time it was the summer again. I was now 10 years of age. As I remember, I worked at least part of this summer at a filling station again. My dad bought a farm and ultimately decided to go into the dairy business. He, with me often along with him, went all over with Mr. Walker, whose first name I believe was Bob and whom my dad relied on as his expert. They were looking at milk cows to put on my dad's dairy farm. I believe that during part of this summer and all of the following summer, I plowed on this farm. As I remember it was all summer when I was 11.

Above is a painting by the author of his horse Shadow painted in 1949 when the author was 18 years of age.

Also, I was able to buy a horse from a man named Mr. Norris, I believe. I loved this horse. He was a 2-year-old gilding when I got him. This is much younger than horses were when they were broke back where I had come from. As I remember it, a black cowboy broke the horse. In fact he came to visit and showed me about the horse. He was very good. I don't remember his name. I named the horse Shadow because he was the color of his shadow on the ground on a sunny day. Late in the evenings, I had wonderful times with that horse. He would run through the woods with me on his back missing all the obstacles, such as tree trunks, limbs and branches. I would bring him apples to make him like me. He decided I was another horse and would try to "horseplay" with me. He would lay his ears back and bite me and even kick at me. I had to put a stop to that. I hit him and told him no, and he stopped.

One day I decided I was going to ride him from the farm, which was a few miles from Cisco, Texas, to Breckenridge. Shadow didn't want to go and I knew nothing about lining a horse out in a smooth, fast gate. It was late at night and Dennis Wimberley, the man dad had employed as his man on the farm, came with a pickup pulling a horse-trailer and said, I'm going to have to take you and Shadow back to the farm. We had a terrible time getting Shadow on the horse-trailer. This taught Shadow a lesson he never forgot. At a later date after dad sold the farm, Shadow was moved to the 35,000 acre Whittenburg ranch in Hutchinson County. Martin and his hands loved Shadow because instead of riding for hours to do various cowboy jobs, they could just get Shadow to jump up in the back of the vehicle, drive to the place, jump off, do the job, jump on and come back in a fraction of the time.

Somewhere along about this year or the last my Uncle Roy came to visit us. He was very impressed with my working every summer. He then came up with a plan for all cousins of my generation descending from George A. Whittenburg to work through the summers, and they would supposedly accumulate a cowherd of their own by the time they were grown. The cowherd part never actually materialized, but that was the initial incentive. I believe this actually started when my first cousin Basil Eugene Walker, Aunt Annie's oldest son, went to work out there when I was 11 years of age. He was actually about a year and a half older than I was. He was already working on the Spool Cattle Company ranch or ranches called the Cross L ranch, which was a leased ranch 75,000 acres in area, and its adjacent ranch the Baker ranch, which was a 50,000 acre ranch owned by Uncle Roy, Basil's dad, Uncle Bill Walker, and Uncle Joe D. A British entity owned the Cross L ranch. Spool Cattle Company leased both ranches and operated them as one. They used the Cross L headquarters as the ranch headquarters, I believe.

Anyway, I got through the summer after my fourth-grade year and it was time for my fifth-grade year to start. This year we did not just have one teacher. We had several teachers. I will always remember Mr. Abernathy, who had coached our football team up until that year. East Ward always came in second. North Ward was always first and South Ward was always last. I had gone out for football my third and fourth grade years, but was really not big enough yet, but I had my days. When almost anybody of that age carried the football, they could not run as fast as otherwise. I could catch almost anybody when they carried the ball and made several tackles in football practice. I don't remember or never knew the reason, but football was discontinued for my fifth and sixth-grade years.

Following I will describe events that took place mostly out of the classroom which may have taken place during my fifth or sixth-grade years. I am not sure which.

The biggest and toughest boy in the school at that time was named Jimmy Spencer. I thought he was Superman, and he was the best football player in the school. One time I remember he and Mr. Abernathy put on the boxing gloves. They were not mad or anything such as that. I don't know why they did. Mr. Abernathy was a small man. He was not even as big as Jimmy Spencer. I thought Spencer could whip him, or virtually anybody, easily. But, very quickly Mr. Abernathy, who was very nervous and likely thought Jimmy would whip him, knocked Jimmy Spencer out cold. Nobody could believe it. Today, in the year 2003, Mr. Abernathy would have probably gone to jail for that.

This was the year World War II had started. I was 10 years of age on Sunday, December 7, 1941, and I was in the fifth grade when World War II started for Americans and we said the pledge of allegiance, truly constitutionally and correctly the way the founding fathers intended. At that time, unlike the way it is now in 2003, the Hamiltonian statism brought back to life by Roosevelt's new deal had not really materialized yet and if you were white, this was a relatively great Jeffersonian country that more greatly recognized the inalienable rights of man for which the American Revolution was fought and the first amendment of the Bill of Rights of the U.S. Constitution.

"I pledge allegiance to the flag of the United States of America and to the Republic for which it stands, one nation, indivisible with liberty and justice for all."

I have now learned the significance of inalienable rights; see "Giants of Political Thought" by Simon and Schuster (Audio).

Tyranny by definition of the Jeffersonian enlightenment thinkers, is a condition caused when the ruling being forcibly deprives its citizens of an inalienable right. Jefferson meticulously set forth how King George was a tyrant in war with the colonies since he forcibly withheld their inalienable rights. Tyranny of the majority, which Madison said is the worst kind, is happening today with congress forcibly depriving citizens of their inalienable right of freedom of religion in the pledge and forced school prayer. It should be noted that this inalienable right is the first right set forth in the Bill of Rights.

There appears to have been great effort to cover up the enlightenment and the true meaning of tyranny at this date in time. There was a girl in our class named Neva Summers, I believe, who would not say the pledge of allegiance. I believe it was because her church forbids reverence to a flag. She was Jehovah Witness in religion, I believe. The teachers just ignored it, but it made a huge impression among members of her peer group such as me. Some of the kids, I remember a boy named Billy Waldrop, would argue with her for hours over that. I note that it is today, in 2003, said that time in our history, before "under God" was inserted in the Pledge, is when our greatest generation existed. I personally think that's truly the greatest except for the generation of our founders who wrote the Declaration, fought the Revolution and wrote the Constitution. But I agree that the generations have deteriorated since the insertion of "under God" in the pledge. In fact, we never failed to win a war until about the time they put "under God" in the pledge and I believe we have failed to win a war since then.

It was along about this time in Mr. Abernathy's class when, what I think is dyslexia got me in trouble again. Mr. Abernathy said he was going to give us a very simple test a "trualflalse test." I couldn't tell what that meant, but he said it was simple; so it must be simple. He would ask a question and say "trualfalse." I couldn't figure out how to answer the question, but I wrote, "No" when I thought it was wrong and "trualfalse" when I thought it was right. We had the procedure of passing our papers to the person in the seat just in front of us to be graded, and the teacher would call out the correct answers. When Mr. Abernathy said the answer to the first question was false, the girl, whose name I don't remember, in front of me held up her hand. When Mr. Abernathy asks what it was she said, "What do I do when he answers no?" Mr. Abernathy stood there dumbfounded and finally he said, "I guess you can count that right." When Mr. Abernathy came to a question in which the correct answer was true, the girl in front held up her hand again. When Mr. Abernathy asks what it was she said, "What do I do when he answers trualfalse? Mr. Abernathy stood there dumbfounded again and finally he said you have to count that wrong. When, after that, we went out for recess, a boy named Joseph Mitchell said to me, " If I ever flunked a test like that, my dad would give me the hardest spanking you could get."

My mother would get me tutors and she said they all told her I was a very intelligent boy and they didn't understand why I didn't do well in school. They didn't really help me in my schoolwork. They just gave me extra schoolwork to do under their verbal tutelage.

Quite often Mr. Abernathy loved to let people in the class get up before the class and sing. Several girls would get up and sing songs. These songs were very beautiful.

These girls could yodel beautifully and do all kinds of things very beautifully. Wanda Lane was probably the very best. I never got up in front of the class. She had a single mother who was a beautician, but she was by far the most popular girl in the class with the girls and the boys and by now even with Mr. Abernathy. Everybody, especially the girls, had long made it clear they wanted him to favor her over that other girl. Sure enough by this time he had dumped the beautiful little blond-haired, blue-eyed girl who sat in an even lower intelligence seat than I.

By this time I was a good friend with Jimmy Pate and alternatively Howard Henderson. I even became good friends with Tommy Smith for a short period of time. I didn't notice that Jimmy was in a gang like it was with Ray and Kay Graves. With Jimmy Pate we played one-handed touch football from the time school was out until dark just about every day. I would ache all over every night from playing touch football. I never saw football played like that any other place in my life. It was probably the most fun way to play football I ever encountered. Under the rules of this way of playing a touch with one hand was equivalent to a tackle in regular football. You had to touch a person while the ball was still in his hand. I don't remember a girl playing with us. If he passed the ball before you touched him, it didn't count and was not the equivalent of a tackle. A person could pass the ball after he had gone in advance of the scrimmage line. It was a very fast game. You moved all the time. You learned how to pass and catch on the run. It was fun. The leader was a big boy, a couple of years older, named Gene Slaughter.

One time we played this type touch football with Jimmy Spencer playing. I don't remember who the other people playing were, but what I do remember is that every time anybody tried to throw the ball to anybody Jimmy Spencer caught it. Nobody could throw a pass to anybody that Jimmy Spencer didn't catch. Also, Jimmy Pate and I would be with a boy named Jack Hesston. He had a big fat mother who always called us "little girls" to tease us. Jack Hesston seemed extremely good at caching the ball. We played a game sometimes with Jimmy and I against him in which if he threw or had thrown the ball in the air before we touched him and caught the ball running away from us it counted as a no tackle. He always won the game against Pate and me combined and the team. that had him on their side nearly always won the game when there were several people playing our regular version of one-hand touch. I never saw him up against Jimmy Spencer though.

One time I copied Jack Hesston's one against two game against my two cousins Jimmie (J.A. III) Whittenburg and Jimmy Walker, Aunt Annie's youngest son, and beat them both badly. They couldn't believe it.

One time I went down to Jimmy Pate's house, which was three blocks south of my house in the northwest corner of the block. That was the position of my house in the block of my house. When I arrived, his mother said he was out in the "shed." I went out there and he met me at the door and said, "will you join our Model Airplane Club." I said sure. The other boys who were sitting there said, "Hey, you said you and Harvey were forming a Model Airplane Club and you just now asked him to join." Jimmy looked very sheepish. I don't remember how he responded. I guess it was because I was taken aback by his manipulation. I had already made several model airplanes, and we had been spending a lot of time flying them. I never made model airplanes with gasoline motors, just the ones with big rubber bands as the source of power.

Jimmy Pate had a dog named Chubby that I thought was a great dog. He was part Chow and the only dog with Chow blood that I remember liking. This dog was bad news for cats. He could kill a cat in an instant and sometimes did. In general he was a very sweet dog though.

There was a sort of gang up there too. It included a boy named Bobby Ray Clark, his older brother Russell, who played center for the Breckenridge High School Buckaroos, a boy named Dee Gault, Jimmy's neighbors in the house just to his east named Bobby and James Walker and that Gene Slaughter mentioned before. The Walker boys were the sons of the man who was my dad's supposed expert in starting up a dairy farm. I found out while being around them while working on the farm that they had many sick ways that were certainly unpleasant. These ways were so sick that I have driven them from my memory.

At intervals I would do things with Howard Henderson, whom I have mentioned before. He lived on a ranch, I don't know how large, east of town about five miles out on an extension of Walker Street. I spent the night with him a lot. We would camp out a lot and dream and talk about quitting school. He was an even poorer student than I was. He was actually an intelligent boy. He may have had dyslexia as I may have had. My dad would take us fishing, and Howard always caught more fish than I would. My dad said, "oh well he is just a little older and smarter than you are." Howard had a dog named "Satan" that I thought was one of the greatest dogs I had ever seen.

One time I was out there, and we took Satan hunting with us. He cornered a skunk. There was a lot of skunk perfume in the air. We finally killed the skunk. People could smell skunk on me for weeks after that and they did complain profusely about it even though my mother had done her very best to clean me up.

One day I went down the street to play with Jimmy Pate. I don't believe Jimmy Pate joined in, but Russell and Bobby Ray Clark, Jack Hesston and others whose name I don't recall had soldier uniforms on, were in some kind of homemade fortification and were playing war. It seemed to be an exclusive affair. This went on for a few days and somehow Howard Henderson and I were talking about it, I think he asked me what I knew about it, and he said, "take me over there I want to watch them." We went over there and watched. Howard talked about that with some of his other friends and they decided if those guys want to play war, let's give them something real. Howard wound up shooting Bobby Ray with a B.B. gun and we had started a B.B. gunfight that lasted a few weeks. I don't remember how we got that fight stopped. Finally it did stop and luckily nobody got seriously hurt.

Howard Henderson loved to fist fight. He and I never fought but I'm pretty sure he would have whipped me if we had. One time he said I just want to have a fistfight. Somehow he got a boy named Jerry Jackson, actually one of his friends, into a fistfight with him. This fight would go on for a few hours every day at school over a period of time of more than a week. The entire class watched and seemed to love watching it. I don't know why the school didn't put a stop to it, especially with all the kids watching it. Somehow the teachers seemed to not know about it.

This was all going on during my fifth and sixth grade school years, as I recall after Ray and Kay had moved to the North Ward district.

My dad loved to go fishing at Lake Brownwood in this period of time. He often took Virginia and I along with him. I had always been terrified of the water in the past. I think it was because my dad had actually drowned and was resuscitated in his earlier life. One time while fishing with Dad, I fell into the water. I had my life preserver on since we always wore life preservers in the boat. Somehow that struck a cord in me, and I swam around for a while in the life preserver. Dad often went fishing with a couple, Mr. and Mrs. May. Mrs. May had worked with me earlier. She tried to get me over my fear of the water, which had really helped. One time later along with Jimmy Pate I decided if I hold my breath it is just as though I had a life preserver on. We went out to an earthen tank outside of Breckenridge, and I just started swimming and could swim from then on.

The principle of East Ward was a man named Mr. Tatum. Everybody was scared to death of getting in trouble with him and Mr. Abernathy both. Mr. Tatum had a huge paddle in his office that everybody knew about. When he punished somebody, you could hear it all over the building. There were no mass murders in schools in those days. He taught math in my class in at least one of and I think both of my fifth and sixth grade classes. He actually gave me one of the very few compliments given me by a teacher. One time while teaching math to us he said, "Harvey tell us how you solved this problem." I told him and he said "very good thinking Harvey. I can't believe it, very good thinking." When he would see me in later years and he had heard good news about me, he would always tell me the good things he had heard.

At some interval during this time period, Wanda Lane lived in a house across the street and about two blocks east of my house. Jimmy Pate and I would ride our bikes east on Walker Street in front of her house and show off in front of her. She would sit on her porch and watch us. It seemed to me that nearly all the boys in our class had a crush on her. If I got up close to her, I could not say a word. One time while being in a dark movie I saw her. For some, unknown to me, reason I thought she was my sister and walked right up to her and touched my nose to hers and said "what are you doing here?" Then I realized who she was and ran away. She always liked me a lot better after that. I have no idea what happened to her in later life.

The summer after my sixth grade year I was 12 years of age and I went to work up on the 125,000-acre ranch in New Mexico as described above with its headquarters at the Cross L headquarters. Basil's assigned horse was our Uncle Joe D.'s horse named Sport. Sport was a good-looking buckskin horse, which I understand Uncle Joe picked over another buckskin horse named King, which was the favorite horse, reserved for the ranch foreman, Martin Beasley. My assigned horse was another buckskin horse named Smoky. I was thrilled to have Smoky. I think the reason I loved Smoky is the fact that Will James, a Creator and Genius and the best Horse Painter and my very favorite author and the only real cowboy to write a book, wrote my very favorite book about a horse named Smoky. I have noticed that today it is very hard to get a book written by Will James and especially one with his really great pictures in it.

My Uncle Roy and Uncle Joe had a much different mode of operating than my dad had used. The dominant principle of their operation was to save money, keep the operating cost low. They employed minimal hands, paid them minimally and gave them much less leeway. Using more strict supervision while expecting much less initiative and ingenuity from the employee. The place was much more run down in appearance. The 125,000-acre spread employed the ranch foreman, Martin Beasley, and two hands named Lloyd Winfred and Sam Moore. Whereas on the 35,000-acre ranch my dad was overseeing in Texas, he had a blacksmith, a truck driver and it seemed to me he had around a dozen hands.

I believe the first thing we did when I started working on this ranch was bail hay for about the first month of the summer. I think there was a cooperative effort with some of the other ranches in bailing of the hay. Also, as I remember it, my Uncle Dick Windsor, Aunt Nannie Mae's husband and the father of my three first cousins, Clair, Deanie and Nancy, helped. There needed to be two "back wiremen." I was one of them, and most of the time Basil was the other one. One of the back wiremen would stick one end of the wire over the top of the bail and the other end under the bottom of the bail. There were two wires binding each bail. The other back wireman would tie the two ends together tightly. One end had a readymade eye in it and the other end was just the wire itself. This back wireman would stick this wire through the eye, pull it tight and wind it around the wire soundly so that it would not get loose.

A sketch by the author of Martin Beasley, ranch foreman, made in about 1943 when the author was 12 years of age.

My job was usually not the tying part of the back wiring job. I don't really remember all the jobs required to bail hay, but I think the back wiremen had the dirtiest job, which required the least strength. One job was to stack the bails, which weighed about 100 pounds each at times when wet enough. That required more strength than I had when I was 12. Another job was driving the "buck rake," which picked up the hay and brought it to the bailer. Basil got to do that sometimes. Somebody had to drive a different rake; I have forgotten its name, which gathered the hay into piles from which the buck rake picked up. I think Basil got to do that sometimes too. Somebody had to pitch the hay into the bailer as the buck rake brought it in. These are the jobs as I remember them. However, my only job was back wiring.

When the bailing was finished, we rode. I will never forget the first time I rode all day on this ranch. Basil rode with Sam Moore, which I know from later experience riding with Sam, was much easier. Sam Moore was a very short and thin man. He was about 5 feet tall. His parents in payment of debt had sold him as an indentured servant or slave, whichever word you prefer, when he was a small child and he had had a terrible childhood. That just couldn't be legal in this great "land of the free"; it seemed to me. I don't know if it was legal nationwide or just in New Mexico. I don't even know for sure that it was legal at all. I just know it happened to Sam Moore. Naturally Sam was a very bitter man, but I think he liked children a lot, the younger the better. His favorite was Nelly, Martin's youngest daughter. He also loved to tell stories and talk when Basil or I rode with him. I don't remember Sam's assigned horse, but he only covered whatever ground he covered in a walk anyway.

I rode with Lloyd Winfred. Lloyd was an excellent cowboy. He would not have been working on the ranch at all-- especially for the lower than average wages of $21.00 per month plus room and board-- if he had not wanted to stay out of the military. Lloyd had several assigned horses in his string. He seemed to have all the smooth gated horses. His favorite horse was named Brownie, which was a beautiful bay horse. Brownie was the smoothest gated horse on the ranch. That day Lloyd was on Brownie. He lined Brownie out in his very fast and very smooth gate and just sat upon that horse as if he were floating on a cloud. You couldn't tell it was two separate beings. It looked as if it was one being just floating along above the ground. I would trot in a very fast, rough trot to catch up with him then I would walk my horse, Smoky, for a while. Then I would trot very fast and rough to catch up. This went on for what seemed an endless period of time. My sides were killing me. My legs were getting rubbed absolutely raw. I developed thick scabs on the inside of my legs that didn't heal for weeks. I thought I would die then and for about the next three weeks afterward.

Lloyd covered about twice as much ground as Sam did. The headquarters house was down in a valley surrounded by very tall mesas. All the cattle were up on top of these huge mesas. We always started out climbing one of these huge mountain-like mesas. Then we would ride traversing these huge pastures up on top and come down slightly before dark. I loved Lloyd Winfred. He was such a beautiful person to watch and such a good hand. However, I was miserable for about the first month when I rode with him. I believe Lloyd was only working the first summer or two that I was there.

After we were through riding or haying at night Basil and I would saw logs for firewood during the wintertime. I remember sawing and sawing with Basil. Basil had always been proudly the toughest of the cousins. To me it was not that pleasant since in my view he overdid it. Sometime earlier I did get to where I could whip Basil. I remember the event when I first whipped Basil. He, Jimmie Whittenburg, Jimmy Walker and I were together one time doing, I've forgotten what, and Basil said "come on I can whip you all come on." First, both of the Jimmy's went up against him and were whipped by him, then I went in there reluctantly, but I whipped Basil. He couldn't believe it and neither could I? It was very difficult for nearly anybody close to my size to throw me down. I'm not really sure why, but I think I was quick and had a long neck, which in combination made it difficult to get a hold on me. I would let Basil keep trying unsuccessfully to throw me down and watch him. When he made various mistakes which I could instinctively take advantage of, I would get a neck hold on him that made him give up time after time. He just couldn't get over this fact and just about as soon I came to the ranch he would beg me to go out in the barn to wrestle. He couldn't believe I could whip him I guess. It didn't make any sense in a way. He was a year and a half older, out weighed me 20 pounds and could lift considerably more weight than I could. I did get tired of wrestling him every evening, but finally he did too and we quit.

My Uncle Dick Cline, who was then the husband of mother's youngest sister, my Aunt Tennessee and father of my first cousins Charlene, Catherine, Whitt and Ditt Cline, came out to the ranch with Uncle Dick Windsor often and by himself. He was the source of having a lot of fun. He always wanted to hunt the big mule deer on the ranch. Martin and maybe even some of the hands would go with him, and Martin would let Basil and I go with him too. All of us usually did it on horseback. One time, I think it was that first summer but it may have been a later summer, Uncle Dick's gun went off accidentally and he thought he had hit his foot. He pulled his foot up and looked and looked at it. He said it burned badly. We all had a good laugh. We concluded the bullet had come close enough to create an intense burning effect.

One time Basil and I were in his car with him at night and we caught several deer including a huge buck in his headlights. They just stood there blinded by the light. He took his pistol out with him and emptied it trying to hit that buck. Finally, he did hit and kill that poor buck. That was strictly against the law, I believe. Then we had the no-fun chore of cleaning and dressing the buck.

One time after Lloyd had left --a different hand-- whose name I don't remember, but they may have called him Arizona, bet Uncle Dick he could win a 100-yard dash with him while giving Uncle Dick a 20-yard head start. Uncle Dick very deceptively looked as though he was fat and couldn't run. I think every hand except Basil, Martin, and me bet on the cowhand over Uncle Dick. I actually only remember Sam Moore being the other hand but Martin's two older daughters, Frances and Betty also bet on the hand, I believe. They probably never even asked and didn't know that Uncle Dick could run the hundred in 10 seconds or less. He was an outstanding football player on the Amarillo Sandie football team.. And he had won many 100-yard dashes in track meets. Anyway, the race went on. When the race was run, Uncle Dick won by 30 to 40 yards. Uncle Dick would not take the hand's or anyone's money. He said they worked too hard for their money to lose it that way. The hand still wanted to race again without giving Uncle Dick a head start. But it was over. Martin wouldn't allow more.

I wasn't present when it happened, but there is a good story about Uncle Dick Windsor too that went something like the following. Uncle Dick Windsor was out with a cowboy once, and they saw a rattlesnake. The cowboy, in relaxed fashion, took out his rope and just popped the snake's head off. Uncle Dick thought," boy that was neat." One time later when Uncle Dick was alone, he saw a rattlesnake, got his rope down and tried to do the same thing. The snake struck the rope, stuck its fangs in the rope and came right up in the saddle with Uncle Dick. Uncle Dick learned right then how fast he could still move out of that saddle.

One time, I don't know whether it was while helping Uncle Dick hunt or during a roundup, but it was my first summer out on the ranch. We were moving fast, but for some reason we had to get off our horses and tie them up for something we had to do while dismounted. I tied Smoky to a log. I thought he would be all right. I think Smoky moved that log while grazing. It scared him and he ran a long way off, pulling the log along with him. I was beginning to learn that he was a very easily spooked horse. Most good cow horses are. We all spent a lot of time retrieving Smoky. Basil teased me about that for years.

I remember participating in driving big herds of cattle up and down those high mountain-like mesa's trails many times out on this 125,000-acre spread. I remember rounding the cattle up and branding, ear marking, vaccinating and castrating the calves. We would throw the calf on its side. One boy would set on top of the calf and hold its front leg in a bent position so the calf couldn't get up. The other boy would put both feet on the bottom leg pushing it forward and use both hands to hold the top leg back so the calf couldn't kick or get up. There was an adjacent rancher named J.C. King whom I remember well. He had two sons. One of them was named R.V. King, whom I remember well too. He looked a lot like Ray Graves with his black hair and brown eyes. These neighbors and others would pitch in with us, and we with them, for the branding occasions. R.V. always wanted to team up with me and exclude Basil to bull dog and hold down calves for branding, etc. This upset Basil pretty bad. He sometimes would love it if he could exclude me as we had somewhat of a rivalry. I think passed events that happened before my time on the ranch were behind R.V.'s actions. Anyway R.V. and I had a lot of fun at these brandings.

R.V. and his brother liked to go off out of sight and smoke cigarettes. I lost peer standing with them because I wouldn't do that, but R.V. still wanted to team up with me. This made me feel good.

There was a swimming hole within walking distance of the ranch headquarters that Basil and I would also go swimming in after hours. I believe it was either in the Cimarron River or in a stream feeding into the Cimarron. The days were very hot as it was at home but much more humid there than I had been used to. We had a lot of fun swimming in that hole.

I am not sure of which summer some of the ranch experiences took place and may get some in the wrong summer, but for now I feel it is time to relate my seventh grade school year and first year in junior high school. Unlike East Ward, junior high was located a long way from our house. It was several blocks west and north of the downtown area, which was about a mile west of our house on Walker Street. By down town area, I mean the area where the Birch Hotel, movie theaters, and several stores were.

I spent a lot of time riding my bike and walking to and from junior high. There was a long hard hill to climb on the way home. This was the general area where my violin, piano and drama lessons were, also. In junior high we had a different teacher for each class. I don't remember all my junior high teachers. I do remember Mrs. Welch. She was a very good teacher. I remember her teaching Texas history. I learned more under her than virtually any of the other teachers. She had a big bad looking paddle hanging behind her desk. It worked. I don't remember her ever having to use it. She looked a lot like Laura Bush, wife of president Bush as of 2003. I remember she presented the Ku Klux Klan as a good organization. I thought it was good for years. I also remember a Mrs. Pritchett. She was a good teacher too. I don't remember what she taught.

I also remember a Mrs. Baggett. The things I remember about her were she wrote everything we had to know upon the blackboard and we could, and better, copy it into our notebook. I copied everything she wrote in my notebook, memorized the notes cold and made the only A I had ever made up until that point. However, I don't think that was a good way to teach because I certainly didn't retain it over the long haul. I also remember a Mr. Laughlin who was the principle of junior high. He taught math, I believe. I also remember a Mrs. Boles who was the mother of one of my new friends from South Ward named Bill Boles. I don't remember what she taught. My English teacher in junior high was Mrs. (or Miss) Ratliff, who was completely unrelated to me.

It was along about this time period that my mother bought me an erector set and started telling me she thought I should become an engineer. I didn't know what that was and had been asking for a chemistry set. I did enjoy the erector set a lot and made lots of things with it, exactly what I don't remember.

It was also along about this time period that Jimmy Pate's parents, along with strong encouragement from Jimmy and his younger brother Jack, decided to sell their interest in the cleaning business they were in and buy a farm southwest of Breckenridge. Jimmy Pate's dad's name was James Owel Pate with the initials J.O. He went by "Joe" Pate. Actually Jimmy was a junior. Mr. Pate had a brother named Leland who had two daughters. The oldest was named Margaret. She was about a year younger than we were. I had a crush on Margaret for a few years, but nothing ever came of it. My friend Dick Atkins married her. I believe Jimmy's parents sold their interest to Leland because they sold the farm and went right back into the same cleaning business in two or three years. Jimmy and I had a lot of fun on that farm. We camped out a lot and hunted and swam together.

At Junior high Ray Graves introduced me to a lot of new friends from both North Ward and South Ward. I'm not sure how he knew the people from South Ward but he knew just about everybody in our class in junior high and was, by far, the most popular boy in the class and the best athlete. The best North Ward football player of my fourth-grade year was Ray's good friend Dale Witcher. Another good friend of his was the football coach's son, whose name was Cooper Robbins. I'm sure Ray's father recruited, or played a big part in recruiting, his dad the coach. Dale was one or two years older than we were. I met a boy named Bobby Douglass who talked me into playing my first tennis game with him on a tennis court at junior high.

There was a slightly rundown tennis court about three blocks north and one or two blocks west of our house at 1101 East Walker Street. Sometimes Bobby Douglass and I would play tennis there, but Jimmy Pate and I played tennis there a lot. None of us had any tennis lessons or really knew anything about tennis except that we had fun playing each other. A boy named Jimmy Gallagher would often come out and try making friends with Pate and me before and after we played. His big brothers, Gus and Charlie were football legends at Breckenridge, but his mother was very disenchanted with her boys playing football because of the health problems Gus and Charlie had and she was, I suspect, pushing her Jimmy to make friends with people like Pate and me. She had long talks with my mother complaining about those health problems.

Although it shouldn't have been so, I never really found a good way to eat lunch at junior high. I didn't like the school cafeteria. Looking back, the cafeteria was wonderful, having very good food at a bargain, but for some reason, still not understood by me, I didn't like it. A very popular place was Hood's, which upon looking back is ridiculous. A person would go in there and hundreds of kids would be screaming "Mrs. Hood, Mrs. Hood, Mrs. Hood" on and on. A person couldn't get her attention. When one finally got her attention what they got was a hamburger that was cold bread and meat with wilted, nearly spoiled, lettuce and tomatoes on it. Looking back what I wound up doing was unhealthy. I would go to a drug store next to the Birch Hotel downtown and order a chocolate malt and a package of Cheese Ritz crackers with a peanut butter filling inside them. At first a Mr. Cary owned it. Later he sold it to the Bowsers. The former Mrs. May, that loved to fish and hunt along with her husband, dad and me, had remarried a Mr. Bowser, since her husband Mr. May had died.

Along about this time period I was becoming as thin as a rail. I was a virtual anorexic. People would put food in front of me, and I just couldn't eat it. They would say "that is your favorite food," which it was at one time, but I must have gotten sick of the same old food all the time.

Ray and Kay's dad was the Boy Scout leader of a Boy Scout troop, the number of which I don't remember. An older prior East Ward Boy named Neil Bullock kept trying to recruit me to his Boy Scout troop. I kind of got tired of it; so, I decided to join Ray's troop. For quite a while after that, every time Neil Bullock would see me he would say, "Hey boy, you're a traitor." Anyway I met new people from North Ward and South Ward, some of whom I liked a lot at the Boy Scout meetings.

At junior high I met a South Ward boy named Phil Pitzer. His dad was Paul Pitzer, a man who was quite successful in the oil business and a good friend of my dad. A man named Cary K. West and Paul Pitzer formed a company named "Chemical Processing." It was one of the most successful businesses in Breckenridge as far as net worth goes. They obtained the chemical process from its inventor for a song. This was a classic *Ellsworth Toohey* (described better later) victory in which negotiators legally negotiate a creation from its creator and make a fortune off the creation with the creator receiving virtually no reward whatever and maybe humiliation to boot. C.K. West got his entrepreneurial start by noticing that at various harvests a lot of the crop was left after the harvest. He hated waste and asked the owners if he could gather the remainder for half the net profit it brought. He built a lot of capital that way to enable him and Paul to start Chemical Processing. Phil had me over to his house a few times to spend the night. I enjoyed it, but it wasn't as much fun as staying with Jimmy Pate or Howard Henderson had been. Other South Ward boys that I liked were Billy Hannah, George Webber and Chouncie Thompson.

At junior high physical education classes and recess, we would often play the two-hand variety of touch football. Ray Graves was always the quarterback. Phil would really cater to Ray and always wanted to run a play where Ray threw him the ball, but he wasn't really very good and Ray would get quite aggravated with him. Ray liked to pass to Billy Hanna, who could catch better and run much faster and better.

Ray started a recess game he had noticed four upper classmen do. Looking back it was a terrible game. It was called Spanish Leapfrog. Two guys would bend over perpendicular to the runner with their rears touching. Two other guys would put their heads between a leg of each of the two with their rears together and wrap their arms around the two legs in line with the runner with one in front and one in the rear. The object of the runner was to hit the rear guy as hard as possible with his back. If a person missed he became the rear guy the runner was trying to hit and the other guys would rotate one person. After four misses the person got in line as a runner again. One time while playing this "game," the bell rang while I was in the process of doing the flip and the rear guy ducked out of the position. As a result I hit the ground very hard and sprained my tailbone. I never before realized that your tailbone is involved in virtually anything you do. It hurt every time I moved to do anything for about a month.

In study hall at Junior high we were seated alphabetically. I was seated next to a boy named Harley Rogers who was a very fast runner and later became a star football player on the Buckaroos. We became fairly good friends. He had a friend named Louie Lee something. Louie Lee taught me how painful and hard to counter it was when a guy quickly grabs a single finger on one of your hands and twist it backward all the way back to your wrist. That knowledge served me well in years to come. With it you can bring almost anybody down to your size. I have very little memory of what I learned in school then. I wasn't really interested and virtually didn't study and didn't know I could study.

It was about this time I was 13 years of age and the seventh grade was over, and I was headed out to the Baker-Cross L ranch. By this time Lloyd Winfred was gone. I think the second summer out on this ranch a man named Verne Walker had replaced him although it may have been "Arizona" as mentioned before. Verne Walker was a good cowboy, but he was much different than Lloyd Winfred. I never again saw a cowboy who could cover such vast territory so beautifully, gracefully and with such apparent ease as Lloyd could. Nobody including Verne could even come close. Verne was actually a Coble and had a close blood relation to Tom Coble, Jimmie Whittenburg's granddad through his mother.

Martin Beasley's wife's maiden name was Christine Walker, and her youngest sister Minnie Walker was visiting this summer. Verne had a big time crush on Minnie Walker. That was obvious even to me, but Minnie couldn't stand him. He probably took a bath once a year and, as my mother said, he smelled like a dead horse; so, it was obvious why she couldn't stand him. Verne was full of advice for Basil and me and he meant well, but his advice was for somebody who was going to follow in his footsteps. Verne had the reputation of being a great bronco rider in his earlier years. He was now about 30 years of age and hobbled around like an old man. Basil and I weren't very impressed with Verne, but in my opinion he was head and shoulders above Sam Moore in his proficiency as a cowboy. I think my mother had taught him in her earlier years when she was a teacher. She, at least, had an encounter with him and did something positive for him.

Anyway Basil and I made it through that summer without much that distinguished it from the prior summer. This may have been the summer that I started having a string of horses and was given individual riding assignments. The horses I remember in my string were Brownie, Smoky, a Sorrell horse named Billy, and a black horse I will call "Blackie." I have talked about what a good horse Brownie was. Billy was a great horse and very lively, but every time I rode him he would lose about 100 pounds. This was a so-called horse disease that has a name, which I have forgotten. Blackie was a good cow horse, but he had rough gates and had a horse disease known as "ringtail." He had been ridden too hard too often in his early life and had developed the lifelong habit of ringing his tail when you needed to speedup or move for some sudden reason and was hard to get moving.

This also may have been the summer that I was also the wrangler. When I was the wrangler, I had to get up before everybody else, go down to the corral, saddle the wrangling horse, which was the horse in my string whose turn it was to be the wrangling horse, ride him to gather everybody's horses for that day before daylight early enough that each cowboy could get started riding at daylight. I remember one time I was on Blackie wrangling, and the saddle slipped too quickly for me to respond to and I woke up later with a big knot on my head and cactus quills all over my body. I had hit my head on one of the igneous basalt rocks, which were all over the pasture. This was because we were in close proximity to "El Capitan," an old Volcano that had erupted millions of years ago probably, but I actually don't know when it last erupted. I thought what am I going to do! Luckily I had fallen in a tree cactus whose quills were not nearly as bad as prickly pear quills are. I was able to pull all the cactus quills out with my fingers in a few minutes, but could I catch Blackie out there free in the pasture? I was no match for him in speed or anything, and he had my saddle under his belly. Luckily, he let me walk right up to him. All the horses in my string liked me because I loved them, and they had experience with other riders. He gave me no resistance when I fixed the saddle back correctly, and I brought the horses in almost on time.

One time while working on the Baker-Cross L spread, Martin said to me: you are going to ride 65 miles today. I often wondered if I had ridden 65 miles with Lloyd Winfred before. Anyway this exited me. What I remember about that was Martin was to ride King, his favorite horse, and round up a herd of horses along with another hand, whom I think was Verne. This was to place King, his horse, 30 miles from Folsom, New Mexico, our destination. Then I was to ride King behind the horse herd the remaining 30 miles to the shipping pens in Folsom with Verne, or whomever the other hand was, leading the way. When we reached Folsom, Basil and I were to ride the two other horses back home, which was 35 miles, as I remember.

So this is what I did. It is much different herding horses than it is herding cattle. You are never in a walk when herding horses as you are when herding cattle. You are in a high trot, lope or run all the time, and you have to respond correctly and quickly to what the horses do to keep them going where you want. Finally we had them penned in Folsom, and Basil took over the other horse, I'm sure it was his Sport, and we started the long 35-mile ride home. It was pitch dark and after midnight when we got back to the ranch headquarters. One thing that is really nice about being on a horse, he knows the best way to go home and you don't have to worry about it. After we left the road and started through the pastures in the pitch dark, King would go to the right gate, and Basil or I would get off and open it. This went on until we arrived at the headquarters. It was a great relief to arrive home and nice to know that I had measurably ridden 65 miles.

Meanwhile back in Breckenridge, Texas, my dad had by now lost hundreds of thousands of dollars of my mother's money. He had only had six years of schooling with each year comprising only three months or less of his being able to get off his dad's farm and attend school. He, therefore, was very lacking in education. He couldn't seem to understand many crucial things about running a business. He insisted that my mother not be involved in the bookkeeping or day-to-day operations. He always hired far too many employees. He knew nothing about accounting, and I personally think his bookkeepers embezzled a lot of my mother's money that she had turned over to him. The Phillips jobbership was really designed to be a husband and wife operation. If they had done it that way, they would have made good money. Instead my dad had five to six hands employed all the time plus he went through two or three different bookkeepers and some of them appeared to be embezzling money. He paid them all top wages. Also the Cisco farm had failed and had to be sold. Anyway, my mother decided she had better get hold of her financial situation or he would lose all the money we had. She turned to her brother, my Uncle Roy whom she trusted more than anyone. This required one-way 285-mile commutes back and forth between Breckenridge and Amarillo during most of my life while we lived in Breckenridge.

By this time it was time for me to start my eighth-grade year of schooling back in Breckenridge Junior high. I was 13 years of age when it started and 14 when it was over. Somehow during my eighth-grade year, my mother talked me into going, next year, to Principia Upper School in St. Louis, Missouri. Principia was a private Christian Science school, the only one in the United States or the world to my knowledge. I was in disarray with all my passed friends anyway during my eighth-grade year. Howard Henderson had clanned up with other boys, including Rex Eubanks. They all decided that it was cool to smoke and do other things I thought were wrong. Basically they ostracized me. The only friend I had left from East Ward was Jimmy Pate and he was ostracized too. However, I still had a few friends from South Ward and North Ward. Ray was still my friend, but he was way too popular with everybody else by now to have much to do with me. Phil Pitzer was still my friend, but he lived much too far away as did the other North Ward and South Ward boys. I felt very isolated during my eighth-grade year. So, I was really kind of relieved at the prospect of going to Principia.

I am sure that in my eighth-grade year I was the most difficult for my teachers to deal with than at any other time in my life. I don't really have memories of specific events, but I do remember making the largest number of "clever" remarks not appreciated by my teachers during that grade; however, I never was in trouble or had to go to the principal or anything like that. Anyway, I did finally get through eighth grade, even though it was one of my most miserable years in my schooling experience.

It was now time to go back out to the ranch in New Mexico. I believe this, the summer I was 14, was the year the lease on the cross L had expired and the lease asking price was increased too much or the equivalent. Anyway the Cross L was not available for Spool operations any more. I really missed the Cross L spread. I also believe the third summer on the ranch was the last summer Martin Beasley spent, and therefore I spent, working on the New Mexico ranches and the future summers were to be spent on the 35,000 acre spread in Texas to which Martin and Sam Moore were transferred. This summer I was also given those more advance assignments described earlier. Basically the events that I have previously described took place this summer or last summer in New Mexico. Anyway, I got through this summer on the New Mexico ranch, and it was time to start my ninth-grade year at Principia.

Chapter IV
Life While Attending Principia Upper School

The Principia experience was an unforgettable experience and had a huge impact on my life. Although I hated many aspects of it at the time, the experience had a very positive influence on my later life.

Above is a picture of the author about the time he started at Principia Upper School.

I will first attempt to describe my memory of a weekday at Principia. I am not certain of the exact times the various activities took place, but as I remember it: at 6:45 am the bugler blew "first-call" that meant, "be prepared to arise from your bed," at 7:00 a.m. he blew "reveille" that meant arise and come out into the hall for role count at which time we would report "here" or the suite chief would report "in" for someone sick, whom the school nurse would visit later. After role call, we had a given period to get dressed, clean our room, bathroom and make our beds, which had to pass a later inspection or we would receive demerits. After a time period thought sufficient, the bugler blew "first-call" again which, this time, meant assembly was going to be in 15 minutes. Next

34

"assembly" was blown, and we went down to be personally inspected and then go into the assembly room. The inspection was to make sure your fingernails were clean, your tie was correct, your suite was acceptable, and your shoes were shined. It was more military than the military was. If you failed the inspection, you received demerits. At assembly the dorm faculty discussed various things they wanted to impress on us that day. After that first-call was blown which, this time, meant be prepared for "soupy" in 15 minutes. Next "soupy" was blown, which meant go to the chow hall and eat breakfast. After breakfast I believe we had another first-call, then assembly from which we went to our various classes. Classes were structured similar to the way it is in college. Each class was in a special room with a number. The teacher, in general, stayed in the same room. You were assigned a class schedule and you were to be at each classroom at a specific time until lunchtime. Before lunchtime first-call would be blown, then soupy and we would go the chow hall for lunch. Next, there would be first-call; assembly and we would go back to classes until about 3:00 p.m. or so. Then we would go to practice whatever sport we had chosen to participate in for whichever season it was. I chose football in spring, basketball in winter and track in fall. After practice, we went back to the dorm, first-call was blown, then assembly, at which role call was taken and after which we went to "dinner." This was a "fancy" dinner in which we were assigned formal tables and seats. We dressed up for this. Certain students, including my suite-chief, Jerry Gillespie, were the "waiters." It was a fancy affair. Before dinner there was a role call in which I was supposed to report "Gillespie Waiting" since Gillespie was waiting and therefore not present. I was one of the few people there whose voice had not yet changed and I took a lot of ribbing about my high-pitched "Gillespie Waiting."

After dinner we went back to our dorm, dressed in our bedclothes and ready to study, first-call was blown, then the bugle call for studying, I have forgotten its name, was blown and we would study for about three hours. Then first-call and after 15 minutes assembly was blown. We would go down for assembly. There was a role call, and the dorm faculty would make speeches. Some students would ask questions and make comments. We were then allowed a recreation period in which we had some snacks at the snack bar, played games and relaxed. The main game I remember being played was pool. I mainly just remember talking to my friends down there. Some people jokingly called it the "Bar and Pool Hall." Then there was first-call blown, and then taps, and we were in bed at 10:00 p.m., which gave us nine hours sleep.

Friday nights were slightly different, as I remember; every Friday night there was a dance in which both the young men and women of my age group attended as well as all the other four grades at the upper school. I think this took place during the time normally allotted to the study period.

The athletic program. was kind of neat. Principia was in a league with private military schools and prep schools. I remember one, which was outstanding to me, Western Military Academy. Another was Thomas Jefferson something and there were several others. The league comprised three team's that stood on their own: the A team., the B team. and the C team.. I don't know the exact criteria, but its formula included the factors of age, grade, weight and height. The older higher grades had to be smaller in size to remain on the C team.. Some smaller members of the C team. were high school seniors or twelfth-graders. Some midsize members of the B team. were high school seniors. I don't believe any freshmen or ninth-graders were on the A team., however.

In my freshman year at Principia, I was on the C team. I was probably the smallest member of the team, thin and uncoordinated. I didn't know it then but I was beginning a growing stage of gaining 10 inches in height and 90 pounds in weight. At first the coach, Mr. Craig who also taught some of my friends and me geometry, ignored me completely. He had his favorite way of tackle practice though. He had a triangle of dummies. One leg of the triangle was perpendicular to the tackler and the other leg of the triangle was perpendicular to the runner-ball-carrier. The ball carriers would change places with each other to avoid being up against me because I would knock the feet out from under them with everything I had. I specifically remember being up against the star athlete Wade McClusky once with him the runner-ball-carrier and me the tackler. I remember knocking his feet out from under him, he telling me "nice tackle Tex" and from then on he would change places in line so as not to be up against me. Anyway the coach put me on the first string at right tackle and I played every minute of every game on offence and defense during that season with one exception. In one game after we kicked off after half time, I think, to the other team. I made the tackle, but got knocked completely out. I could hear Bill Kelly's voice and feel his hand on me and hear him say, "that was a great tackle," but I couldn't get up or even move. That was one of two times I had the weird experience of living in "slow motion" where your mind speeds up giving the sensation of slow motion. In the slow motion I remember hitting the runner's knee head-on with my head. I didn't know it then, due to adrenalin I think, but in the tackle I had sprained both my ankles and couldn't walk after a few hours and it took me a long time to completely recover. In that game I was carried out and stayed out for the duration. I have since wondered if I may have undetectably damaged my neck in that incident since I remember in slow motion hitting the runner's knee with my head head-on. I now at age 72 have peripheral neuropathy and nobody has as yet figured out why.

In football practice I began making friends. The person everybody was carried away with was the big, great athlete, at that level, named Wade McClusky. He played quarterback on the team, but his favorite sport was basketball. His dad was a war hero in World War II. In the Battle of Midway he had sunk the most Japanese ships of anybody, as I understand it. He was from the state of Washington as I recall. Another running back, Wade's best friend, was named Bobby Mayor from San Angelo, Texas, and he played either halfback or fullback. They had become inseparable friends while attending Principia in the eighth grade in the prior year. We played the "T" formation. Don Rishoi played the left tackle; he was much larger than I was. The guards were played by: Bill Campbell and Bill Drake. The other halfback was Dave Parsons, a small senior who was very fast and known as "crazy legs." As I recall the fullback was Harvey Glor or he may have been the other halfback. Nobody called me Harvey. They all called me "Tex." Bill Kelly and Bill Wixson were also on the team. I think they played end. I believe end was also sometimes played by one of my very best friends named Stedman Smith. He was known and wanted to be known as Sunny Smith, not Sonny. Sunny was probably the first person at Principia that I had a friendly conversation with, friendly meaning with the possibility of becoming real friends. He was fairly tall for that age, very well built with lots of natural athletic talent. He could kick and pass the football beautifully. He had sandy hair and hazel eyes and was from Los Angeles, Cal. He later told me that the first words I said to him were "you sure do talk funny." The laugh was on me. Everybody at

Principia thought I talked funnier than anyone. There were other players, in fact some 14 others, but they were not on the first string.

The picture above is of the C football team. On the first row from left are Bill Kelly, Dave Parsons, Amberg, Ratliff, Bill Drake, Bill Campbell, Harvey Glore, Tony Ling, Don Rishoi, Bobby Mayer, Wade McClusky, Bill Wixon, and Allen Burdsall. On the top row from left are Ned Shepard, Parker Jackson, Mel Owen, Miller, Conrad Byrd, Sunny Smith, Weisenberger, Dick Turner, Nelson, Hills, Douglass Woodward and Austin Treworgy.

A good friend of Sunny and probably the best friend I met while at C football practice at Principia was named Melville Owen and was known as Mel Owen. He was not on the first string and may not have ever played in a game. Mel was an unforgettable person to me. Mel was maybe a little taller than me but about my height. He had virtually black hair and hazel eyes and was quite a handsome young man. He was from Berkley, Cal. near San Francisco. He and I had a lot of good times and some bad ones. I was a little bit stunned at first, he seemed to have a lot of friends, but just out of the blue picked me out and wanted me to go with him everywhere and do everything with him. He would even check up on me during the dorm study period, against the rules. My suite chief, Jerry Gillespie, would tell me to stay away from him. "He will get you in trouble." Jerry Gillespie was probably the nicest person I met while at Principia. He was a senior and would be gone after my ninth grade year. He acted as though I was his kid brother with an interest in everything about me that I have very seldom seen in this life. I heard one of the other upper classmen named John Watkins call him "SS" after the two had a long whispering conversation in my presence. I asked Jerry, "what does 'SS' mean." He said, "Ask him." I didn't ask John but, although I don't remember how, I learned later that "SS" meant super sensitive.

In general Jerry was a very encouraging positive person that stood for hard work and doing the right thing. I was very fortunate to have him as a suite chief. He seemed to be too sensitive according to some of his classmates though.

The picture above is of Jerry Gillespie, who was my favorite suite chief.

Mel, Sunny and I would do everything together we could during what time we had available to do it. I believe it was before we would get ready for bed, we would go down to the large dorm shower room in our bathrobes and with our soap in its container and take a shower at night. We would always go to breakfast and lunch together and just about everything we could. We would also take our shower after practice of the various sports. For a while we had a gang or clique that included another boy named Tony Ling, whom I had a somewhat distaste for. After some period of time, it was probably six to seven months, I reached a point that I felt I was just tagging along with Mel all the time and couldn't make other friends or anything. It also had begun to dawn on me that people in general and Mel in particular had hidden agendas. What you saw wasn't exactly what you got.

I, like everyone else, would have loved to have been friends with Wade McClusky and tried to do so at some time with little success even though he was always nice and friendly toward me. Wade really liked, and I gathered used to date, the young lady nearly everyone thought was the prettiest in our class. Her name was Marline Wetzel. A guy who was a grade ahead of us with the reputation of being a great athlete was named Dick Hedges. He would tell Wade in front of everybody. "I'm going to steal Marline from you." One time at a Friday night dance I, like a fool, went up to him while dancing with Marline and said "get away from Marline; she's Wade's girl." They both turned red-faced but nothing happened, and Wade just embarrassedly laughed it off. However, I did notice that neither Dick Hedges nor Marline disliked me after that. Marline would congratulate me after football games and was one of the few people at Principia who called me Harvey, and Dick Hedges would call me the school artist after that. One time Wade's father had a party and invited several, maybe all, of Wade's classmates. What I remember about that party was that out of the entire group there at the party, Wade's dad wanted me to give the speech. I stood up and tried, but I was totally unprepared and couldn't give a speech. Mel later sarcastically said, "Hey you gave a great speech there Tex."

I didn't really understand fully the concept of "hidden agenda" at that time, but I knew something not liked by me was going on. I had the feeling that Mel was playing me in a way directed at making himself very popular maybe even the student leader of the entire school, which he later became. Anyway I started resisting Mel's continuous invitations to do everything with him. During that period I remember with great regret making a very stupid mistake, which was probably fatal to our continued close friendship. During the peak of my resistance period, his parents were visiting and Mel invited me to be his special guest and dine with him and his parents. My big mistake was that I made my lack of desire to do this very obvious in front of his parents. Actually, Mel's father, even though I didn't know it until 57 years later was a United States patent attorney. This was something since in my later life I would patent 28 of my inventions. Back to the subject of Mel's and my friendship, he got tired of me resisting, and one day he dumped me. That was it. Our friendship was very casual ever after that. My life at Principia was not nearly as much fun after that. He was the only one who ever put me first at Principia even though he nearly certainly had a hidden agenda. To everybody else I was just another guy except to some extent Norman Evans, whom I will describe more later, and Jerry Gillespie, but Jerry was a senior. Sunny was then kind of like Mel. We just had a casual friendship and did virtually nothing together anymore.

There were many more facets to Principia life. I have yet to describe the weekends. On Saturday we had our morning reveille, roll call, inspections, assembly, breakfast, lunch and dinner. Saturdays were completely planned by the faculty of Principia, but we had various recreational and cultural activities planned for us. We would have to attend concerts and operas, which until this day I really don't enjoy very much. We had planned outings that I think of as sort of like picnics. We would attend museums and the like. We had compulsory dancing lessons that lasted several Saturdays. Sundays were different. For breakfast we arose later and stayed in the dorm and went down to the snack bar and had a sweet roll and milk for breakfast. We went to the Christian Science Church after this different breakfast and in the afternoon we had the privilege of being able to do something off campus on our own, if we had no demerits. We had to sign out and accurately write down where we were and when we would return. For the first six to seven months, Mel, Sunny and I virtually always did something together off campus on Sundays. Mostly we went to a movie.

Everybody at Principia did not live on campus. Some students were "day students." They lived in St. Louis and attended Principia. Don Rishoi, the left tackle was a day student. When I was first at Principia, Don's girlfriend was another day student named Bonne Bloss, whom Mel later took away from him. After my relationship with Mel became only casual, I, along with J. Walter Bell and others, spent a lot of my spare time with a day student we knew as "Stubby" Stubblefield. He was a brilliant model airplane builder. He built gas engine models that he flew and controlled from the ground with a string or cord apparatus. He could put one together in a day. His planes had gasoline motors, were covered with beautifully sanded balsa wood and beautifully painted with dope. We had a lot of fun with him flying his planes. We couldn't do things like making model airplanes in the dorms and didn't have the spare time it took.

Principia was the first school I attended since Canyon, Texas, in which I could be in an art class. My art teacher's name was Miss Evelyn Pattison. She was not nearly as encouraging as Mrs. Nichols had been, but due to Mrs. Nichols no teacher could discourage me to any extent. I thought in my heart that I was a natural artist regardless of what anybody else thought due to Mrs. Nichols. I did have a classmate whom I liked a lot and whom I greatly admired as an artist, and the feeling was very mutual. His name was Norman Evans and he was from a ranch near Gillett, Wyoming. I would love to look him up but never have. In a way he was my best long-term friend while at Principia. We would sometimes take on individual projects and compete with each other to see who we mutually thought did the best job and would sometimes ask the other art students and Miss Pattison their opinion. Later while I was at Prin., members of the faculty, usually a Mr. Lake always picked me to decorate various events to take place, mostly Friday night dances. I would almost always ask Norman to help me out, and he always did. Norman had a big brother Dick, whom I also liked very much. He dated Mel's big sister, Christie Owen. Both Dick and Norman were very good wrestlers on the school wrestling team, also.

In that class we also studied lots of different art and artists. It was probably there that I developed my lifelong love for the Creators and geniuses: Michelangelo and Leonardo da Vinci. We also visited the St. Louis museums of art, which I greatly enjoyed. Mel, who was considerably more advanced than me in many ways, especially with the female of our species, had a girl friend named Bonne Bloss, as mentioned before, for a while whom he later broke up with. One day he just dumped her like he dumped me. Actually, in the early months I was really more popular with the young women than Mel was, but I was just too shy and utterly unable to pursue one enough to have her as my girlfriend. I remember a beautiful young lady named Roxanne Campkin that Mel really pursued, but she made it clear she much preferred me; however, I just was unable to bring myself to pursue her. I still don't understand why that was. I was also unable to pursue the only Principia young lady that I really had a crush on whose name was Glenna Bowman. To continue about Bonne, she was in the art class that Norman and I were in. Miss Pattison was very good friends with her mother who visited her in the class virtually every day. She picked Bonne to give the best artist of her class award. Norman and I did not think that was an unbiased choice since it seemed mostly because she liked Bonne's mother so much, but as I was to learn again multiple times throughout the rest of my life, that is life in the world outside the free enterprise system as, for example, I participated in as an entrepreneurial Petroleum Engineering Oil and Gas operator. In most worlds advancements and decision-making are some 90 percent political and 10 percent merit when one is an employee inside a corporation, governmental agency or branch or the like.

One of the many projects of the art class was for each student to individually make a Marionette, dream. up a play or skit for the Marionette and dream. up and paint the proper stage props and background for the play. What I remember about this was that after making my Marionette, I dreamed up a play in which Norman helped me out. I played the hillbilly son and he played the hillbilly father inside the house. When everyone presented the plays, the crowd went wild over my play. A lot of people told me it was the best one.

Principia had a very positive effect on my eating practices. Before coming to Principia I was very picky about my food to the point of almost being anorexic. It had reached the point that whoever prepared my meal would give the same thing and tell me that was my favorite food with the result that it was very hard for me to force the food down. At Principia it was different. Except before bedtime there were no snacks. We had three meals a day. These meals were your only chance to eat. One day I cut loose and ate more food, by far, than ever before. I remember thinking to myself, that is the first time I've been really full, and it is wonderful. From that day forward I began really healthy eating and started my 10-inch, 90-pound growth period.

I had many other suite chiefs at Principia after Jerry Gillespie. I believe the next one was named Austin Treworgy, who was also the manager of the C football team, which I was on. He did not rate, in my esteem, even close to Jerry Gillespie. He seemed to be possessed with a jealousy or anger toward me. I think it was a result of his perception that I was very popular and well liked. He also knew, since he was the manager that I was on the first string. He wasn't bad, but the pleasure as it was with Jerry just wasn't there. His best friend was a guy, whose name was Nigel Pridmore-Brown from Mexico City, Mexico, whom all my friends thought was weird. Austin would tell me "well, he mastered different things from guys like you. You mastered people, but he mastered other things." I guess he said this because he thought I was very popular and therefore I had mastered people.

It may have been in my second year at Prin., but I also had another great suite chief named David Miller. I really liked him. He was great. It wasn't like Jerry though. Dave's mother would send him, what I thought were, the greatest cookies ever. They had this wonderful chocolate flavor, and this butter in them that I could not find. Much later in my life, I decided that these cookies were in actual fact the first chocolate chip cookies I ever had. While in David's suite I first met a guy who was two grades ahead of me but whom would become a very good friend named Eddy Williams. He was the only fairly close friend from Principia who actually came to visit me afterward. We got him a job, and he stayed with us in Amarillo for a month or two. Actually, I would later be in Eddy's suite. I felt very lucky to be his friend because he was a tyrant to everyone else in his suite. One of the people in the suite that he was a tyrant over was named Marco Wolf. Once Eddy made me hit Marco. Marco was a concert level piano player, but he was very arrogant, obese and in general obnoxious. He and I greatly disliked each other. Eddy was from Warren, Ohio. I once ran into him at the Washington National Airport later in life while researching prior art, i.e., searching the patent files for prior inventions, at the U.S. Patent Office search room. I recognized him, went up to him and asked him if he was Eddy Williams. With a frightened look in his face he said, "Yes." I was by then considerably bigger than he was. He said he would have never recognized me in a million years. We spent a couple of hours talking and having a great visit. He had been at the same search room doing a patent search and was a practicing engineer.

While being with Dave Miller, I also had another interesting suite mate named Conrad Bird. He was from California, and his father was a movie actor. I had even seen a movie with his father in it. It was just a class B movie though. Conrad was also one of my classmates. We never really became friends. There were actually two boy's dorms at Principia as I recall: the main large dorm and a smaller dorm across the street from it known as Howard House. Dave Miller's suite was in Howard House and he was my first, and maybe the only suite chief I had while living at Howard House. I do recall being in Stanley Grau's suite and I believe it was in Howard House with Harvey Glor and Bill Kelly as suite mates.

Another suite chief, or he may have just been my suite mate, that I really liked was Dave Parsons, who was also the great C team running back mentioned earlier. I really liked him and we got along well, but he was a twelfth-grader when we were together in the suite as was Jerry and this did make a difference.

Principia had a completely different system of nomenclature from other schools. One such difference was in how they described the grade you were in. They didn't define a ninth-grader as a high school freshman. They defined a ninth grader as a "1st Ac," a tenth-grader as a "2nd Ac," an eleventh-grader as a "3rd Ac" and a twelfth-grader as a 4th Ac. Another difference was in the description of the grade a person made. The highest grade there was not an A but an S, which meant superior. The second highest grade there was not a B but an M for mastery. The third highest grade was the lowest passing grade and was not a C D or "E," but a P for passing. The failing grade was not an F but a "U" for unsatisfactory.

Art was, of course, far from the only subject we studied at Principia. Another subject I took there was aeronautics. My aeronautics teacher was Mr. Paul Dietz. Mel and Sunny were also in the same class. Another young man in the class who was Mel's best friend after dumping me was named Parker Jackson Parker was over the top crazy about Mel. Mr. Dietz's favorite student's name was Bill McGrew. He was probably Conrad Bird's best friend. I was good at building model airplanes, but I was just not, in general, a good student. I think this is because I'm dyslexic. Aeronautics is where I believe I was first introduced to the "slide rule," which I used later extensively while getting my engineering degree in later life. I remember when first attending aeronautics, Mr. Dietz went on and on about how brilliant my sister was in front of the entire class. She had attended Principia Upper School the year before as a 4th Ac and was now attending Principia College. I found out from her later that she had been in one of Mr. Dietz's classes, and he hardly even noticed her. But, when it came time to take the nationally rated achievement test she made, by far, the highest grade of anybody. This made Mr. Dietz look good and really impressed him.

English was, of course, a subject we had to take. My English teacher's name was Miss Irma Eareckson. She was a good teacher. Mel, Sunny, Parker, Bonne, Glenna and Marline were all in that class also. At some point while I was at Principia, my mother employed her to give me special tutoring. She would have me write stories, which wound up being about experiences I had working out on the ranch as I remember it. She wrote my mother telling her she never knew anyone who knew as little about nursery rhymes as I did. Later on in her regular classes we would do plays about the various subjects we were studying. When I acted a part in one of these plays, she would always send a "superior" report over to the dorm. Those were the only "superior" reports I ever received.

My geometry teacher was the C football coach, Mr. Craig, whom I liked very much, and the algebra teacher was Mr. Jack Eyerly. Mr. Eyerly was physically impaired in his walk and had a limp. Mel, Sunny and the rest were in these classes also. Mr. Eyerly was a concert level pianist and often performed in concerts we attended. I really felt that I did pretty well in the math classes and my mother never told me about a bad report in my math. I don't remember my grades, but they weren't "S."

I had other teachers, but I really remember very little about them. One other teacher was named Mr. Hugh Semple. The only thing I remember about him was that one time he told me "Tex, you are just careless. You spelled the same word four different ways." I later learned from reading "Patton A Genius For War" by Carlo D'esta that is a sure sign of dyslexia. Patton, a true genius and probably the greatest general we ever had, sometimes spelled the same word more ways than that. I don't even remember what subject Mr. Semple taught.

Another teacher I remember was, I think her name was, Miss Paul. I seem to remember only funny or embarrassing things that happened in her class. She always used her middle finger to point with. One time Bill McGrew volunteered to point out a group of places on a map which locations we were all supposed to know. He pointed to each place with his middle finger, and the class just roared with laughter. Miss Paul kept saying, "What is funny." One time I had to give a speech in that class, and the class laughed and laughed. I never really understood why.

I met and went on Sunday free time with some other interesting people. One of them was named Bill Wixson. He was a really nice guy and we had a great time but never became close friends. He had attended Western Military Academy the year before and was actually a grade ahead of me but played on the C football team. And we were mutual admirers of each other.

The picture above is a group of my class members of the years 1945 to 1946; some people such as David Clark are missing. I will point out the people I remember from left on the top row are Tony Ling, myself, Dick Arthur, Skipwith something, Parker Jackson, Mel Owen, Sunny Smith and Douglass Woodward. On the next row down Glenna Bowman is seventh from the left, then Marlene Wetzel is eighth, Bonnie Bloss is ninth, and Dawn Leonard is twelfth. On the third row, third from the left are Ned Shepard, fourth Don Reshoi, fifth Joan Ostenberg, sixth Nancy Sue Stitt, seventh Marco Wolf, and ninth Charlotte Robeline. On the bottom row from left is Susan Tripp-Secretary, Wade McClusky-President, Bobby Mayer-Vice President and Bill McGrue-Treasurer.

Another interesting person I once went on Sunday free time to town with was named David Clark. David's father was a quite successful candy manufacturer and

David was thought to be arrogant by nearly everybody in my class, but I liked him a lot. We got along really well. He didn't go out for football, basketball or track; however I remember him going out for wrestling. In his first wrestling match he was up against Erwin Stoner who was a big-time athlete on the A teams: football and basketball I believe. David won the wrestling match and stunned everybody. Nobody could believe it.

When it became basketball season, Wade McClusky was in his heaven on earth. The Principia C basketball team. won every game and became the league champion, as I recall. Wade was by far the best on the team. I didn't even play in a game, as I recall, neither did Mel, but Sunny did quite a bit. I remember very little about track except I was too clumsy at that point in life to do well. However the discipline and calisthenics of the three sports did me a lot of good. School athletics and "athletes" were way behind the learning curve on the use of weights, not recognizing them at all in those days. However, there were individuals at Principia that appear to me, in hindsight, to have been advanced body builders. One such person was named Jim Hathaway. Anyway another effect Principia had on my life was to create a desire in me to be a body builder.

Finally it became the end of the school year and was time to go back out on the ranch. Until now I haven't mentioned the fact that I traveled back and forth from home to Principia and vice versa by way of a Pullman car on the railroad train. That was really great. You could take long walks on the train and did every time you went for a meal. At night what were seats in the daytime were made into beds at night. One bed was on top of the other. It took two to three 24-hour days to make the trip, but the way we traveled was fun. It was also by far the safest way of travel ever in existence in the United States.

I was 15 in the summer of 1946 and it was time to go back to work on the ranch. This summer it would be on the 35,000-acre spread in Hutchinson County, Texas. Whereas my dad's ranch headquarters was south of the Canadian River on Section 56, Block 47 as I recall and known as the Bear Creek headquarters, the new headquarters was what was left of the town Plemons, Texas, which was also on the 35,000-acre spread but north of the Canadian River on a Section and Block I have forgotten. It could have been Section 14, Block 47. This was the town of my mother's childhood as it was with all her brothers and sisters. Bear Creek was now resided in by one of the ranch hands other than the foreman. Since my Uncle Roy now oversaw the operation, the ranch was very rundown in appearance as compared to how it was when my dad oversaw it.

My memory of working on the Texas spread is not nearly as clear as it was of working on the New Mexico spread. I remember Martin Beasley and Sam. Moore were there. Sometimes I went with Sam., and sometimes I had individual assignments or assignments with Basil. In general we rode the pastures checking the water, the fences and the cattle in the pastures. Sometimes we built fences or repaired fences. Sometimes when a pasture was too well grazed, we moved the cattle from that pasture to another pasture. Sometimes we repaired windmills, which were the main source of water in most of the pastures. Sometimes we would round up and brand, vaccinate, earmark and castrate the cattle. Sometimes we would sort the cattle by holding one group in a corner of a pasture and cutting another group out and holding them at another location or just letting them stay in that pasture while moving the sorted cattle to another pasture, branding the remaining cattle or moving them someplace like to market. There were different cowboys who stayed at Bear Creek, whose names I have forgotten, who rode over and helped us sometimes. There was a hand that stayed in the Plemons area whose name was Curtis Cimmons. Martin was critical of him, but I liked him. He taught me the words of "Strawberry Roan" which I treasured the rest of my life. He was actually a college graduate. He said Sam. Moore use to always be critical of him until he helped him with his income taxes, and Sam was never critical after that. I don't remember why a College Graduate was working as a cowhand, but I believe he said he needed to because of his or his wife's health.

The words to Strawberry Roan as I remember from Curtis are:

I was bumming around town just spending my time; out of a job, not earning a dime; when up steps this stranger and says I suppose, that you're a bronc rider from the looks of your clothes, well you guesses me right and a good one I claims, do you happens to have any bad ones to tame; he says I've got one and a bad one to buck; a throwing good riders, he's had all the luck; I gets all excited and asks what he'll pay, to ride this old pony for a couple of day; he offers me ten and I says I'm your man; the bronc never lived that I couldn't fan; well get you a saddle I'll give you a chance, we'll hop on the buckboard and head for the ranch; I waited until morning and right after chuck; I stepped out to see if that outlaw could buck; standing in the corral out there all alone, was that cabillo a strawberry roan; he had a ewe neck and a long lower jaw; I could tell with one eye he's a regular outlaw; little pin ears that touch at the tip, a map of chewawa all over one hip; his legs were all slathered, they touched at the toes, little pig eyes and a big roman nose; I buckled my spurs on, I was sure feeling fine; I pulled down my old hat and I picked up my twine; I loaded the rope on him and well I knew then, that before I had rode him I'd sure earn my ten; first came the bridle, it sure was a fight; next came the saddle I screwed it down tight; then I got on him and slipped up the blind; then it was look out he's going to unwind; he bucked all around there, he went high and wide; I don't see how he kept, from losing his hide; he went up to the east and came down to the west, to ride this old pony, I sure did my best; I lost both my stirrups and also my hat; I grabbed for the leather just as blind as a bat; with a phenomenal jump, he went up on high and left me a setting up there in the sky; I turned over twice then I came down to earth; I lit up to cursing the day of his birth; I know there are ponies, I'm not able to ride; all of those lions; they haven't all died but I'll bet all my money there's no man alive, that can ride old Strawberry when he makes that high dive.

Jimmy Whittenburg was sometimes out on the Turkey Track Ranch adjacent the Whittenburg spread to the east. He would sometime come to visit us and work with us at whatever our assignment was. There was an old Chevrolet pickup on the ranch that Martin let Basil drive, and we did various jobs in that pickup. I don't really remember what the jobs were but what I do remember is that Basil had a wreck once while I was with him but nobody was hurt. The steering mechanism had a lot of play in it and this threw him off and he lost control and went into the ditch, but we didn't actually turn over as I recall. We sometimes got to go swimming at the Bugbe place that was on Jimmy's folk's property. Another thing I spent a lot of time doing while working in both Texas and New Mexico was getting somebody unstuck while they were driving a ranch vehicle. By doing that, I learned a lot about how to not get stuck and how to get unstuck, which served me well the rest of my life.

I never met a cowboy who compared with Lloyd Winfred in my opinion. Since this was the summer of 1946, good hands for the wages paid were virtually non-existent.

We had three or four miserable hands from back east that knew nothing about what they were doing.

Anyway, I got through the summer of 1946 with nothing very remarkable happening and it became time to go back to Principia for my 15-16-year-old year as a 2nd Ac. My parents or one of them would deliver me back and forth from the ranch to home, and I rode in the Pullman car of the train back to Principia for the 1946-1947 school year.

I remember two suite chiefs mainly during that year. One was named Ben Armstrong. I remember him well but don't remember many specific things about him except that it was while I was in his suite that Miss Eareckson sent over my superior reports. Another thing I remember was a suite-mate, whose name was Bill Jareo, who had a "runaway heart." He was quite a nice guy, but some thought he "wasn't playing with a full deck." Then again there was a guy named Bill Butler who thought I "wasn't playing with a full deck." I remember Ben Armstrong gave very deliberate instructions but was not anything like Jerry Gillespie or as high in my esteem. To Ben everybody was just another rather insignificant person. Another suite chief I remember was named August Jansen, who was from Holland. He was a very serious student and studied every spare minute he had and loudly complained at everybody making noise in the time periods that were not allotted by the school for studying. At the end of the school year however he received, by far, the most scholastic awards. This was the year Dave Parsons was a 4th Ac. He was definitely my roommate and probably my suite chief during this period. I definitely liked him the best of any upper classman I was with while being a 2nd Ac. Another upper classman that was my roommate and maybe my suite chief was named Dick Gillespie, who was not related to Jerry. This was his first attendance at Principia, but I did like him a lot.

There were some new students I remember and liked: Chuck Capcioppo, Bubs Whitney and Jane Dull. Another student I liked and have not mentioned before was named Dickey Arthur except in the above picture. His mother was a Hollywood insider. I think she was the movie star named Jeanne Arthur that was a star in "Shane" with Alan Ladd and a John Wayne movie "The Lady Takes a Chance." Anyway through him we got to go to "screenings" that were movies in the testing stage before they were actually released, and they were free to us. This is where we went on our free time Sunday afternoons a lot.

My art class was actually attended by all four grades. I believe Norman Evans was actually one grade ahead of me. When I was a 2nd Ac, he was a 3rd Ac. That year I think Norman's big brother Dick had graduated and gone since he was a 4th Ac the prior year. That year also there was a 4th Ac in the Art Class whom I liked a lot and was a good friend with named Dick Adams. I think he was a half brother to Jane Dull or at least related to her. He was a great athlete, a running back on the A football team., a good wrestler and boxer. I remember one year we had a wrestling program., and a boxing program. and Dick Adams boxed Dick Hedges. It was close. I don't remember who won, but they were both good. Dick Adams loved art and admired my art talent.

When I was a 2nd Ac, I was way too big to play on the C football team under Coach Craig and had to play on the B football team. The B team had a different coach named Mr. Phillip Edwards, whom I didn't like. He cared nothing about "guts." He only cared about how good of an athlete a person was. At that time I was in my 10-inch, 90-pound growth streak and quite uncoordinated. He would not play me in games and further he had a lot of anger toward me because, evidently, many team members pressed him to play me. Some on the team really liked me and thought I had the most "guts" of anybody.

I believe this was the actual year Miss Eareckson was hired by my mother to tutor me in English, since it was this year the superior reports were sent to the Dorm. Mr. Remington was the principal of Principia and although I didn't like him, he would have a huge influence on my life.

When it became basketball season, Wade McClusky was promoted up to the A Basketball team and was their best player. Bobby Mayor was also promoted to the A team.. They went 5-10, scoring a total of 508 points and allowing 524 points. So even though they only won 33.3 percent of the games, they scored 49.2 percent of the points scored. I know this by looking in my copy of the 1947 Principia Annual. I heard that in Wade's 3rd and 4th Ac years Principia won the league championship in basketball.

Above is a picture of the author about the time he finished Principia.

The above is a picture of Virginia and Harvey Ratliff in St. Louis, MO. in about 1946

All I remember about my 2ⁿᵈ Ac track season was that, due to my fast growth and accompanying clumsiness, I did no good.

By this year I seemed to have become the school event decorator of choice and would nearly always, with Norman's help, be decorating for some event. It was during this year that Principia, the human source I don't know, wrote a letter to my mother, which essentially said, "don't send your son to college. He is not college material." This is also the year that Mr. Remington, the principal, called me into his office and essentially told me that I should take no more math or science and from now on concentrate on becoming an artist to the exclusion of everything else. I had always thought I was good at math. My mother and my Uncle Roy had told me many times that I was. Further, my mother had told me that I should be an engineer, and that artists seldom were able to make a living or have a wife and family. Mr. Remington's assertions left me totally stunned and actually very angry. Principia in general had made it abundantly clear that my education was in terrible shape, and I had to get a hold of myself, and concentrate on repairing my education, but Principia had definitely given up on me. I would have to repair my education some place else.

Above is a photo of the author and his lifelong wife and sweetheart Clara Ratliff
at the Principia Reunion of June 2001.

Principia had done something else for me. I had been able to think back at events
of my passed life back at home from a much more objective perspective and began to
realize that it was my mother who was my real mentor, not my dad. She had always
given me the unconditional love that I desperately needed. My dad had always been
impossible for me to please, and I could feel no love from him. I don't think he had
much personal self-esteem and certainly had a very negative influence on my self-esteem.
My Uncle Roy, on the other-hand, had a very positive influence on my self-esteem,
which I needed badly. All of these things began to formulate in my mind.

Above is a photo of Mel Owen and the author at the Principia reunion of June 2001

Anyway, I got through my 2nd Ac year at Principia realizing I must drastically repair and work very hard on improving my education and preparing to be an Engineer. And, Principia was not the place to do the repairing because they had pegged me as a person, whom I didn't want to be. I still did not really understand what an Engineer really was. I only knew my mother had told me many times that an engineer is what I should be. I was also left with anger toward Principia that I didn't get over for years. It caused me to do something I will always regret. Once a prior Principian named Rodney Lee, whom I had liked while at Principia, was staying in Amarillo and wanted to associate with me, which I refused to do out of my great anger toward Principia.

By the time of my 16th summer, about all of my aunts and uncles except the youngest two, Aunt Helen and Tennessee, had joined Uncle Roy who had joined Uncle S.B. in trying to make the struggling Amarillo Times successful. It was a very difficult, ruthless and "for blood" battle against the Amarillo Globe News of that day. The Whittenburgs ultimately won the battle, but at a very high cost. My mother and most of her sisters and brothers including Uncle Roy accumulated huge debts during the process.

Part II

The Story of an Entrepreneur Who "Is Not College Material"

Rather than working on the ranch during the summer, my sister had been working for the Amarillo Times. I think Basil had worked for them last summer also. Anyway I decided to work for the Amarillo Times during my 16th summer. Uncle S.B. assigned me as an assistant photographer. It turned out that I was the assistant to a man named Maurice Leblanc, who was French. This was my first experience with a Frenchman. I did learn the process of taking and developing black-and-white pictures and various other things. But the main thing that really sticks in my mind about him was the strong effort he made to convince me that I was his complete inferior. He would demand that I scrub the photo lab room floor on my hands and knees. It wasn't so much the dirty job as it was his attitude, but I had never seen anybody do that before. The janitors used a mop. I was convinced that he did that and other things to show me how superior he was to me, and I resented it. "All men are created equal." Jefferson himself said so.

I think I must have complained to my mother, because I was living at home with her. Anyway, Uncle S.B. reassigned me to work in the engraving department with a man named Virgil Welch, whom I really liked. He was a full-blooded, red-blooded American, in those days that was a precious word. Life was much better and I learned more and did more constructive helpful things working with him. Through the engraving process we would prepare the pictures for printing on the newspaper. It was very interesting work. Virgil and I were friends ever after that. Some of his sons always entered a "Derby," the name of which I have forgotten. In this "Derby" boys, and maybe girls, would build cars which were big enough for the boys to ride in and were only powered by the earth's gravity to roll down a long, I think some 2 miles long, incline at the fastest rate. As I remember it his boys often won. The Amarillo Times sponsored the event.

Roy Whittenburg
Born Jan 11, 1913
CAPRICORN

A sketch made by the author July 11, 1948, when he was 17 years of age of Roy Whittenburg his Uncle as he sat and posed.

It was along about this time that my parents got knowledge of an artist, named Simon Michael, I believe, working out of Mineral Wells, Texas, near Breckenridge. My parents and I went to one of his shows and exhibits and were very impressed with his work. My parents worked it out for him to give me one or two three-to-four-hour periods of instruction. Those one or two short instruction periods were among the most valuable of my art instruction. I don't know what became of that artist, but I thought he was great. He taught me how to get depth in a picture just by realizing that light scatters and you must have more pale colors, as the depth gets greater. At Principia and from him I had learned to look at and really notice the sky.

The above photo is of the author and Mel Owen on his yacht the "Pat Pending" in June 2001.

Chapter V
Life After Leaving Principia Upper School

It became time to start my 11th year of schooling as a junior in high school. I don't remember why, but I started my junior year a Breckenridge High School. Looking back, the unsatisfactory results of this should have been predictable, but I vaguely remember my dad wanting me to go there really badly. Ray Graves had moved away. I think it was down to Stephenville, Texas. The instant I started back to school at Breckenridge, I was very popular. I was still real good friends with Jimmy Pate and was very welcome in two different gangs. One gang comprised Jimmy Pate, George Webber, Bill Boles, Jamie Bilhartz, Bobby Douglass, James "Smitty" Smith, Ralph Bufkin, Jimmy Gallagher, and others, whose names I have forgotten. These guys represented all three of the ward schools, east, south and north. The other gang comprised: Billy Woods, Henry Sorelle, Floyd Payne, J.L. Kite, "Booger Red" Nixon, Bob Vaber, and others whose name I can't think of. I had actually known Billy Woods and Floyd Payne back in the third grade at East Ward, but had not really been friends with them at that time. My friends even talked me into going out for the Breckenridge Buckaroo football team. Needless to say I was not repairing my education at Breckenridge. We had a great deal of fun. Maybe the most I ever had, but I was not repairing my education. It was along about this time the Possum Kingdom Lake had filled up and my dad had a very nice lot and boathouse on it. We also had many good times using that boathouse on that lake. We had an inboard Chris Craft Motor Boat and rode the surfboard and later the water-skis. I took my cousins: Jimmie Whittenburg, Claire, Deanie, Nancy, and the Walker boys, Basil and Jimmy, to that boathouse and lake. I, and some friends, loved to swim under water and underneath the boathouse. I loved to pull my self on the sub-structure pipes underneath the boathouse, which enabled much faster movement underneath the water.

My mother had an apartment; I believe it was in the Tallmadge Building quite close to Amarillo High School in Amarillo, Texas, where all her brothers and sisters were and where the ruthless business struggles were taking place. Therefore, it was possible to attend school at Amarillo High. I decided this was the only chance I had to repair my education. When I had a lot of friends and good times, I just couldn't study. Further, I found the math teachers at Breckenridge very inadequate. So, the second semester of my junior year I transferred to Amarillo High School. At this school I made absolutely no attempt to make friends and studied all the time available. Amarillo had much better math teachers than Breckenridge. I don't remember my algebra teacher's name, but she was excellent and was impressed with my performance. Breckenridge had never offered any art courses, but I took art all the time I attended Amarillo High. I took the entire math I could, art and all the required courses. I had started Spanish as my language option at Breckenridge, but was just not capable of being good in that subject although I tried hard but never liked it. We basically only studied Spanish vocabulary, which I have virtually forgotten. Also, soon after moving to Amarillo to attend school there, my aunt Nanny Mae Windsor talked me into going to her ophthalmologist, Dr. Frank Duncan. He examined my eyes finding me 20-400 in vision and told me that if I didn't wear glasses, I would go blind. I thought he was lying, but I was concentrating on studying now and not trying to make new friends; so, I did start wearing glasses and continued to the rest of my life. Aunt Nanny Mae's daughters Claire and Deanie were less than a year different in age from me. They were both good students, very popular and winners of many beauty and other honors at Amarillo High. Nancy was younger but also very popular, a good student and beautiful. About this time my mother bought the house that the Windsors had been living in at 2206 Hughes St. in Amarillo. Also, since I had long wanted a Doberman Pincher dog, I finally bought one shortly after moving to this house in Amarillo. I named him Satan after Howard Henderson's dog that I liked so much. He proved to be my lifetime favorite dog, but I never thought he would have been good around children and he was therefore the last Doberman I ever had. Anyway, I finished my junior year at Amarillo High and felt that I was finally making some headway in repairing my education.

It became time for my 17th summer. I believe this was the summer that Martin was transferred to a farm east of Amarillo, which was approximately 800 acres in area, and I was put to work plowing on that farm for all or most of the summer. Uncle Roy had a dream that Amarillo was going to be a cattle feeding center of America and on that farm he was beginning the building of a facility to be right in the middle of it. He was partly right. Amarillo did become the cattle-feeding center of America but for some reason we missed out on it. I believe it was because he priced us out of the market for our service. Anyway, I spent a summer plowing on that farm and digging a cesspool for the house Martin was living in.

"The Magnificent Cat" painted in oil by the author in 1949 while attending Amarillo High School.

I got through another summer. It was time to start my senior year in Amarillo High School. I took the required courses plus art, physics and trigonometry. What I remember most was my physics course, which changed my entire life. The teacher's name was Mrs. (or Miss) Walden. She was apparently not greatly impressed with me or I with her at first, but she, and physics, changed my entire life. She was a brilliant physics teacher. The book we used was "Modern Physics" by Charles E. Dull, copyright, 1939, 1943, and 1945 by Henry Holt and Company, Inc. At first, I hated the subject. She kept saying "its just common sense," but if you didn't understand certain things, it made no sense at all, I thought. However, after working hard for about a month, the subject started hitting a deep cord in me that I had been hungering for all my life. I just loved it, but it was a lot of work. I started telling everybody that I was going to be a physicist. My Uncle Roy certainly didn't like to hear that and immediately started trying to convince me otherwise. He equated physics to "looking at the stars," which I always thought was totally wrong. However, I settled back to becoming an engineer, which I see as being a physics artist or the application of physics to create or produce things that serve mankind.

There are interesting things I remember about that physics class. I was in the class with the valedictorian and salutatorian of the class, James Garner and Hubert Ralston respectively. As I remember it, James Garner, who was also a great athlete, made the highest grade average ever made at Amarillo High. Nearly everybody in the class sat at the same table with those two and checked their answers. I was mostly on a table by myself competing with them. Once a student and school athlete named Charles Seaber sat at the table with me and checked answers with me. I also found out many years later that the guy, Billy Creamer, who was president of my homeroom class and later became a good friend of mine, got through physics by having one of his friends break into my locker and he and others copied my work. He told me this shortly before he died "to make me feel good," he said. I had wondered why Mrs. (or Miss) Walden gave me funny looks sometimes, as if she thought I was cheating. Despite all these circumstances I received a 92 percent average which was still a B since an A was 93-100, a B was 85-92, a C was 77-84, a D was 69-76, an E was 61-75, and an F was 60 and below at Amarillo High.

I also remember my trigonometry teacher of that year named Mr. Underwood. I did well in that class too. I also remember sitting next to Hubert Ralston, who somewhat irritated me with his superiority attitude. Everybody loved James Garner, who was very modest in attitude. I thought he would be president of the United States. He played end on the Sandie football team., but he called all the plays, and the team went all the way to the state championship, but I think they lost that game. I did have one recreational activity that Principia had caused me to want to do. My sister dated a guy named Ben Waggoner for a while, whom I became good friends with. I had ordered the Joe Wieder Weight Lifting set and program, and so had he. We decided to work out together and become body builders, alternatively at his place, the Key Furr residence, and in the basement of our house at 2206 Hughes St.

Anyway I got through my senior year and graduated receiving my diploma from Amarillo High School feeling much better about the shape of my education and feeling as though I was a much better student. I was also much happier with the shape of my body. However, I now knew I would always have to work very hard at every endeavor I was to succeed in.

It became time for my 18th summer. This summer I decided to go back to work at the 35,000-acre spread in Hutchinson county. As I remember, this was a rather miserable summer since Martin sent me over to work at the Tarbox place under a man named Leonard Jones. Leonard was a brother-in-law of my Uncle S.B. whose wife had died, she being the sister of my Aunt Frances, Uncle S.B.'s wife. Apparently unknown to Uncle S.B., Leonard had a great amount of jealousy and anger toward Uncle S.B. since his wife had apparently been pointing out how much better her sister's life was. This anger was transferred to me through him and his son Ronald to the extent that it made life quite unpleasant for me. That summer was not a jewel.

In a time period between getting out of school and going out to the ranch my mother arranged for me to have a couple of my wisdom teeth pulled in Ft Worth, Texas. This is where Bill Williams now lived. He couldn't get in the military during World War II because he was burned all over his body; so, he found work in a defense plant in Ft Worth and he and his beautiful wife, Jane, were still there. I'm not sure whether the plant was still operating then or whether he was now working someplace else in Ft. Worth. Anyway, a big memory about that visit was once when Bill was talking to my mother about how he was always held in high esteem by his employers, or a similar conversation. I remember popping off and making the assertion that "you will never get ahead unless you go into business for yourself." You could have heard a pin drop for what seemed to be several minutes. My mother was put out with me for saying that and I felt bad about saying it, but apparently Bill really took that to heart because sometime later while visiting Breckenridge, Charley Hitchcock, one of Bill's many old friends, apparently made a special effort to come and tell me that Bill had been in Breckenridge looking for me. Bill was now in business for himself in Decatur, Texas. I never got to look Bill up after that and have always regretted it.

Another thing happened to me on that Ft. Worth trip that I'll never forget. I believe it was the first time I was robbed. Although I didn't figure it out until quite a while later, looking back I can remember how I was set up for the robbery. The porter was somehow tipped off that my wisdom teeth had just been pulled and I remember him specifically telling me to "hang my pants on this hook right here" pointing to the hook "and lie down right there in that bed." Like a fool I did what he said. I vaguely remember briefly being awake enough to vaguely remember some shadow of a person going over and fooling with my pants. When I tried to pay for a haircut later I noticed that I had been robbed of all the cash in the billfold. This was a pattern that would be similarly pulled on me in the future and, at some future date I would start looking for.

Chapter VI
Beginning My College Education

It became time to go to college. I'm not sure why, but I decided to attend Amarillo Junior College during my 1949-1950 year. Amarillo Junior College had a good reputation as a good place to get well founded for engineering in the freshman and sophomore years. I continued to concentrate on nothing but studying and bodybuilding while at AJC. I took the recommended freshman course for an engineering major. I received probably the most compliments from teachers while attending AJC. Dr. Bruce who taught trigonometry and analytical geometry gave me several and Dr. Devani, who taught descriptive geometry, was quite impressed because I solved the problems with the completely correct solution drawings quicker than anyone else, although my neatness was at B level along with my A level solutions. I remember my first semester English teacher was Miss Lucille Lynn and her course was entitled "College Rhetoric I." I remember being apprehensive about giving her a book report on a book about Thomas Paine, whom I highly admire. I tried hard but had not completely read the book, but the report actually went much better than I expected and I remember her telling me I should be an A English student. I don't believe I ever made above C in English and did make a C under her. I also remember my second semester English teacher was named Miss Doris Gail Crownover. I remember once in her class we were supposed to have read a book or a long article about Henry Ford and in the class after we were to have read it, she asked a question relating to what impressed us about Henry Ford? A girl held up her hand and when called upon she answered, "he said I don't like to read, it musses up my mind." Miss Crownover was very irritated with that answer, but couldn't refute it. I also remember clashing with her because, at that time, I was taken with my Uncle Roy's political views, which were Republican and she was clearly a Democrat in those days. I later found out that she was once engaged to Dr Allen Early, my sister's future husband.

Amarillo Junior College had mostly great teachers; however, they did have a teacher who was either the worst or second worse teacher in my esteem ever encountered by me in my college endeavors. I thought his purpose was to simply make life miserable for our class, mostly pre-med students who were the largest percentage of his chemistry students. Anyway, I don't believe anybody learned a thing in his chemistry class even though it was a nightmare. The class average was very low; I think about 22 percent before the curve. I think everybody passed after the curve, but learned nothing and was miserable doing it. He presented it in such a way that there was no way I could find to study and learn the subject. Anyway, I did get through my freshman college year doing well and feeling good with my grades except for that chemistry course. Unfortunately and sadly, while I was attending Amarillo Junior College my aunt Nannie Mae Windsor died of cancer and it was hard to get through that.

My 19th summer was the last spent working out on a ranch as a cowboy in Uncle Roy's program. I worked again out on the Hutchinson County ranch. To tell the truth I have very little memory about that summer on the ranch except that I had lost my enthusiasm about working as a cowhand on a ranch and in ranching in general. I was not very impressed with the caliber of people out on the ranch, and I didn't feel there was a good future in this field. I had my eyes on engineering.

It came time for my 1950-1951-college year. I don't remember why, but I did decide to go to the University of Texas in Austin, Texas. My then mentor, and near a personal idol, Uncle Roy strongly thought I should join a social fraternity while attending the University of Texas. Down deep I very well knew from passed experience that it was a mistake, but due to his opinion I did pledge Pi Kappa Alpha fraternity. I really liked the guys in the fraternity, but the result was the same as it had always been in the past, if I'm not studying to the point of excluding or minimizing the interaction with people, my schoolwork is inadequate. As a result of this and even though I did finally break my pledge, my grades were too low with the result that I was drafted into the army during the Korean "War," I think it was really a war but the politicians were not honest about it. It also didn't help that I encountered what I thought was the worst teacher of my career as a student. He was very angry that he had to teach at all, as he wanted to only do research. His writing was totally illegible with the result that I could never figure out what the assignment was or whether there was one. His speech was much too fast and unintelligible. It was virtually impossible in his class to learn or accomplish anything.

There were positive results of my attendance at U.T.; I took my last English course. This course had a major influence on my life. The official name of it was "Technical Writing," however there were two unexpected but very significant results of this course. If I had realized how important this course would be to my later life, I would have remembered the fortuitous teacher's name, but I'm sorry to say I've forgotten it. One of these results was we deeply studied evolution in that class. That subject was very interesting to me. This was the first place I remember ever even hearing of evolution. This had a big influence on me. I believe, from the apparent evidence, the education system of my experience had until then suppressed the teaching of certain science, especially the science involving evolution.

This actually is unconstitutional, the Constitution states that congress "shall have the power to promote progress in science and the useful arts" but the Constitution does not say the Congress or any governmental branch shall have the power to promote the Christian or any religion at all. The Constitution, in the first provision of the "Bill of Rights" strictly prohibits the making of any law establishing a religion. The Constitution, in its body, also strictly prohibits the use or regard of religion in selecting any person for any governmental position having any power at all.

Another very positive result of that technical writing class was that I was required to write a technical paper. While at U.T., I also took weight lifting to meet my physical education requirement. In that class were most of the people who turned out to be my real friends while at U.T. One of my friends of that class was named Billy Barnes. He was an electrical engineering major. At that time I thought I was going to be a civil engineer as recommended by Uncle Roy. In talking with Billy Barnes, he gave me some electronic papers on the details of how the television works. From reading these papers I worked up my technical report. In the process I solidified a lot of knowledge in my mind about electronics, which caused me to score high in electronics tests when I joined the army. This proved quite significant as to my future in the army.

Another positive thing happened to me while attending U.T. I saw two movies that proved to have a huge influence on my life. One movie was entitled "The Fountainhead" with Gary Cooper, Raymond Massey and Patricia Neal. This movie was based on Ayn Rand's magnificent book of the same name and made a huge impression on me, haunting me the rest of my life because it struck at the very core of my being.

Briefly, this was a story about a very original deeply thinking creator of architecture named Howard Roark in a world dominated by altruistic, parasitic negotiating collectivist epitomized by Ellsworth Toohey who detested true creators of wealth and sought ultimate power including power to make people such as Howard Roark their unrewarded slave. The story was reinforced by a beautiful romance between Howard Roark and Dominique Frankon, and, also, reinforced by a newspaper owner named Gail Wynand.

As a result of this movie, I determined my life long goal, which was to create and principally to use science to create or produce things to benefit mankind. Strangely, I just happened in on that movie and didn't learn the name of the movie or its author and although it continuously haunted me, it took decades after I was married for me to locate it. My Uncles Roy, Joe and maybe S.B. seemed very unimpressed with my new goal and showed the ugly face of Ayn Rand's *Ellsworth Toohey* about it. My Uncle Joe, who I believe was always my Uncle Roy's spokesman when he knew I would deeply dislike what was said, told me *there is no significance or value to such a goal.* This highly negatively impressed me. It starkly looked like they were on the side of *Ellsworth Toohey* to me. Another thing happened at U.T. While taking a break once, I started a conversation with a guy and he went on and on about what a great man Thomas Jefferson was. I also saw the movie "Born Yesterday" with Judy Holliday and William Holden. I believe it was here that I began to gain my life long great esteem for Thomas Jefferson. Some of Jefferson's words as I remember them follow:

"I have sworn upon the alter of God eternal hostility against every form of tyranny over the mind of man." And

"We hold these truths to be self-evident that all men are created equal and endowed by their creator with certain unalienable rights and among these rights are life, liberty and the pursuit of happiness; in order to secure these rights, governments are instituted among men, deriving their just powers from the consent of the governed, and when governments become destructive to these ends, it is the right of the people to alter them or abolish them." These words would burn in my mind for the rest of my life.

To me the perfectly naturalist essence of the Declaration of Independence and the Bill of Rights is each citizen of America has the right to be oneself to the greatest extent

possible without interfering with each other citizen's right to do the same thing. It is even better if one enhances other people's rights and happiness by being oneself, which is the essence of free enterprise at its best. I have never been able to reconcile this essence with that of the supernaturalist belief that each human is born evil, i.e., a sinner, and can only be saved from his evilness, i.e., sin, by the grace of God, a supernatural being, who died on the cross because each human is born evil, i.e., a sinner, and by believing certain things one undergoes a change giving him or her the God-like supernatural power of eternal life, but in the meantime one can never actually be good and God does it all anyway.

I was politically confused for a long time. The Democratic Party was supposed to be the party of Thomas Jefferson and Franklin Roosevelt had the Jefferson Memorial built, which to me is the greatest memorial of all time. So, I thought they must have been trying to do what is right. It didn't occur to me for a long time that *they were actually replacing the Jeffersonian Republic with Hamiltonian Statism. The Republicans seemed to be on the side of the same group of people that Hamilton was for, i.e., the rich parasitic negotiators who negotiate the wealth created by its creators away from them and unto themselves, whereas Jefferson seemed to be for the true creators of wealth, i.e., the individual farmers, scientist, inventors, educators, miners, engineers, fine artists, builders and laborers.* And, the Republicans also have since joined the Democrats to transform the Jeffersonian Republic into Hamiltonian Statism.

Also while at U.T., I believe I attained the greatest physic and physical strength of my life. I was doing 12 repetitions of dead lifts with 400 pounds, 12 repetitions of overhead presses with 135 pounds and 12 repetitions of bench presses with 150 pounds. The dead lifts that I did were the Joe Wieder type, the ones in which your legs are straight and you entirely lift with your spinal erector muscles. Today it appears to me that some modern "athlete," who is afraid of being sued in this litigious society, has ruined untold numbers of backs by teaching that one should develop all the muscles in the body except the spinal erector muscles. The terrible results of this should be obvious even to lawyers, some litigants of which have strengthened the *Ellsworth Toohey* element destructive to creators and made life in the United States much worse these days. I attribute my strong spinal erector muscles as the reason I have never had back problems in my 72-year life.

By the time I had realized that my grades were too low I made a futile attempt to join the Navy, but it was too late. I was drafted into the army. I was processed by the draft board in Amarillo, Texas. Although it was set that I was drafted, it wasn't until after my 20th fall in October of 1951 that I was actually taken into the army. During the summer of 1951, I talked Uncle Roy into letting me observe him through the summer to get an idea of what I might expect if I did the things in later life that I thought he was preparing me for. Ayn Rand's *Ellsworth Toohey* kept showing his ugly face. Although I remained in denial for years, that summer I began to gather evidence that my Uncle Roy had many hidden agendas that he wanted me to know nothing about. This is really the prominent thing I began learning that summer.

Chapter VII
In The Army During The Korean Conflict

It finally did come time in October 1951 for me to be inducted into the army. The woman in charge at Amarillo was related to Ray Snead, who was by now the husband of Aunt Nannie Mae's oldest daughter, Claire. The result of this was that I was put in charge of the draftees while we were transported from Amarillo to Fort Sill, Okla. On the trip to Fort Sill, I became good friends with a fellow inductee named Rex Foster, whom I never saw after leaving Fort Sill, but I still have a photograph of him and me while at Fort Sill.

The above is a picture from left of Harvey Ratliff and Rex Foster shortly after being tested into the Army while being tested at Fort Sill, Okla.

We arrived at Fort Sill Oklahoma and were awakened at 5 a.m. the next morning, as I recall, we started an extensive battery of tests that lasted for, it seemed, two weeks. Those tests opened a lot of doors for me. From them, I had the opportunity to become an officer by going to Officers Cadet School. This I chose not to do because I would have had to sign up for four active years and I really was not struck with desire for a military career in a war that we were forbidden to win. What I really wanted to do was create things, anyway. I didn't know it then, but from those tests, they would send me to radio repair school (principally because of my technical writing course and high school physics course) after basic training. After going through these tests they sent me to Camp Gordon, Ga., near Augusta for my eight-week basic training course.

At Camp Gordon, our Sergeant, whose name regretfully I can't remember, was known as "Sergeant Gig" because he gave out more demerits than anybody there. He was from Connecticut and really conscientiously did his job very well, but he was hard and demanded a lot from us. I don't really specifically remember what we did, but we only averaged five hours of sleep a night, marched many miles, set through many training classes, went on many bivouacs and obstacle courses, had shooting practices with various weapons, M-1, Carbines, various automatic (machine-gun type) weapons and other things. We would have to crawl under arrays of bullets zooming inches above our bodies. When I would get still, I could hardly stay awake. It was hard. It seemed to take forever but I finally got through basic training in the first two months and was sent through the radio repair program. At Camp Gordon, which was supposed to take eight months.

The above is a picture of the author while attending Radio Repair School in Camp Gordon, Ga.

Our first course was "Direct Current," or D.C. I had a 100-percent average through that course mostly because of my high school physics course. The second course was "Alternating Current," or A.C. I had a 99-percent average through that course for the same reason. This was mostly due to my high school physics really, but it was somewhat due to that Technical Report. After that we got into "Capacitors" (sometimes known as "Condensers"), "Induction Coils," resistors and resistance, ohm's law, i.e., $E = IR$, e.g., 1 volt equals 1 amp times 1 ohm, harmonic frequencies, radio waves, audio waves, modulating audio waves onto radio waves, frequency modulation, fm, and amplitude modulation, am, transmitting the modulated radio waves, receiving radio waves, tuning by harmonic frequencies to their frequencies and detecting the audio waves off of the radio waves and reproducing them on the speakers. We got into vacuum tubes, which actually is what the Cathode Ray tube of the early television sets were. At that time all radios had to use vacuum tubes. There were no transistors, which came later. Next we studied all the radios in use by the army at the time the course was planned out. My grades were never as good as they were in the first two courses but my average was well over 90 percent. The teaching method was that the teacher would lecture a certain amount of time on each subject. After the lecture was finished, with no study opportunities, we were given a multiple-choice test afterward, which was the basis of our grade.

We went through a period that we were switched to night school, which meant we went to school during the night and slept during the day. The first night hardly anyone could stay awake. The redeeming feature about night school was we would get three-day weekends. It was on some of these three-day weekends that I went to visit Glenna Bowman in South Carolina, her home.

At the eight-month school I developed several friends and acquaintances. I remember John O. Webb, who was my best friend while there, and in general a great friend. He was from Dearborn, Mich. I wanted to go visit him but never have. He invited me to his wedding even, but I failed to attend that also. I forget why. He had three other friends, the Steinman twins, William and Wilber, and a guy whose last name was Roose. I was more or less included in their gang. I also had acquaintances that weren't really friends. One was named Joe Sweeney who was about six-feet tall and weighed at least 400 pounds His dad was the police chief in Lawrence Mass. I don't know why but from later experience I learned that Joe developed a secret hatred for me that I was not then aware of but would learn at high cost later. At that time I was caught up in my Uncle Roy's Republican philosophy. This may have contributed to his hatred for me, and if not, he could later use that against me because almost everybody in the army was a democrat at that time.

While in radio repair school, I had an appendicitis attack and was subsequently operated on to take it out. During the process my mother came to visit for which I was very grateful. While there she did some nice things for John O. and his wife-to-be. This operation set me back a month. Fortunately for me, in the class I graduated in, I was second in the class and therefore had the option of spending the rest of my army career teaching, which I probably should have done, or going to fixed station radio repair school in Fort Monmouth, N. J., which I chose to do. The only negative thing about my eight-month, (that turned into nine months actually) radio repair course was, although I knew the theory very well, when it came to fixing the sets the only one worse than me was the one who was first in the class. Actually when one thinks about it, the principles of how a radio actually works are of little help in repairing a radio which involves looking at the radio with the cover removed for a damaged part such as a resistor, condenser, coil or vacuum tube. The guy who was best at repairing radios barely had a passing grade in the course. His last name was Evans. I can't remember his first name. It may have been Tom.

By now it was September 1952, eleven months had passed since I was inducted into the army, and I was 21 years of age and was stationed in Fort Monmouth, N. J., to attend the two-month Fixed Station Radio Repair School. All I really remember about this school was that I got through it with over a 90-percent average and did well. It was either while here or while at the radio school at camp Gordon that I did contact Glenna Bowman the Principia girl whom I had a crush on but upon thinking about it I'm almost certain it was while in night school at Camp Gordon that I visited her. I visited Glenna at her home a couple of three-day periods and we had a lot of fun, but she was too attached to someone else. I didn't know it then, but that was a blessing.

It was while I was in radio repairs school and mostly fixed station radio repair school with some spare time that my mother and I collaborated to write the article of **Appendix B.** I wrote letters in longhand and she corrected and typed them. As one can see my ideals have gone through some changes since then but are still much the same. I never knew why but my aunts and uncles and maybe my mother didn't want it published, but J.C. Phillips published it anyway in the Borger News Herald. Recently I have read on audio Ayn Rand's "Atlas Shrugged" and was amazed to find that it was on the same theme.

Including about a month leave, I wound up only spending about nine months overseas in Germany.

On the ship going overseas I remember being set up for a robbery and being robbed again. While on KP duty I remember stupidly asking the sergeant where to put my jacket. With a stunned look on his face, he said on that chair right there and pointed to it. I did what he said. After KP, I could not find my jacket anywhere. Later over the intercom of the ship someone said they had a jacket, which was described such that I thought it was mine. I enthusiastically and gratefully went up to retrieve it. After I exhorted my enthusiastic gratitude and explained how someone had changed my inititials on the jacket, the Lieutenant, with a strange look on his face he said, "You know you have been honest with me, and I'm going to believe you." Only then did I realize that that sergeant didn't want my coat. He wanted the officer's coat and had switched my jacket for the officer's jacket and was trying to convince the officer that I had stolen the officer's coat. In short the sergeant was trying to frame me for his crime Soon the Lieutenant got his jacket back and the gig was over. Whew, that was a close one.

After having leave before going overseas I wound up at 322 Signal Corps in Darmstadt, Germany, in December 1952. I could not get used to the German cold weather and didn't warm up until spring. The German people were very nice. I liked them. I could have and probably should have enjoyed my stay in Germany more than I did. I don't know how I wound up in Germany but felt fortunate to be there, since I was not sold on the idea of dying in a war we were prohibited from winning. However, I went through some unhappy times while there. It worked out that right after I arrived, a Sergeant Fisher came over to our radio repair unit and I made the mistake of smiling at him. He asked the sergeant in charge of the repair unit, who's name I've regretfully forgotten, if he could take me over to his small motor repair unit. This resulted in my being transferred over to become his assistant. The effect was that all my expensive training was for nothing. Instead of having the MOS of a radio repairman that I was trained to be, I was then to be reduced to the MOS of a small engine repairman, which I was not trained for and didn't really like. I liked Sergeant Fisher as a person but thought it ridiculous that I was not doing what I was trained for. First of all, this made Sergeant Fisher my enemy. Second, this got me into a lot of trouble otherwise and made my stay there miserable.

I went to the only person there I knew, Joe Sweeney, who secretly hated me and who had an inside track with the sergeant in charge of the radio repair unit and was well liked by him because he had been there long enough to be good at his job and who was in the first group with me at Camp Gordon Radio Repair School as described before. I think he also held a grudge against me for getting to go to Fixed Station Radio Repair School and maybe he was an Ellsworth Toohey disciple; who knows? I asked him if he knew a way to get me transferred back to the job I was trained for. He said he thought so and did but in the process he really set me up for a lot of misery. I had virtually no friends that could or did help me over there after that. I did have a pleasant experience while overseas in the army. My sister, who had just been married while I was overseas, as I recall, and her new husband Allen Early came overseas, and we met in Paris. We went to London for the Queen's Carnation; saw Switzerland, Belgium, Holland and other places. It was great. However, I had more unpleasant experiences with Frenchmen while waiting in Paris to meet Allen and Virginia. To me the movie "European Vacation" with Chevy Chase describes the French person perfectly.

I will describe some of the things that did happen to me over there. While we were on bivouacs we were under Sergeant Grady King, who was black. Actually he was probably the nearest thing I had to a friend while there. He really kind of sympathized with me, but he wanted to shed his responsibility of being the driver of the bivouac truck. So, guess who got sent to truck driving school. It was I, of course, even though I didn't want to. Joe secretly thought for sure he could get me in real trouble if I drove the truck. In Grady's bivouac crew was Joe Sweeney, a guy named Walter Burkman, and a guy named Pete Gonzales and me. They made bivouacs as miserable as they could for me. I remember on one bivouac trip, Sergeant Fisher, who was the caravan leader and I suspect Joe Sweeney had a plot to get me lost. As a result, they got the truck behind me lost, which meant they got everyone in the battalion lost except me. Once they tricked me into backing into the repair unit sergeant's car. A truck driver must have a person outside properly guiding him while backing up. The truck driver is totally dependent on the one guiding him. However, that was actually the beginning of this sergeant's coming over to my side, against Joe. Joe gradually began to lose favor with that sergeant because of his vendetta against me. They, Joe and others, tried to get me in trouble with the officer in charge of all of us. But, that backfired. I noticed that for some reason the officer had me drive him around long enough for him to take a good look at me. Later I noticed the officer was always quite nice to me every time he saw me after that and once when he saw me at the Post Exchange he introduced me to his daughter. But the hatred of Joe and some of the people he had influenced over to his vendetta just made life unpleasant. There was a guy named Clayton Reynolds who lived in the same barracks that I did, but who had another MOS (military occupational status) from me and therefore couldn't help me much, but he sympathized with me. He loved to call Joe Sweeney "Sidney Greenstreet", a the character in the Bogart movies such as Casa Blanca. There was another little Italian American named Jimmy Morocco he loved to call him "Peter Lori." He would call them Peter Lori and Sidney Greenstreet all the time. They didn't like that much, but I it secretly tickled me. However, I had nearly worked my way out of the problem when I was shipped back to the states.

Another unpleasant thing happened while I was overseas; my dad, at 55 years of age, had the first of his many strokes. My brother-in-law, Allen was with him when it happened at a fishing lodge in Pearl Lakes, Co., which lodge my dad and his friend Cliff Haggard owned. Although my dad did not die from either a stroke or a heart attack, he had some three heart attacks and over a dozen strokes before he did die of something else.

Chapter VIII
A Civilian Again

Finally I got through that most miserable experience in Darmstadt and they shipped me back to the states in September 1953 when I was 22 years of age. I was really drafted for eight years, two of which were active duty and six of which were in the inactive reserves. As soon as arriving back in Texas, I enrolled in Texas Technological College as it was named back then as a petroleum engineering student. While in the army I decided that is what I wanted to be. Mr. Phillip Johnson of the Petroleum Engineering Department enrolled me. He saw how poor my record had been during my bad year at U.T. and would hold that against me during my entire attendance at Tech, but apparently never told anybody else. He was also the man, in petroleum engineering, whose job it was to "sort the men from the boys." I missed two days of class and was on track to continue my college education.

I had now been in the United States Army. That had several effects on me. It reinforced the discipline learned at Principia. It made it very clear to me how important it was to obtain a college education. It had strengthened my technological skills. It had bred a strong determination to do well in school. It even went a long way toward paying for a college education.

The first semester curriculum at Texas Tech as, it was often called even then, included a 5-credit hour differential and integral calculus course, a 4-credit hour physics course, a 4-credit hour chemistry course, a 3-credit hour physical geology course and a 3-credit hour economics course. I arose at 6 a.m. every morning spent the day either in the classroom, eating breakfast, lunch and supper or in the College Library until 10 p.m. every night studying every chance I had. When I returned to the dorm I went right to bed. I had very little human involvement. I basically never had any problems with my roommate, whom at that time was a guy named Jack Arbuckle or later roommates, we went to bed at 10 p.m. every night and I was up at 6 a.m. the next morning.

At the end of that semester I had made an "A" in calculus in which I had a 100 percent average going into the final and made a 93 percent on the final. This was the first "A" I ever made in a math course. The teacher, Mrs. (or Miss) Roberts made a lot of requirements that a lot of students took a dim view of such as knocking off 10 points if you didn't put your name correctly on the assignment or test paper. To me these were just easy points. We had a pop quiz at the beginning of each class. This was a bonanza for me because I would study for an hour just before attending class and it gave me an easy 100 percent pop quiz average and reinforced my knowledge for the six-week tests. I made a "B" in physics, but only one student did better than me in the class of some 40 students, and he beat me by only one percentage point. His last name was Wine, but I can't remember his first name. The book we used was "Physics" by Erich Hausmann, E.E., Sc.D. and Edgar P. Slack, S.B., M.S. Third edition-eighth printing, copyright, 1935, 1939, 1948 by D. Van Nostrand Company Inc. I made an "A" in chemistry, which was probably the best-taught course I have ever encountered in a school. The book was "College Chemistry" by Paul R. Frey, Professor of Chemistry Colorado A and M College, Copyright, 1952, by Prentice-Hall, Inc., fourth printing August 1953. Each week, which for this course comprised Monday, Wednesday and Friday, we would be given an assignment from a well-written completely clear Text Book that wrote all the important concepts in italics. The teacher would completely go over all the subject matter emphasizing the important concepts set forth in the book again to reinforce it and the last day of the week we would go to a big laboratory holding several classes in which all the concepts of that week would be demonstrated in the laboratory. That course enabled me to make an "A" in every chemistry course I took at Tech in my future years at Tech. I made an "A" in physical geology and loved the subject. It was relatively easy since non-majors were in the class. I believe the geology teacher's name was Mr. Arper. To my surprise I made an "A" in my economics course and really enjoyed the course. Economics was the only non-science, non-math course (however it was more scientific than any other "non-science" course I took) I could make an "A" in, however due probably to my weak reading ability. So, I started off with a great grade-point average, which really helped me all the way through Tech. That figures: 53 grade points for 19 hours or a grade-point average of 2.79 on the 3-point scale that Tech used.

I really don't remember the other semesters nearly so well and never did quite that well again. I believe in my second semester at Tech I had a 2.50 grade-point average. Later I was in geology courses with geology and petroleum engineering majors which were harder. I was also in Phillip Johnson's petroleum engineering courses and although I did "A" work, he always gave me a "C", which were the only "C" grades I received at Tech. But I graduated in the top 10 percent or at least high enough to get into Tau Beta Pi and Pi Epsilon Tau, the Honorary Engineering Fraternity and Honorary Petroleum Engineering Fraternity respectively.

Also, in the second and third semester I took American history, which I loved but could not make an "A" in, making only "B". The textbook was "The Stream of American History" Volume One and Two, by Leland D. Baldwin, University of Pittsburgh, Copyright, 1953, by American Book Company. An interesting thing to me was that it devoted a large number of pages to the relatively short period of time that the struggle between Jefferson and Hamilton had during Washington's presidency. This to me was certainly justified because it has been playing through American history ever since.

While pledging Pi Epsilon Tau I did have to stay up all night with the pledges a couple of times. I think it was while in my third semester at Tech that while in the pledging or joining procedures of Pi Epsilon Tau that I made a big impression on the upper classmen. They elected me as their most outstanding pledge or a similar honor. One of them was named Alan Olsen. He was very impressed with me. I was also very impressed with him. He built models of oil drilling derricks. He had great ones that he built. I think his dad owned a drilling company. He was in charge of the Petroleum Engineering Show that year and he caused me to be selected as the one in charge of the Petroleum Engineering Show the next year. They were also talking about making me president of the AIME at Tech, which was the national organization for petroleum engineers at that time since there was then no SPE. All my newfound popularity really shook me up and put me in a dilemma I didn't figure out how to solve. I knew the history of my grades capitulating when I tried to mix studying with heavy human involvement and what is worse I didn't know how to explain my problem to anyone without ruining my effort to get a degree in pet. eng. Additionally, I had just met a girl while on Christmas vacation or some occasion back at Amarillo whose name was Rachel Stanford.

Due to these dilemmas and pressures and the grind of studying virtually all the time, I dropped out of Texas Tech after these three semesters probably using Rachel as a scapegoat reason for the time period of January 1955 to January 1956.

One thing that happened after dropping out was that I read a book about Johnson O'Connor's Human Engineering Laboratory. Johnson O'Connor was actually a Physicist and started working on his system while General Electric employed him, as I understand it. Mrs. Early, Allen's mother, gave me this book. I liked Johnson's approach to human ability. Regardless of the reason a person has their abilities or what is now known as DNA? There are only two choices: to nurture the DNA or not nurture the DNA. If the DNA of human abilities is like the DNA of a rose, one can't change the rose into another flower such as an orchid. That only amounts to not nurturing the rose. Likewise one can't change one's ability or DNA that just amounts to not nurturing your ability or DNA. A person can't even change their DNA by being a born again Christian into eternal life or by becoming a member of the Christian faith. There is no supernatural change in the DNA. DNA is like a fingerprint in that one cannot change it. To me, this is conclusive proof that either a person is already born with access to eternal life regardless of his or her belief or a person has no access to it regardless of his or her belief. The tyranny of belief control has no truthful basis. The science of DNA has proved a lot of truths that the astronomical human ego has a very hard time accepting. The huge human ego loves to believe things like a supernatural God made humans in his supernatural image and gave us supernatural powers such as access to eternal life, with its implied supernatural DNA change, that other animals don't have access to and basically put us on an earth that is flat and at the center of the Universe with all the heavenly bodies rotating around it and further gave human's dominion over all the other animals, plants and minerals of the earth to do with as we please. In Christian States before the birth of our wonderful United States, untold numbers of people have been murdered merely for telling truths such as the earth is spherical and is not the center of the universe. In the 30 Year War over differing supernaturalist beliefs, i.e., not based on reason, in the State of Germany, alone, some 16 million Germans met their death, which was half its population. The greatest loss sustained by the U.S. was 0.6 million in the Civil War. We lost only some 0.45 million in World War II. Even though there were over 22 million military deaths reported and over 33 million civilian deaths estimated in that war, these numbers don't look very big as compared to, for example, losing half the U.S. population in a supernaturalist war like the 30 Year War. DNA science actually reveals that man's DNA differs from a Chimpanzee's by less than 1 percent according to "DNA The Secret of Life" by James D. Watson, who along with Francis Crick received the *Nobel Prize* for their scientific work with regard to DNA and who was rated the greatest *living* human in the last 1000 years by A&E's list of the top 100 of the millennium. In that list Edison was first, Jefferson second, Washington third, Lincoln fourth, Ford fifth and Watson and Crick sixth among the Americans in the list. The first five of these are deceased. Worldwide Edison was 14th, Jefferson was 15th, Washington was 21st, Lincoln 23rd, Ford 29th, and Watson and Crick were 31st. All the people ahead of Watson are deceased. (Crick did die in about July 2004). This book's copyright was in 2003 by DNA Show LLC. DNA science also shows man branched off from the chimp some 5 million years ago, the gorilla branched off from the chimp some 10 million years ago and the orangutan branched off some 17 million years ago. That puts man, as a species, right in the middle of the great apes. Can man's astronomical ego ever swallow the truth? Anyway I took the Johnson O'Connor tests and concluded from them that I was laying the foundation for pursuing my true abilities from wherever they came. Please note that in America you have the inalienable right to be yourself as long as you aren't stopping others from doing the same thing and Johnson O'Connor intended to help you do just that.

Johnson's test broke abilities down into, not just one "IQ." He broke them down into many aptitudes with different aptitude patterns determining the type of work or activity a person should pursue. He worked hard to assure that aptitudes as measured by him had no relationship to knowledge. He also tested vocabulary, which he equated to knowledge levels (general and specialized), and recommended techniques for improving the levels. In his vocabulary tests a person has to know the exact meaning of a word to answer correctly. His Laboratory knows all the stages of learning the meaning of the word and puts a choice in the multiple-choices on the test for every stage. The tests aren't like many multiple-choice tests where most of the wrong choices are obviously wrong. His aptitude-based approach makes sense. From what I knew then, IQ tests made no sense to me and were ridiculous. My highest aptitudes were foresight 100 percentile, drawing 100 percentile (my score was perfect), which was then measured by the laboratory, subjectivity 89 percentile (100 percentile on one test and 78 percentile on another) and tonal memory 96 percentile. Unlike Ayn Rand's system, in Johnson O'Connor's system subjective people are individualist or individual workers and objective people are collectivist or group workers. Put another way subjective people see a human as the wheel itself while objective people see a human as one of the many cogs in the wheel. My second highest aptitudes were structural visualization 84 percentile (wiggly-block-69 percentile, cube-82 percentile, form-board-98 percentile and paper-folding-85 percentile) and memory-for-design 87 percentile (it was actually rated "A" which means anywhere between 75 percentile and 100 percentile). They later found that the drawing aptitude was structural visualization and memory for design in combination. It is interesting that: $(1-0.84) \times (1-0.875) = 0.02$, which would be 98 percentile. I was also high in ideaphoria (rate of idea flow) 60 percentile. They found me low in analytical reasoning, 20 percentile, and inductive reasoning, 32 percentile, which I was shocked about. However, this was an excellent aptitude pattern for a creative engineer (creative people are virtually always low on their inductive reasoning test) and foresight is the key aptitude for an entrepreneur, and I think it helps an inventor. It is actually a form of imagination. The aptitude was discovered while the laboratory was looking for an alternative test for ideaphoria that didn't depend on writing speed. In what I thought were the "good student" or "high IQ" aptitudes: silograms (language ability) and graphoria (clerical ability) I scored a low 16 percentile in silograms (14 percentile in the "not-isolated" and 21 percentile in the "experimental" section of the tests) and 47 percentile in graphoria. I was slightly below average in graphoria but far below it in silograms. This revealed to me why I was a poor reader and student having to work so hard. I think a 16 percentile score in the silograms test is also a good indication that I'm dyslexic, but this is just a layman's opinion on that subject. My sister scored 99 percentile in silograms. My below-average graphoria was why it was hard for me to make an "A" in math although "A" math students would seek help from me even when I could not make higher than a "B" in subjects such as analytic geometry. But, with enough cleverness and study it was good enough that I still was able to, with hard work, at Tech later. It is interesting that during December of 2003, I was on line and noticed the opportunity to take the "Emode IQ" test. I took the test and from my score they said my IQ is 131. They said 95 percent of all the people who take the test score with an IQ between 70 and 130. This leaves 2.5 percent above 130 and 2.5 percent below 70. So, I scored in the top 2.5 percent. In their description of my type of intelligence, they said: "You've got a very experimental way of learning and a strong mathematical mind. You're able to whittle even the most complex situation down to comprehensible component parts. In short, you have mastered the art and science of precision. That's what makes you a Precision Processor." They said: "Because of the way you process information, these are just some of the many careers in which you could excel: scientist, mathematician, accountant, data analyst, musician, astronomer, researcher, physicist." They broke my intelligence down into four parts: Mathematical Intelligence, in which I was 100 percentile, Visual-Spatial Intelligence, in which I was 80 percentile, Linguistic Intelligence, in which I was 90 percentile, and Logical Intelligence, in which I was 100 percentile. At this time of writing, 12/2003, I am 72 years of age and have been listening to lots and lots of audio books on tape and CD (some 50 or more books). I was very pleased, but shocked, that I had scored 90 percentile in Linguistic Intelligence. Other than that, this test actually depicted my mentality more like I, in my gut, had always thought it was, but nobody else seemed to think so except maybe my mother. My rhetorical question is: "Where was this test when I needed it?" I believe this is the first time I knowingly scored over 50 percentile in linguistics on a test.

Rachel had lived in Amarillo and was a friend of my double-cousin Pattie Whittenburg, whose dad was my dad's first cousin and my mother's second cousin. We had met while she was visiting Pattie. I drove to Eugene, Ore., her new home that she claimed to hate, in my 1955 Bell-Air Chevrolet, my lifelong favorite vehicle, and tried to convince Rachel that we should marry. To make a long story short, this finally brought out the fact that she was in love, or at least thought so, with a man named Tom Laird from Eugene and they wound up getting married. Which again was a blessing for me even though I didn't realize it until later.

During part of this time period and during some of the summers while at Tech, I would do surveying and mapping work, known as cartography in some circles outside Uncle Roy's, for my Uncle Roy on the Baker Ranch and on the Hutchinson County ranch in Texas. I checked out all the section surveys and made various maps of these ranches.

I knew that I really had to wait until January 1956 to start back at Texas Tech; so, I decided to enroll in the Kansas City Art Institute in Kansas City Mo. Art was one subject I could successfully take and still be highly involved with people. I developed several friends while there. My best Friend was named Darrell Dishman from Lawrence, Kan., as in "Dark Command" with John Wayne, Roy Rogers, Walter Pigeon and Claire Trevor. I went to Darrel's home in Lawrence a few times and we had a lot of fun there. We had a lot of fun in general and I learned some things about art that I hadn't known before. There always were a lot of other students watching me, with apparent awe, every time I drew or painted anything. We, art students, spent a lot of time painting and drawing models in the classroom. We also would spend a lot of time at the Kansas City Zoo drawing animals there.

Darrel and I lived in the same boarding house. We ran around with several other people who lived there most of whose name I've forgotten. One was named Cecil Whitley from North Carolina. Another was named Dan Kinkler, I think. The others I can't remember. When it was approaching time in January 1956 for me to go back to Texas Tech, I checked out of the Kansas City Art Institute. They got mad and gave me "withdrew failing marks" in all my subjects. That was just an immoral lie as my true grades were "A's" and "B's". But, I have run into a lot of those type lies in my life.

Back at Texas Tech, Alan Olsen was now gone. When I checked out of Tech, he asked me whom I recommended to take my place as head of the Petroleum Engineering Show. I told him Joe Bohanan whom had been my friend and fellow pet. eng. major since I started at Tech. Joe did take my place. Joe basically had tagged along beside me even though I was trying to avoid or minimize interaction with people, but we talked pet. eng. virtually all the time. He graduated the coming June at the end of the 1956 semester. Some of my other old fellow classmates were Robert Powell, Sid McHamey, Jim Asbell, Bob Herd, Wallace Pounds, Leslie Carnes, Paul Gaston, Andy Lyle, Len Walden, Chick Smith, Freddy Smith and others I don't remember at this writing. Andy Lyle was a pretty good friend of mine and we took many breaks together. Bob Herd was not an outstanding student but may have been the most successful Independent Operator in the class at a later date. His operations were in the East Texas area, as I understand it. I think he had contacts there before coming to Tech. Robert Powell had been a teaching assistant and had graded my physics papers when I first came to Tech. After that he zeroed in on me and came to me for help all the way through the first three semesters I was there. That is how I knew how close I was to first place in that physics class. He and Sid were close buddies and went to work as Petroleum Engineers in Argentina. Some of my new fellow pet. eng classmates were Noel Rietman, known as "Bud" Rietman, Lucian Dudley Sipes, known as "Buddy" Sipes, (Bud and Buddy were probably the two best pet. eng. Students of the class) John Weaver (who was also very talented), Verl Downey, Cloice Talbot, Scott Hickman, and many others who's name I've forgotten. Talbot was not really a talented engineering student and had a friend and classmate, whose name I can't remember, who basically tutored him through school, but he was the "executive" (*Ellsworth Toohey*) type and became one of the most financially successful graduates. Among other things he is head of the production part of the company known as Patterson Drilling Company.

My petroleum engineering instructors were, Mr. Phillip Johnson, who always gave me "C" even though my work was "A", Professor Wilber L. Ducker, the head of the Department, who always gave me "B" regardless and Dr. Harold Blum, who always gave me "A". People, who knew me or thought they knew me *well* always would *peg* me and I could never get out of the *"peg"* they put me in. That is why I'm not fond of small schools.

An Instructor that impressed me the most was a civil engineering professor named Dr. George Whetstone. I was required to take several courses under him. He was very impressive to me. His teaching technique was supreme. He drew perfect pictures, i.e., perfectly straight lines, perfect squares, perfect circles, in the solution of each problem on the blackboard, which was actually green. His writing or printing was perfect and as legible as it could be. Watching him at work was more beautiful than any symphony I ever witnessed. His solutions were brilliant. His teaching technique was to give the class a problem, send them to the board to solve it, and after they had a short time to think of the solution, send them to their seats and show them how to solve the problem. I could learn quicker and more completely under him than any instructor I ever had. The one subject under him that I was the best at and which is at the heart of my type of petroleum engineering was his course in hydraulics. I would always have the problem solved before his short chance to do so was over and he always used my work to explain the problem to the class. That was the only class of his that I saw anybody do that. Dr. Whetstone had earned his doctorate from the University of Washington (or maybe Oregon) as I recall.

In my senior year and maybe the last semester of my junior year at Tech, several of us were given a pet. eng. project, which required us to stay up all night to accomplish it. I went all the way through Texas Tech without knowing how to type and many times my mother would type papers for me that had to be typed and weren't a group project. In rare occasions I had to hire somebody to type a paper for me.

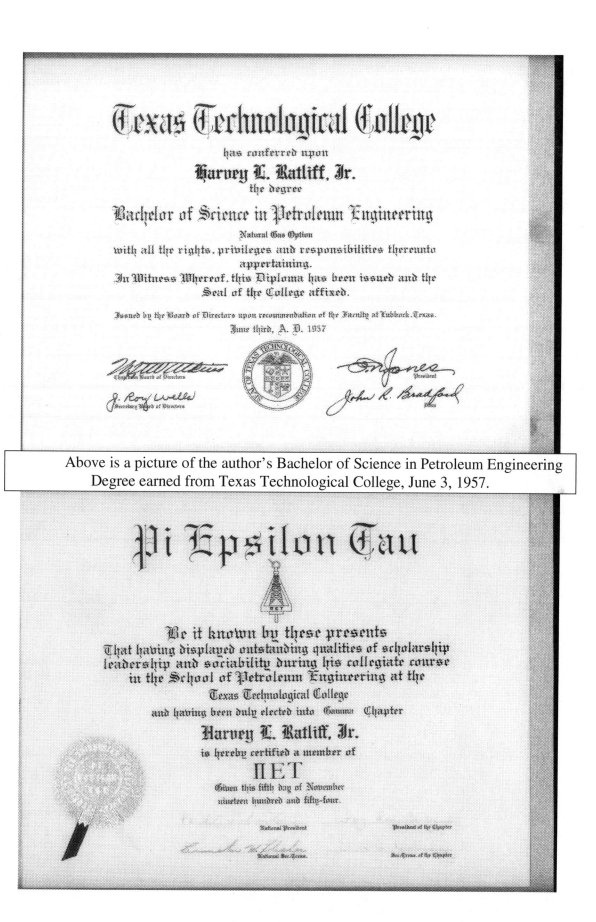

Above is a picture of the author's Bachelor of Science in Petroleum Engineering Degree earned from Texas Technological College, June 3, 1957.

Tau Beta Pi

Texas Beta

Be it Known, That having maintained a rank in Scholarship in the first fifth of his class during his collegiate course at Texas Technological College and having been duly elected by the above Chapter

Harvey Ratliff

of the Class of 1957 is hereby declared and certified a member of

T Δ Π

and is granted all the honors, insignia and privileges of this Association.

Given this eleventh day of December 1956.

Harold M. King
President, Executive Council

Robert H. Nagel
Secretary of the Association

Elder J. Reynolds
President of the Chapter

Ray Aylsworth
Secretary of the Chapter

Above are pictures of certificates of membership in the honorary fraternities of *Pi Epsilon Tau and Tau Beta Pi.*

74

Above is a picture of Clara Hedwig Schneider, who would later change the author's life, standing left of Maria Stein.

Finally, after many hard hours and days of work and achieving some 158 credit hours and a grade-point average of some 2.2 overall at Texas Technological College and membership in Tau Beta Pi and Pi Epsilon Tau, the day came in June of 1957 in which I received my degree in petroleum engineering. I remember my mother and aunt Georgia attended the event. It was a wonderful feeling to have finally attained that degree.

Chapter IX
Civilian Life After College

I was very excited after receiving my degree in June of 1957. Uncle Roy had been telling me what great plans he had for us in the oil business. The Whittenburgs had won the bitter battle of the newspapers and now the Globe News Publishing Company was theirs. They owned the Amarillo Globe News, the Lubbock Avalanche Journal, the Borger News Herald, KGNC radio and television of Amarillo and KFYO radio and television of Lubbock. While I was overseas, they had built the first television station ever built in Amarillo. I had my degree in hand and we were going to do great things in the oil business. While working there, I was actually employed by Plains Radio, I believe, anyway it was the parent company of all the newspapers etc. I was actually working for Uncle Roy. I did, however, gain a much closer relationship with Uncle S.B. during this time period. We played a lot of chess. I don't think he could believe that I was better at chess than he was.

However, at that time I started learning difficulties of working with Uncle Roy that I had, at best, only an inkling of before. Although Uncle Roy had never had the Johnson O'Connor tests, it was clear to me that he, like me, had an extremely subjective personality, which he totally didn't understand. That meant it was "his way or the highway" as a son, I later had, loved to put it. I continuously ran into the ugly face of Ayn Rand's *Ellsworth Toohey* while trying to work with him. He was very skilled at negotiating. He seemed to me to have loved power and control over people and knew exactly how to keep it and exercise it over his brothers and sisters along with their spouses. I had, not a chance, to win a political or negotiating battle or argument with him. In my view, being correct or right had no weight whatsoever even though he never even recognized that fact either. In my view he had absolutely no understanding of or ability in petroleum engineering matters. What is worse, he thought he was a genius in that and just about everything else and neither realized nor accepted any of his weaknesses. He also had multiple hidden agendas that he wanted me to know nothing about. That, to me, meant I could be getting involved in something I absolutely did not want to be involved with. He seemed to me to be extremely exploitive of employees, by skillful negotiating he underpaid them way below the going free-market rate, and in general did not treat them right at all. He negotiated underpayment to me, but I overlooked that for a while. Most of the work I actually did was cartography although he or anyone there did not use the term cartography. He did have me complete a couple of wells but *Ellsworth Toohey* showed his face there and there was way too much interference from him virtually nullifying my decision making power. He really didn't know how to use a petroleum engineer. He would only lease acreage for drilling that had no geological or any scientific basis and only if he could get it for $1.00 per acre or less. He seemed to think engineers were supposed to magically pull rabbits from hats on demand in the oil business without the aid of any science at all.

Actually, I was in denial for too long because I really loved and nearly idolized my very charismatic Uncle Roy throughout my growing up period. I couldn't bring myself to tell him how I really felt or actually really understand how I felt at that time.

The first thing that happened was I was put on a leave of absence for a while. Back in 1955 or '56 a man named Jack Grimm, of later "Big Foot" fame, talked my dad into drilling three wells. My dad actually used Virginia and my money from a trust for us to illegally do it, but he found a small shallow oil field in Palo Pinto County Texas. The field produced over 350,000 barrels, which at an assumed price of $20 per barrel would have a gross value of some $7,000,000. But, as usual my dad did way too many wrong things. He drilled about 20 wells whereas one or two wells would have drained the whole field. Although he had complete control, he gave way too many people way too big of a cut. I don't really know, for sure, where all the money from that field went but it just seemed to have evaporated. This field was in the Strawn sand at a depth of some 1850 feet from surface. My dad had gone through an up hole zone in the Pennsylvania Strawn at some 1550-foot from surface with strong shows in it. I don't remember the reasons why but with my mother's help, we decided to sell our house at 2206 Hughes St. and Virginia and I would drill a well too that depth. This is what we did. Virginia and Dad would decide later while I was working at the patent office to plug that well. We really didn't know the right legal procedure and used a way one of our lawyers wanted us to use, which I learned later is by far the wrong way to do it.

It didn't take me too long after drilling that well to realize that it would never work out with Uncle Roy. It would be impossible for me to succeed in the oil business with him. After I had decided this he put me in a bad dilemma or at least I thought he did. I forget how it was done but what it amounted to is that the entire family, including my precious mother, would conclude that I would divulge Whittenburg oil business secrets if I went to work for a major oil company. So, I couldn't live with that, or even if my reading was wrong, my perception of that. I had gone to the placement office at Texas Tech and, after reading their job possibilities catalog, noticed that there were a lot of job openings for people of my qualifications at the United States Patent Office.

Ever since I was that young boy in Canyon, Texas, looking at the dioramas in the museum there, I had been dreaming up ways to create a greater way to present better wide-angle, stereoscopic views of beautiful, wonderful, historic or great events. By now with my hard gained knowledge of physics and technology, I had many inventions in mind and had long wondered if someone else had thought of them. Here was my long-desired chance to find out. I thought I would be right at the focal point of the creativity of the United States and the world.

I decided to help constitutionally "promote progress in ...useful arts" at the United States Patent Office in Washington, D.C. I would be starting out as a GS9 civil servant and would be paid over 60 percent more than my Uncle Roy had been paying me.

Chapter X
Life While Working at the United States Patent Office

I found out how and applied for a job as a Patent Examiner at the U.S. Patent Office. I was given a 92.5 rating, as I recall. It had helped that I had been in the army to the extent of adding five points to my rating. This was a very high rating and I was immediately hired with no interview or anything. My Uncle Roy wanted to rate me an "A" in every category of their questionnaire, but I asked him to rate me "B".

Even though I was immediately hired, due to governmental slowness there was a long waiting period before I was actually required to move to the Washington, D.C. area and start my job. In April of 1960, as I recall, I actually started working at the patent office as an examiner. I found a place in an apartment complex in Falls Church, Va. to rent as my new abode. Fortunately they asked me in what division of examining I would like to be in. I told them optics since my secret agenda was that was where I thought I might find inventions preceding mine. By then I had learned that in a world of secret agendas, I sometimes must have one too. The Patent Office was then in the Commerce Building at 14th and Constitution, in Washington, D.C.

Above is a picture of the author in front of the White House while working as a patent examiner at the U.S. Patent Office, Washington, and D.C.

At this point I think it appropriate to go into some of the things that were happening with my dad, mother and sister. As stated earlier, my dad had a stroke when he was 55 years of age while I was overseas in Germany. By now, in 1960, he was 63 years of age. I think his stroke and heart attack possibilities created their newfound interest in health food. I am not sure how it all came about, but somehow and sometime during the last eight years my mother, dad and sister became very interested in health food, especially as a way to prevent strokes and heart attacks. My mother was throughout nearly all of her life a very devout Christian Scientist, but she would drift away once in a while. Both my mother and sister were great readers and read extensively on health food "Adel Davis style." They were juicing fresh, ripe and raw carrots and the like enthusiastically; however, it never dawned on them that the juice should be drunk right away. I was not a good reader but loved to try and think originally. I got caught up in the health food mode, which followed me the rest of my life even though my mother, sister and dad soon lost enthusiasm about it. I had decided the key to health food is "fresh, ripe and raw." Get certain types of profit motive out of the food you eat such as the profit motive, which takes all the nutrition out of food to increase the shelf life and thus profit, i.e., sugar, flour, potato chips and the like have very long shelf lives and sugar and flour are in almost every food a person cooks or buys already cooked. So, one of the things I did when I first became a patent examiner was experiment with living on just fresh, ripe and raw fruits and vegetables mostly freshly juiced. If they were fresh, ripe and raw, man could do minimal damage to them. You don't reduce the pesticides by cooking and probably not by processing food. I had researched enough to know that if I had carrot juice, an apple and fresh nuts or avocado I would get all the amino acids and therefore protein that I needed. Anyway I tried this diet then and decided it worked very well. I would get at a good healthy weight and stay there while on this diet. I later moved to 924 Twenty-fifth Street, northwest, apartment 501 in Washington 7, D.C. and walked to the patent office each morning of the workweek.

While at the patent office, all kinds of exciting and wonderful things happened over a period of some 19 months until November 13, 1961, when I left. Upon starting work we were first placed in an orientation class. In orientation class they taught us many things. One thing was the constitutional basis of the patent system. It was not emphasized but in the orientation I was impressed that the United States was the first constitutional patent system on earth. Another thing I remember is that Thomas Jefferson was the first patent examiner in the first constitutional patent system and nobody could have been better at that job. Best I can tell he was the examiner when the first 100 patents were granted from the system. We were taught the "nuts and bolts" that for the most part I really didn't understand until later and some things probably never.

I was put to work in Division 7, which was the optical division at that time. The division head was named Emil G. Anderson. I was seated in a cubical with Ronald Wibert, Ronald Klett and John Duncan, as I remember. Ronald Wibert would become my best friend while at the U.S. Patent Office, but it was Ronald Klett who would do me the greatest favor anyone would ever do for me. These guys were really intelligent people. While in the Army, Ronald Wibert scored the highest in the battalion on a test, which was the army equivalent of an IQ test. I think as high as one could score. The Battalion Commander called him to front and center of the troops and said; "I just wanted to see what an intelligent man looks like." John Duncan showed me his score on the legal "aptitude" (or LSAT) test he took before starting night law school at George Washington University, a few blocks away. It was extremely high like 99.4 percentile. For some reason Ron Wibert took a liking to me right off and put me under his wing and was as nice to me as he could be. We always took our breaks together. He often brought along two to three others, Joel Goldberg from Philadelphia, a guy whose last name was Koenig with two dots over the o, pronounced Kernig, and Walt Williamson who actually started working after I did. Wibert also really liked Thomas Jefferson.

We often had "debates" in which I would find Wibert and me on a side and Klett on the other side. I faired pretty well in the debates even with John Duncan, which surprised me. We got to go to special parades that came down 14th Street. I remember seeing Alan Shepherd in a parade right after he was the first man in space and I saw President Kennedy in a couple of parades. I believe I saw Eisenhower right after arriving too. I would often go to lunch with those same guys, Wibert etc. If I could, I would slip off and have my carrot juice at a juice place near by. Its juice had a lot of pulp in it, much more than the juice from my juicer. When I worked up an *"action"* I was to report to an experienced examiner, which usually turned out to be a man named Bill Mesick. Everybody told me he was terrible, but I really didn't mind him.

The patent office had the system of posting everyone's production. So, everybody knew how many *actions* per week you produced and how many *"disposals"* you produced. Good producers had large numbers of *disposals* per week. An *action* was a letter to an applicant either rejecting the claims and explaining the reasons for the rejection or allowing the claims. A *disposal* was either an abandonment of an application or the granting of a patent to an applicant. The goal was to get a large number of *disposals* with as few *actions* per *disposal* as possible. It seemed to be the standard procedure to try to get an easy abandonment because this was an easy way to have a high *production rate with few actions,* which is the determinant of a "good" examiner. This led to what, to me, was great unfairness to applicants.

The key laws were 35 U.S.C. 101 which stated that an invention had to be *new*. Virtually never did this law prevent an applicant from obtaining a patent. Another law was 35 U.S.C. 110, as I remember, stating that the applicant must "particularly point out and distinctly claim the invention." The law that was the one causing the greatest number of abandonment's was 35 U.S.C. 103, which states that the invention must be *unobvious* to a person of *ordinary skill* in the art at the time the invention, was made. I personally think that is a poorly written law and should be that the invention must be a *new function* to be patentable. This is in fact the determination a good examiner makes because he very well knows that if it is a new function it isn't obvious because there are some six billion people on earth and none of them figured it out before. When Edison invented the electric light that looks very obvious because he merely reduced the size of the filament of a heating lamp. What is spectacular about that invention is that it was a spectacular new function that nobody had before. When the Wright brothers invented flight they merely changed the shape of the airfoil of an old well-known combination, this is obvious looking in hindsight but it is a spectacular new function that nobody ever thought of before. *"Unobvious"* is a very poor criteria.

Once in a while I had to report to Dave Rubin. He was an extremely good examiner, the best in the division for sure and maybe the entire office, but it was murder to have to report to him. I absolutely could not read his writing and can't understand how anybody could. Each sentence looked like a beginning letter, such as B, with horizontal lines or underlines following it. I feel sorry for the poor person who typed his actions. I basically had to remember everything he wrote which I was often unable to do. It was murder. They finally promoted him to a division unto himself with nobody reporting to him. He was much happier with that also. He produced seven to eight actions per week with an excellent disposal to action ratio. Most people couldn't produce three and had a worse ratio. He could read a page about as fast as I could read a sentence.

A claim can only be one sentence, e.g., the invention being the object of I claim. So, in a claim you may have an object, the invention, which could take three or more pages to set forth. It is like nothing else in the world that I have ever seen. To me it is one of the wonders of the earth. *Function, in patent law,* is mode of operation of elements cooperating together to obtains a result, e.g. Edison's reduced filament changed the mode of operation and produced a new result both. It is a new function if the mode of operation is different or if the result is different or if both are different from the prior art. *Prior Art* means inventions described in prior literature or patents. The *specification and drawings* of the patent must clearly disclose and explain the invention claimed in the claims to the point that it is clear what each element does and how it cooperates with the other elements to produce the result of the invention claimed. One key to becoming a good examiner is to be there long enough to master the *prior art* in the classifications of *prior art* that the examiner examines in.

I met a lot of other interesting people at the Patent Office. One was Mrs. Coiner who was actually a beautiful lady considerably older than I was. Her field of examining was exactly the field I was most interested in, Stereoscopic viewing systems. While I was at the patent office she seemed to me to be very hard on applicants. I was afraid I might be up against a brick wall if she examined my applications later. I later surmised that she probably wasn't too mean to applicants. She just liked to obtain the sympathy of her associate examiners. In actual fact, while I was at the patent office she was always very nice to me. Also, to my surprise when I, at a later date, filed for patents in the wide-angle, stereoscopic field, she apparently refused to examine an application of mine that she felt she had to reject for some reason. The only application, of mine, she examined and acted on, she granted in the first action. That was the only time that ever happened to me. It made me feel as though I had offered a car for sale and someone bought it in ten minutes. Nearly all the time I received these ridiculous rejections attempting to invalidly bluff me into an early abandonment. Another very interesting person I met was Dick Wintercorn. His dad was a successful patent attorney. Tom Skeer was another quite interesting person. Ed Connors was another, so was John Corbin, a Mr. Pederson, who seemed to be always talking to Mrs. Coiner, and there were others.

Chapter XI
Meeting My Wife-To-Be While at the Patent Office

In about October of 1960, Ronald Klett invited me on a picnic with a group of his friends. Ronald Klett was very frugal, as in the "Millionaire Next Door" by Thomas J. Stanley, Ph.D. and William. D. Danko, Ph.D., and didn't have a car. I was to pick up a couple of ladies at an address he gave me and they were going to tell me where to go from there. The ladies were both from Germany. One lady was named Clara Hedwig Schneider and the other was named Lisa, whose last name I can't remember.

This meeting turned out to be a momentous occasion in my life. I met my lifelong sweetheart that day. Soon after that day I realized that this is it. There is the lady I have always been looking for.

Anyway, I picked the two ladies up and we went to this park and had our picnic. We then went to an amusement park where Clara and I rode the roller coaster and did other fun things together. At the park we met Ronald Klett, Ed Connors, Edith Zelzer and others that I can't seem to remember. We did several things and Clara and I did them mostly together and one of them was we rode the roller coaster together. It seems Ronald

Klett and Edith had a "fight" at that picnic. Anyway, I really enjoyed myself at the event, which turned out to be a very momentous event in my life.

Later, after this momentous event I luckily noticed that Clara had left her sunglasses in my car. I decided I just had to take them back to her. When she answered the door, she was in her short-shorts and Wow! She was beautiful. I asked her for a date and we were off and running. Clara had first come over to the United States on a diplomatic visa with a diplomat, Mr. Norden, who was the son of the inventor of the Norden Bomb Sight, which was used in World War II. She was now on a visa that allowed her to work for Geico (Government Employee Insurance Company). I thought from virtually our first date that this is the one I want as my wife. It was really love at first sight for me, but I always tried to keep my head and be as logical as I could.

The above is a picture of Harvey and Clara visiting Monticello.

While dating Clara, I met a lot of her friends who were nearly all ladies from Germany who had married former patent examiners who were now patent attorneys. One couple was Christa and Joe Labowsky, later changed to Labow. Another couple was Renate and O.A. Neumann. Also I met Clara's friends who were still single. One was the German lady Clara was then or soon to be living with whose name was Maria Stein. Also I became more acquainted with Edith Zelzer. Before me Clara had been dating a well-liked patent examiner in my division 7 named John Corbin. They had split up, the story goes, because he was Baptist and she was Catholic and O.A., who was also Catholic had convinced John that it could never work; so, that caused her to be more amenable to becoming Episcopalian with me.

The above is a picture of Clara and Harvey Ratliff at their wedding at St. Andrew's Episcopal Church, Amarillo, Texas.

We dated for some five months and on March 18, 1961, we were married in St. Andrews Episcopal Church in Amarillo, Texas. Since Clara grew up a Catholic, and all my life I had been told horror stories about Catholics and didn't really want my kids forced into that or any religion actually. We settled on the Episcopal Church as a compromise. It is enough like the Catholic Church in its worship style for Clara to be happy in and I liked it because Jefferson, a deist as were his heroes Isaac Newton and John Locke, had remained a member and supported that church throughout his life although he was one of the worlds greatest advocates of freedom of religion. I also talked Clara into going along with my "fresh, ripe and raw fruit and vegetable juice" philosophy.

Actually the wedding was a big event orchestrated by my mother with the help of my aunts Tennessee and Helen, I believe. I had limited annual leave available for our marriage; so, Clara had to bravely go down to Amarillo all by herself a week ahead of the wedding and meet all my relatives. This she handled very well as I understand it. Those were an awful lot of names to remember. All my mother's twelve brothers and sisters and their spouses plus 41 of my first cousins, many of whom had spouses and even further some of the Hedgecokes, who were first cousins at my mothers generation and second cousins at my generation.

I was to fly into Amarillo, where it seldom rains, with Maria Stein, her maid of honor, in time to be at the rehearsal. However, we were rained out. We went back and forth to Denver, and back and forth to Dallas, couldn't land. Finally the plane landed in Lubbock and we arrived by bus at a late time such as midnight. Clara had to go through the rehearsal and rehearsal dinner without me. She sat by my two-year-old nephew John Early at the rehearsal dinner, I believe.

The rector presiding over the wedding was Father Evans Mooreland, whom Clara and I both really liked. He was very influential to our becoming Episcopalian. He made it very easy for me to get through the wedding without a glitch even though I couldn't make the rehearsal. We were maybe the only couple he gave the premarital talk to after the wedding. I still remember his saying "it is not the big things that will be a problem but the little things" and he was prophetic in saying that. I had to get our marriage license on a Saturday before the wedding, but luckily my brother-in-law Allen Early had enough influence for us to get that done.

We spent the first night of our marriage in the Plainsman Hotel in Lubbock, Texas. Somehow, in my hick way, I thought that was a nice hotel, but I don't think Clara was that impressed. We were going to spend our second night in our boathouse on Possum Kingdom Lake about 30 miles from Breckenridge. My dad wanted us to arise at 5 a.m. the next morning in order to drive to Breckenridge in time to entertain his friends: Paul and Phil Pitzer and others I can't remember. Needless to say we didn't get up at 5 a.m. the next morning. It was supposed to be our honeymoon. But, anyway I thought we had a good honeymoon. Not as good as my wife deserved but "good."

When we returned to Washington, D.C., fellow examiners and Clara's old friends, the men of which were past examiners gave us a real nice party at the very nice home of Carl Norden's, son of the bombsite inventor. Back working at the patent office I began to realize the prior art was virtually non-existent in the field of the inventions I had in mind. That began exciting me. Somewhere along about this time in June of 1961, I think, we moved to the Fort Bennett Apartments in which Maria Stein lived and O.A. and Renate lived. I don't remember the exact address, but it was across Key Bridge from George Town, D.C., and about a block from Rosalind Circle.

The more I worked at the patent office the more convinced I was that the state of the art was wide open to my inventions. If I stayed at the patent office for three years, I would automatically be qualified to be a patent agent. A patent agent can represent an applicant before the patent office and up to the highest appeal level within the patent office, but if it gets out into the Federal or State Courts, a patent attorney is required. This put me in a dilemma. However, it was on my mind that the longer I put off getting out to apply for patents after one year, the more likely someone else was to kill my opportunity to do so. I just had to leave the patent office and get to work filing applications for patents.

Chapter XII
Raising Children and Filing Applications For Patents

So, on November 13, 1961, I left the patent office. Before I left my fellow examiners gave me, and maybe Clara and me, a very nice party. This brings to mind that Clara's friends all loved parties, but Clara probably loved parties, it turned out, more than anyone I had ever known before. However, she wanted children much more than anything. She always told me she wanted six children. I remember being at some party; I think it was about this time in my life, and hearing some of Clara's old friends, i.e., Jerry Garfinkle, who really hardly knew me, say "we used to have parties all the time, but Clara got married and now we don't have any it seems to me."

The above is a picture of Clara and Harvey Ratliff shortly after they were married.

After leaving the patent office, Uncle Roy agreed to hire me back and I went back to work for him. I couldn't, by law, file an application for patent until I was out of the office for a year. We first moved in with my mother at 5109 Matador Trail in Amarillo, Texas and started looking for a permanent residence. President Kennedy had convinced my mother that she must have a nuclear bomb shelter and she built quite a-bomb shelter underneath that house. We had our first son, Thomas Lee Ratliff, while living there on December 26, 1961. The "Thomas" was for Thomas Jefferson, the great enlightenment thinker, revolutionary leader, inventor, scientist, first Constitutional Patent Examiner in the world, on and on and the "Lee" was a family name, my dad's mother, my dad's and mine. Clara and I had agreed that with the boys we would give them one historical name and one family name. I loved enlightenment thinkers and leaders. Thomas was born in Northwest Texas Hospital in Amarillo, Texas. The delivery doctor was Dr. Howard Puckett and the delivery nurse was named Dorothy Johnson who also was a good friend of our neighbor next door to the south. My mother insisted we hire a nurse, not Dorothy, for caring for the new baby. Clara and I strongly believed in breast-feeding our baby. The nurse hated breast-feeding and set out to convince us not to by waking Clara up every hour, which certainly didn't help. It turned out that Clara almost bled to death that night. We fortunately called Dr. Puckett, probably the best doctor I've ever had, and he came to the house and immediately took her to the hospital and saved her life. That type of doctoring is seldom seen today.

By about June 1962, we found and moved into a house at 5315 Alvarado Street in Amarillo, Texas. Clara loved this house the instant she set eyes on it. I used one of the bedrooms as my office and studio to work on my inventions and to paint and draw pictures. As I recall, I did a lot more cartography work for Uncle Roy during this time of employment by him. I would do various surveys on the ranches and make various maps that Uncle Roy wanted.

On November 15, 1962, slightly more than a year after leaving the Office, I filed five applications for patent at the U.S. Patent Office. I was very excited about it. I still couldn't type and my brother-in-law Allen Early typed these first five applications. I believe I had to quit my job at this time and went to Drougne's Business School for a week to learn typing and at later date bookkeeping. I believe the two weeks training in typing and bookkeeping has been very valuable to my later success. One thing my dad inadvertently taught me was a person could lose it all through the bookkeeper. In fact these two courses of two-week duration turned out to be one of the most valuable parts of my education. I virtually learned to type while typing my applications for patent and prosecuting them to fruition. Of these first five applications filed, none of the ones as originally filed, actually became a patent.

For many years my cousin Tennessee Ann Pickens, who was the oldest daughter of my Aunt Pattie Morris, kept the books of Jetru, Inc., which, upon my mother's direction owned the patents I would obtain. We had developed a good relation that began with me helping her get through a physics course, which I believe she encountered at West Texas while pursuing her degree in accounting.

My first U.S. Patent No. 3,251,284, was the first patent granted to me in May 17, 1966, my second son Franklin Xaver Ratliff's third birthday. The name Franklin is after Benjamin Franklin, the great American enlightenment thinker, revolutionary leader and I\inventor and on and on. This name also smacks of Clara's father's first name Franz. The Xaver is after Clara's father's middle name. We had Franklin while living at 5315 Alvarado St., Amarillo, Texas. He was born May 17, 1963 in Northwest Texas Hospital of Amarillo and delivered by Dr. Howard Puckett with Dorothy Johnson the delivery nurse, as was Thomas.

Back to my patent, this first patent granted resulted from a division of application Serial No. 237,795, filed November 15, 1962. The divisional application was Serial No. 429,317, filed February 1, 1965, while we lived in Lubbock, Texas, which will be described in more detail later. This first granted patent was entitled "Camera For Making Wide-Angle Stereoscopic Pictures" and had five claims, based on adequate specification and drawings, 27 figures of drawings in fact, for a patentable wide-angle stereoscopic camera mechanism. The primary examiner was John M. Horan, who wrote and signed all the actions. The principal prior art he relied upon was a patent No. 2,953,980, to Roger Lenis De Montebello, who used what to me was a vastly different system. For each eye view while taking the pictures, he had an array of small molded short focal length lenses with its front surface a large concave surface and the back surface the array of small highly convex surfaces. To view the pictures he would exactly reverse the lenses with the large concave surface toward one's eye. My system in this patent was to have comparatively long focal length taking lenses producing left and right eye view transparencies which overlapped in the middle with some type of system to allow the right eye to see only the right eye view and the left eye to see only the left eye view in the central overlapping surface. Horan cited six other patents as prior art: 2,063,985, 2,413,996, 2,566,110, 2,568,327, 2,794,380 and 2,883,906.

"The Magnificent Friend" painted in oil by the author in 1962.

"The Beautiful Worker" painted by the author in oil in 1962.

May 17, 1966   H. L. RATLIFF, JR   3,251,28⋅

CAMERA FOR MAKING WIDE-ANGLE STEREOSCOPIC PICTURES

Original Filed Nov. 15, 1962   8 Sheets—Sheet

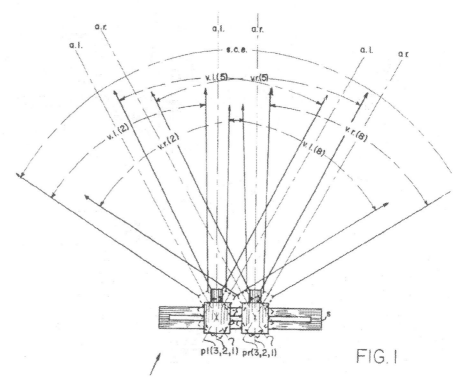

FIG.1

Figure 1 of my first U.S. Patent 3,251,284

My second U.S. Patent 3,272,069, granted September 13, 1966, also originated with one of these first five, but had to be re-filed April 1, 1965, as application Serial No. 447,600. It was entitled "Apparatus For Viewing Wide-Angle Stereoscopic Pictures" and had four claims, based on an adequate specification and five figures of drawings, for a patentable wide-angle stereoscopic viewing mechanism. This patent was for the viewing mechanism for the pictures produced by my Patent No. 3,251,284. It was a viewing device that did not require short focal length oculars to view the two wide-angle pictures, which overlapped in the center and reversed the process for allowing overlapping centers so that the right eye saw only right eye views and the left eye saw only left eye views. The primary examiner was Jewell H. Pedersen, whom I spoke of, earlier and slightly knew while working at the office. The assistant examiner, who signed all the actions as I recall was named Orville B. Chew, whom I had not known before. I still had some "rough edges" then and got into some of my most bitter arguments on this application for patent. Mr. Chew wanted to take me before the board, according to my friend Ron Wibert. However, this patent was finally granted. The prior art cited by the examiner was Ames 1,673,793, Ives 1,882,424, Parsell 2,218,875, Winnek 2,562,077, Welborn 2,627,781, Mahler 2,674,156, Rehorn 2,883,906, Domeshek 2,930,980, Montebello 2,953,980, Heilig 2,955,156, and Van Alabada, col. L.E.W., "A Wide-Angle Stereoscope and a Wide-Angle View-Finder," Transitions of the Optical Society of London, vol. 25, 1923-24, pp. 249-257, 259-260.

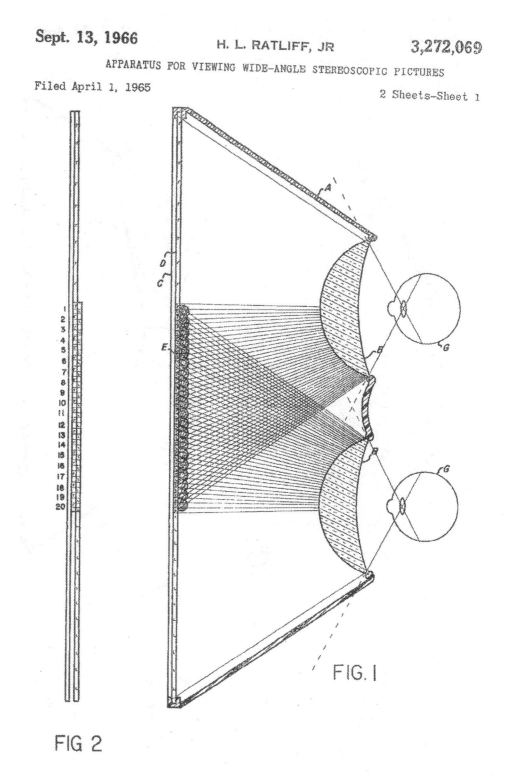

FIG 2

FIG. 1

INVENTOR.

Harvey L. Ratliff Jr.

Figure 1 of my second U.S. Patent 3,272,069

90

My third U.S. Patent 3,291,904, was granted December 13, 1966, and resulted from Application Serial No. 295,792, filed July 17, 1963. It was entitled by the Examiner "Stereoscopic Television System With Special Effects" and had 12 allowed claims, based on 16 columns of specification and 13 figures of drawings for a patentable theatrical system which would give the viewer three-dimensional (stereoscopic) wide-angle, up to 240 degrees horizontally and 130 degrees vertically, of the movie presentation along with stereophonic sound of the event and with the eyes of the viewer completely taken up by the viewing system, it could also provide various odors and tactile sensations of the event. The primary examiner was David G. Redinbaugh, whom I didn't know at all. The assistant examiner was R.L. Richardson, whom I didn't know at all. The prior art cited by the examiner was Madison 1,711,897, Stern 2,540,144, Stern 2,562,959, Goldsmith 2,506,700, Black 2,955,156, and Morton L. Heilig 2,955,156. The prior art cited by applicant was McCollum 2,358,170, Stern 2,562,960, Disney 3,050,870, and Morton L. Heilig 3,050,870 (this, I believe, is the Patent for Imax and Omni Theaters).

The above is a picture from left of Thomas, Harvey Locke, Harvey and Franklin Ratliff soon after Harvey Locke was born.

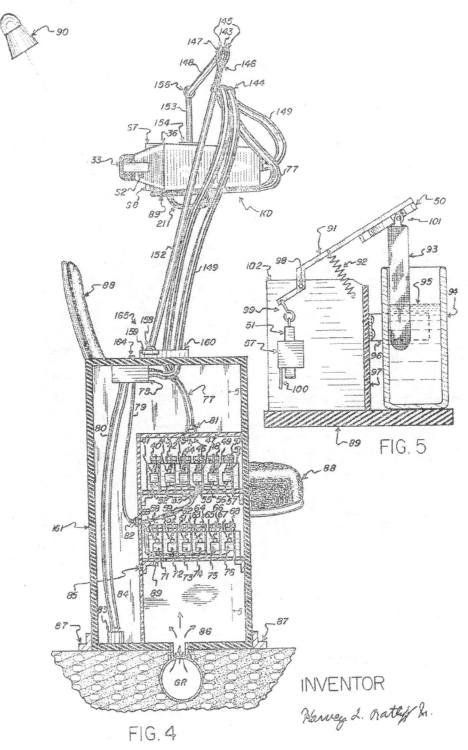

FIG. 5

FIG. 4

INVENTOR

Harvey L. Ratliff Jr.

Part III
The Story of An Entrepreneur Who "Is Not College Material"

My fourth U.S. Patent 3,293,358, was granted December 20, 1966, and resulted from Application Serial No. 250,562, filed January 10, 1963. It was entitled "Cathode Ray Tube Optical Viewing Device For Reproducing Wide-Angle Stereoscopic Motion Pictures" and had five allowed claims, based on five columns of specification and 11 figures of drawings. The summary of the invention was "The converting of electrical signals into stereophonic sound and wide angle stereoscopic motion pictures upon the phosphorescent screen of a cathode ray tube; said screen also being the screen of a wide-angle viewer having an associated reticle or the like; there being up to many thousand separate cathode ray tube wide angle stereoscopic viewers showing said motion picture simultaneously and individually for individual viewing observers." The primary examiner was David G. Redinbaugh and the assistant examiners were T.G. Keough and J.A. Orsino, none of which I knew at all. Ron Wibert told me that Orsino made some remarks about me, whom I have forgotten, but I remember considering them very "snotty." The prior art cited was Zworykin 2,107,464, Carnahan 2,301,254, Schroeder 2,642,487, Calvi 2,701,503, Vanderhooft 2,783,406, Abramson 2,969,426, Heilig 2,955,156, Moulton 2,969,426, Owens 3,020,341, and Schmidt 3,045,544.

The above picture is the author's oldest son, Thomas Lee Ratliff, born December 26, 1961, in Amarillo, Texas.

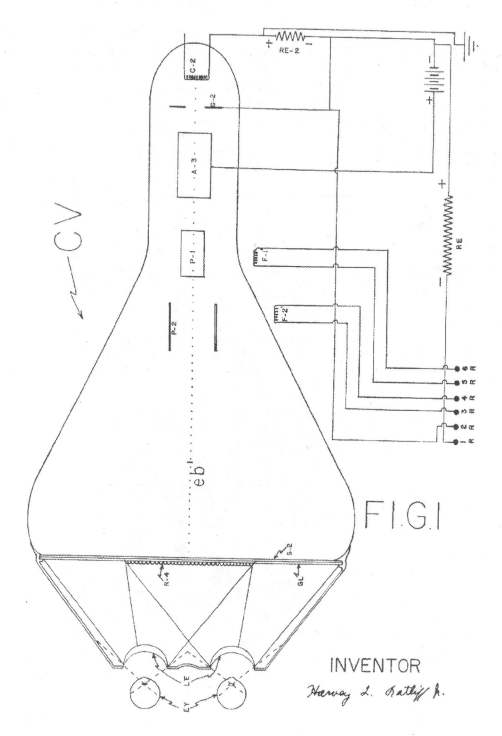

FIG.I

INVENTOR

Harvey L. Ratliff Jr.

Figure 1 of my forth U.S. Patent 3,293,358

My fifth U.S. Patent 3,298,771, was granted January 17, 1967, and resulted from Application Serial No. 275,411, filed in April 24, 1963, divided and resulting in this Application No. 505,119 filed October 18, 1965. It is entitled "Stepped Zone Lenses For Wide-Angle Oculars" and had one allowed claim, based on six columns of specification and nine figures of drawings. It was for a stepped zone lens designed to enable a short focal length viewing lens as the ocular so that an overlapping central portion would not be necessary for viewing wide-angle transparencies. The primary examiner was Jewell H. Pedersen and the assistant examiner was R.J. Stern. The prior art cited was Straubel 934,579, Wolfe 1,802,100, Frederick 1,966,792, Godwin 1,993,272, and Beach 2,405,989.

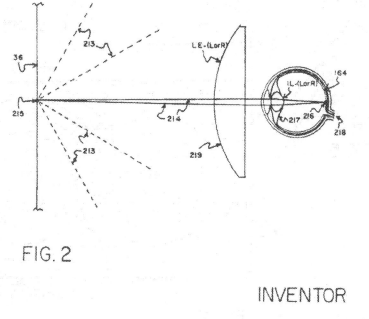

FIG. 2

INVENTOR

Harvey L. Ratliff Jr.

Figure 2 of my fifth U.S. Patent 3,298,771

My sixth U.S. Patent 3,326,106 was granted June 20, 1967, also resulted from the original five applications filed and had some of the exact same figures, but had to be re-filed in Application No. 429,316, filed August 30, 1965. It is entitled "Apparatus For Recording Wide-Angle Stereoscopic Pictures" and had two allowed claims, six figures of drawings and two and a half columns of specification. The abstract of disclosure read "There is a means **39** of placing a right real image **32** and a left virtual image **34'** upon an object plane **41** with the picture centers thereof substantially separated. There is a means

36 or **36'** of focusing the images at **41** upon an image plane **40** wherein the image has three portions: a central portion **28**, a right side portion **27** and a left side portion **29**. There is a means of separately focusing and recording the central portion **28.** Therefore, a picture is produced that can be viewed in a viewer such as described in U.S. Patent 3,272,069 to produce a wide-angle re-creation without viewing a strip between the left and right eye views." The primary examiner was John M. Horan and the prior art cited was France 944,255 and France 977,368.

Sometime along in here I decided I needed to work on a masters degree in electrical engineering, since I thought it would help in succeeding in my inventions. At that time there was a company, I think it was known as Nash-Phillips-Copes, in Amarillo that would take our house in Amarillo and trade it for a house in Lubbock; so, this is what we did and we moved to 3701 46th St., Lubbock, Texas, 79413. The electrical engineering department at Tech told me I would have to do one year of undergraduate work to become qualified for a masters in electrical engineering since my BS was in petroleum engineering. I had to take the graduate record exam. and scored 93 percentile in the quantitative part and 33 percentile in the verbal part. I remember having to take an updated physics course and found physics had changed a lot since I last took it. Edwin Land's inventions had changed some of the emphasis in physics for one thing. The "men from the boys" teacher was Dr. Seacat. He was a very difficult teacher. His tests were never actually over the material we covered in the lecture or textbook. They were some 25 percent over the material we covered, 25 percent over material we covered before the tested period and 50 percent over material not even mentioned in the textbook or by the teacher. I drew on my radio repair training a lot. The solution to all problems was the rote, for computers, Matrix solutions that depended purely on clerical speed (what Johnson O'Connor termed graphoria) and no cleverness at all. I made a "C" in that course.

While we lived in Lubbock my third son Harvey Locke Ratliff was born September 8, 1964, at St. Anthony's Hospital, Amarillo, Texas and delivered by Dr. Howard Puckett. The name Harvey came from my dad's Uncle Harvey Stewart Ratliff, my dad and me. The name Locke came from the great English enlightenment thinker John Locke. Mom, Thomas and Franklin rode the train from Lubbock to Amarillo in order for mom to have the baby. My mother took care of the children before I got there by car in time for the actual birth.

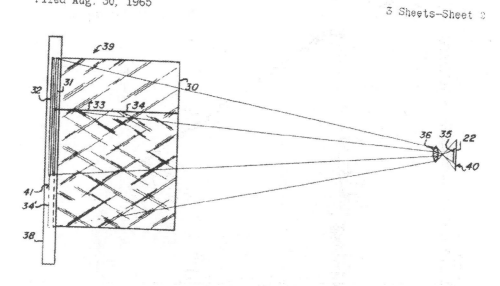

FIG. 3

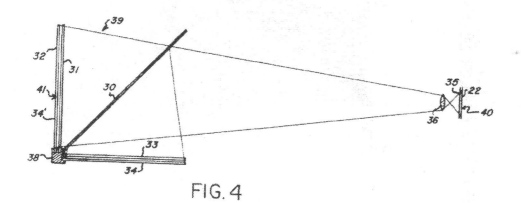

FIG. 4

INVENTOR.

Harry L. Ratliff Jr

Figures 3 and 4 of my sixth U.S. Patent 3,326,106

My seventh U.S. Patent 3,358,078 was granted December 12, 1967, resulted from Application Serial No. 291,198 filed June 27,1963. It is entitled "Apparatus For Making Wide-Angle Cartoons" and had seven allowed claims, eight figures of drawings and 10 columns of specification. This was a device to enable an artist to render wide-angle-stereoscopic cartoons in analogous manner of the single-narrow angle cartoon rendering artists had been doing. The device enabled them to see their creations in three-dimension and at the wide angle it would appear in theaters or viewers later. It was actually more to the point of improving the dioramas of that museum in Canyon, Texas, which had inspired my inventive efforts back when I was 5 or so years old. The primary examiner was John W. Caldwell; the examiner was David G. Redinbaugh and the assistant examiners were P. Sperber, R.L. Richardson and J.A. Orsino. The prior art cited was Barnett 2,933,008 and Heilig 2,955,156.

The above is another picture of the author with Thomas, Franklin and Harvey Locke.

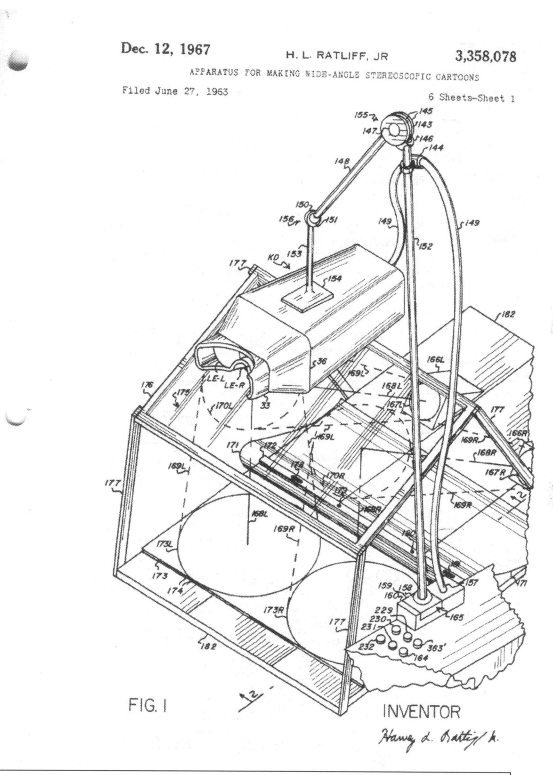

FIG. I

INVENTOR

Harvey L. Ratliff, Jr.

Figure 1 of my seventh U.S. Patent 3,358,078

    I did go to school nine months and did become qualified to enter graduate school pursuing a masters in electrical engineering, but by this time it became very clear that I had to move back to the Washington, D.C., area, because it was necessary to meet with the examiners and explain certain things in order to successfully obtain the sought after patents. There were other problems; the technological level in Texas was just too low for my inventions. I was told everywhere I looked in Texas that you couldn't make an optical quality mold for molding oculars. I knew this wasn't so, but it just showed I needed to be back east. I was not very financially independent and needed a job so I applied for a job with the Department of the Navy as a Cartographer. Obviously I couldn't go back to work as an Examiner. I received the job applied for and was supposed to report to Suitland, Md., for my new job. We had no place for Clara and the children to stay back in the D.C. area so I had to go there by myself, secure a place to stay and report for my new job.

We then moved to the Dennis Grove Apartments in Oxon Hill, Md., into a ground floor apartment where pets were allowed. We had a nice sliding glass back door opening right out to the beautiful landscape in back with a brook within 30 feet of our back door. I used some bookshelves as bookshelves but also as a wall to partition off a little cubicle I could use as my office and studio that I used principally to prosecute my applications for patents.

My eighth U.S. Patent D. 210,326 was a design patent granted, February 27, 1968, resulting from Application Serial No. 3,097, filed July 15, 1966, while I lived in Oxon Hill, Md. The design was revealed with six figures. The primary examiner was Edwin H. Hunter and the assistant examiner was William. M. Henry. The prior art cited was De Vry D. 90,191, Ring D. 136,398, and Fuller D. 175,542.

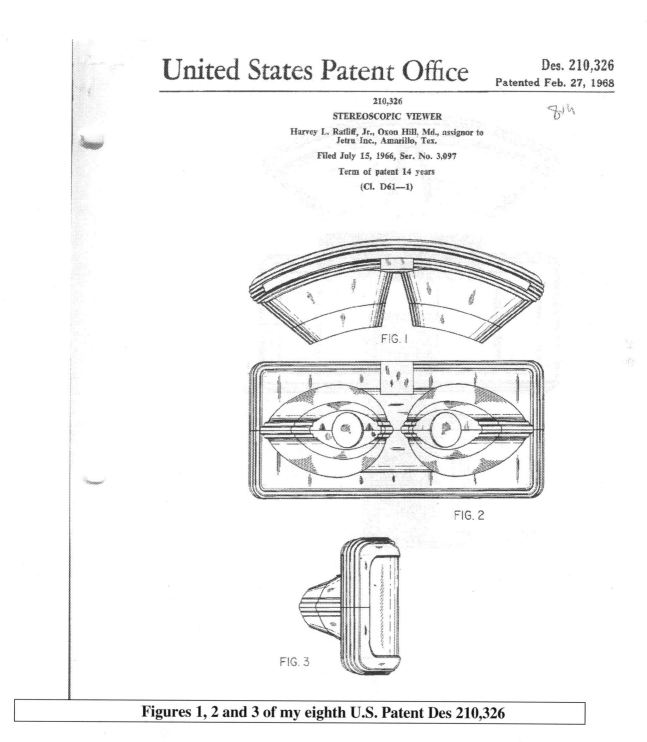

United States Patent Office

Des. 210,326
Patented Feb. 27, 1968

210,326

STEREOSCOPIC VIEWER

Harvey L. Ratliff, Jr., Oxon Hill, Md., assignor to
Jetru Inc., Amarillo, Tex.

Filed July 15, 1966, Ser. No. 3,097

Term of patent 14 years

(Cl. D61—1)

FIG. 1

FIG. 2

FIG. 3

Figures 1, 2 and 3 of my eighth U.S. Patent Des 210,326

My ninth U.S. Patent 3,360,606, was granted December 26, 1967, and resulted from Application Serial No. 287,338, filed June 12, 1963. It is entitled "Stereophonic Systems," had 21 figures of drawings, 23 1/4 columns of specification and three allowed claims. It set forth essentially the stereophonic system for my wide-angle, stereoscopic theatrical presentations. The primary examiner was Kathleen H. Claffy, the Examiner was David G. Redinbaugh and the assistant examiners were J. McHugh and A.H. Gess. The prior art cited was: Schweyer 1,435,339, Gannett 1,850,130, Holt-Seeland 2,655,564, Marson 3,082,295, Camras 3,158,695, Jeliner 1,964,879, and Mueller 2,826,112.

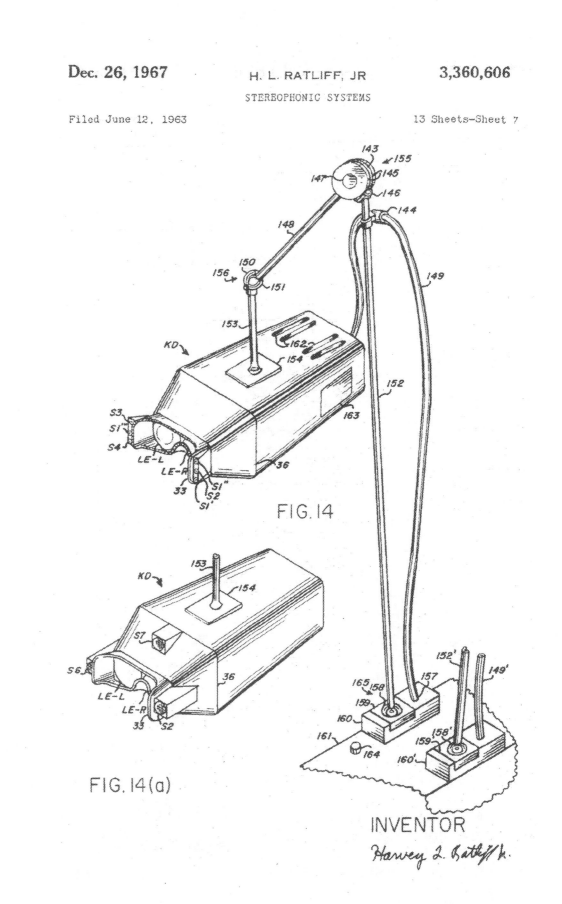

FIG. 14

FIG. 14(a)

INVENTOR

Harvey L. Ratliff Jr.

My 10th U.S. Patent 3,376,381, was granted April 2, 1968, and resulted from Application Serial No. 337,878, filed January 15, 1964. It is entitled "Wide-Angle Stereoscopic Recording And Viewing Apparatus Utilizing Fisheye-Type Distortion And Diverging Lens Axis," had 11 figures of drawings, 9 1/3 columns of specification and five allowed claims. Claim 1 reads: "A wide-angle stereoscopic viewing device for use to re-create substantially distortion-free wide-angle stereoscopic scenes from compressed images having a predetermined amount of fisheye-type, barrel distortion at the ocular object plane with respective right and left picture centers which correspond to the intersection of the axes of symmetry of the fisheye-type compressed taking lenses which introduce the fisheye-type barrel distortion, said axis having a predetermined and operative angle with respect to each other, comprising: a supporting means; right and left wide-angle and expanding ocular lens means for expanding the rays and introducing a predetermined amount of pincushion distortion to nullify the fisheye-type barrel distortion and bring the rays into the eyes of a viewing observer at wide-angles, said ocular lens means having respective axes of symmetry which make an operative angle which is substantially the same said predetermined angle with respect to each other; right and left picture maintaining apparatus for maintaining the right and left fisheye-type, compressed and wide-angle images substantially perpendicular to the respective right and left ocular lens axes with the picture centers of the respective right and left images laterally displaced such as to produce the stereoscopic effect upon a viewing observer." The primary examiner was Robert L. Griffin; the examiner was John W. Caldwell and the assistant examiner was J.A. Orsino. The prior art cited was Levy 2,223,630, Wanner 3,045,573, Smith 3,055,265, De Montebello 2,953,980, and Heilig 2,955,156.

The above picture from left is Lillie, Harvey Locke, Thomas, Franklin, Harvey and George on vacation at Galveston Beach, Texas.

April 2, 1968   H. L. RATLIFF, JR   3,376,381
WIDE-ANGLE STEREOSCOPIC RECORDING AND VIEWING APPARATUS
UTILIZING FISHEYE-TYPE DISTORTION
AND DIVERGING LENS AXES

Filed Jan. 15, 1964   7 Sheets—Sheet 2

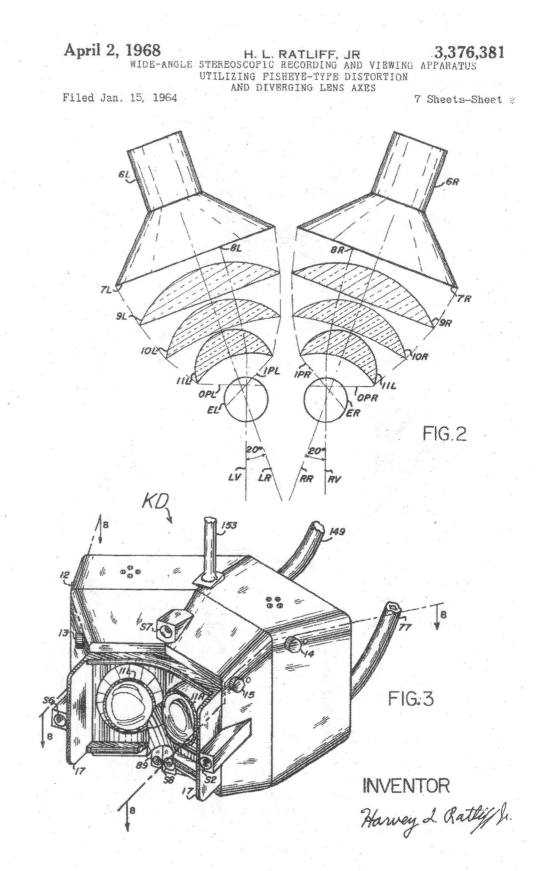

FIG.2

FIG.3

INVENTOR

Harvey L. Ratliff Jr.

104

My 11th U.S. Patent 3,379,489, was granted April 23, 1968, and resulted from Application Serial No, 488,053 filed September 17, 1965. It is entitled "Stereo-Rama Motion Picture Machine," had six figures of drawings, 5 3/4 columns of specification and 16 allowed claims. It was my wide-angle stereoscopic viewing system described in U.S. Patent No. 3,376,381 with the possible addition of stereophonic sound in combination with a coin operated machine. The Primary examiner was Julia E Coiner. The prior art cited was: Macy 1,592,034, Fairall 1,744,459, Montebello 2,953,980 and Heilig 3,050,870. This is the patent Mrs. Coiner allowed in one action, which is the only time that ever happened to me.

The author's second son, Franklin Xaver Ratliff, born May 17, 1963, in Amarillo, Texas.

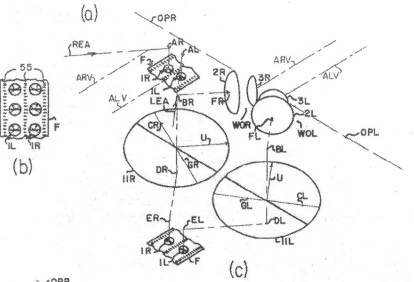

(a)

(b)

(c)

FIG. I

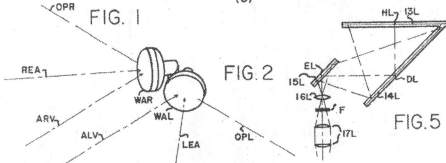

FIG. 2

FIG.5

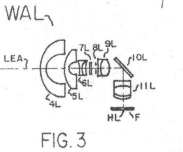

WAL

FIG. 3

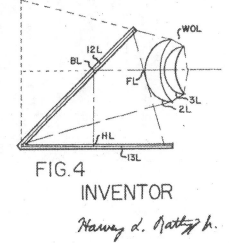

FIG.4

INVENTOR

Harvey L. Ratliff Jr.

106

My 12th U.S. Patent D. 211,421 was a design granted June 11, 1968, resulting from Application Serial No. 9,850 filed December 19, 1967, after we moved to 938 Copley Avenue, St. Charles City, Waldorf, Md. The design was revealed with six figures of drawing. The primary examiner was Edwin H. Hunter and the assistant examiner was William. M. Henry. The prior art cited was Ratliff D. 210,326.

The author's third son, Harvey Locke Ratliff, born September 8, 1964, in Amarillo, Texas.

United States Patent Office

Des. 211,421
Patented June 11, 1968

211,421

STEREOSCOPIC VIEWER

Harvey L. Ratliff, Jr., Waldorf, Md., assignor to
Jetru Inc., Amarillo, Tex.

Filed Dec. 19, 1967, Ser. No. 9,850

Term of patent 14 years

(Cl. D61—1)

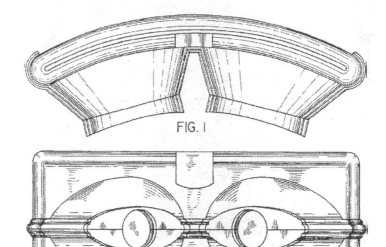

FIG. 1

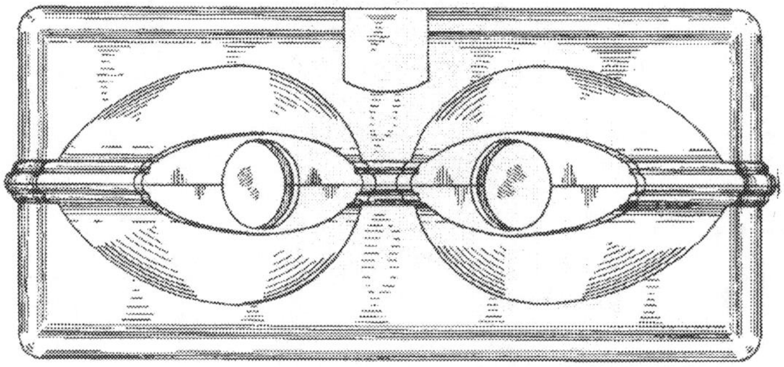

FIG. 2

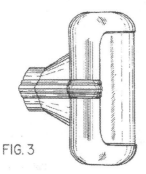

FIG. 3

Figures 1, 2 and 3 of my 12ᵗʰ U.S. Patent Des. 211,421

My 13th U.S. Patent 3,390,587, was granted July 2, 1968, and resulted from Application Serial No. 394,698, filed September 8, 1964 and continued with Application Serial No. 577,091 filed September 2, 1966. The first application was filed on Harvey's birthday but I had actually put the application in the mail a few days before. The filing date is when the Patent Office received it. It is entitled "Aircraft Control System." The government put out brochures of inventions needed in which they said they needed better aircraft control systems, which could control more functions with one control. But, these brochures turned out to be meaningless. I actually thought of this control system while working on my stereophonic sound creation system. The abstract of disclosure reads: "a single lever control assembly which enables many controls from one lever. Axial displacement of the lever can control one mechanism such as the throttle of a fixed wing aircraft. Rotational movement of the lever can control a second mechanism such as the ailerons of a fixed wing aircraft. Lateral displacement of the lever about a pivot point in a first, say horizontal, plane can control a third mechanism. Lateral displacement of the lever about the pivot point in a second, say vertical, plane can control a fourth mechanism such as the elevators of a fixed wing aircraft. And manipulation of a switch or rheostat secured to the lever can control a fifth mechanism such as the flaps of a fixed wing aircraft. The primary examiner was Milton Kaufman. The prior art cited was Stevens 3,266,523.

The author's wonderful daughter Lillie Christine Ratliff, born November 21, 1966, in Washington, D.C.

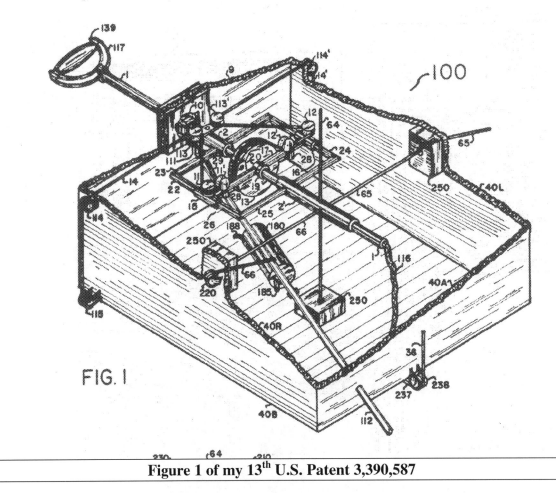

FIG. I

Figure 1 of my 13th U.S. Patent 3,390,587

My 14th U.S. Patent 3,395,498 was granted August 6, 1968, resulting from Application Serial No. 275,411, filed April 24,1963, divided and this application Serial No. 505,117 filed October 18, 1965. This patent is entitled "Method Of Making Lenses For Wide-Angle Oculars." This patent is the method of making the lens of my U.S. Patent 3,298,771, and is divided from the same original application. It had nine figures of drawings, six columns of specification and two allowed independent claims. The primary examiner is Lester M. Swingle and the prior art cited is Laisne 1,286,032,

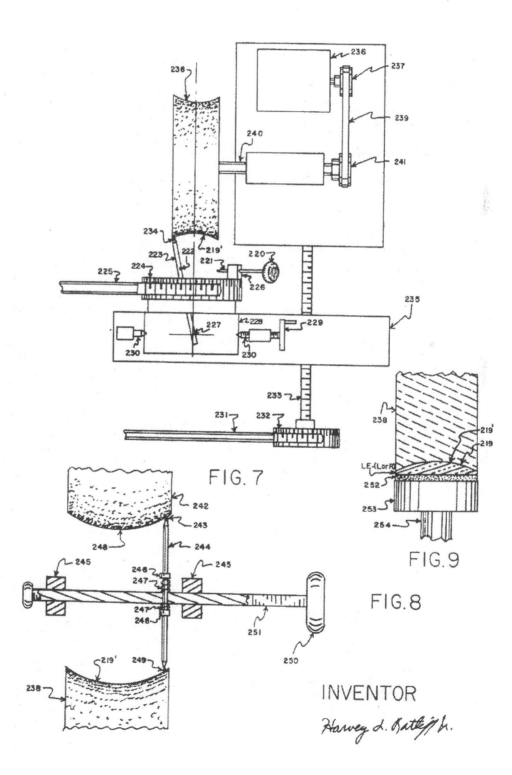

FIG. 7

FIG. 8

FIG. 9

INVENTOR

Harvey L. Ratliff Jr.

111

My 15th U.S. Patent 3,403,576 was granted October 1, 1968, resulting from Application Serial No. 394,698 filed September 8, 1964, and is a continuation-in-part thereof and this Application Serial No. 578,342 filed September 9, 1966. It is entitled "Single Lever Control Assembly." It has two figures of drawings, 2 1/2 columns of specification and five allowed claims. Its abstract of disclosure reads "There is disclosed a single lever control assembly which enables many direct and mechanical controls from one lever. Axial displacement of the lever can directly and mechanically control one mechanism such as the throttle of a fixed wing aircraft. Rotational movement of the lever can directly and mechanically control a second mechanism such as ailerons of fixed wing aircraft. Lateral displacement of the lever about a pivot in a first, say horizontal, plane can directly and mechanically control a third mechanism. Lateral displacement of the lever about the pivot in a second, say vertical, plane can directly and mechanically control a fourth mechanism such as the elevators of a fixed wing aircraft." The primary examiner was Milton Kaufman and the prior art cited was Stevens 3,266,523.

Oct. 1, 1968   H. L. RATLIFF, JR   3,403,576

SINGLE LEVER CONTROL ASSEMBLY

Filed Sept. 9, 1966

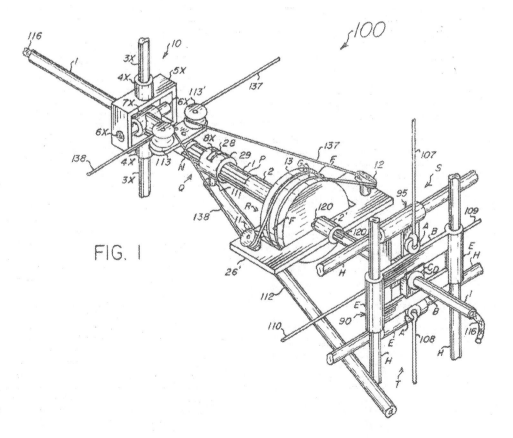

FIG. I

Figure 1 of my 15th U.S. Patent 3,403,576

My 16th U.S. Patent 3,424,511 was granted January 28, 1969, resulting from Application Serial No. 560,531 filed June 27, 1966. It is entitled "Wide-Angle Stereoviewers." It has eight figures of drawings, 5 1/2 columns of specification and three allowed claims. The abstract of disclosure states "A panoramic viewer with a large curved picture slot for panoramic stereo re-creation coacting with wide-angle oculars having divergent optical axes which enables substantially distortion free wide-angle viewing." The primary examiner was David Schonberg and the assistant examiner was P.R. Gilliam.. The prior art cited was Hayashi 2,093,520, Mast 2,326,718, Bennett 2,674,251, Romrell 2,834,251, Montebello 2,953,980, Heilig 2,955,156, Italy Fazio) 546,968 and Van Alabada: "A Wide-Angle Stereoscope and a Wide-Angle Viewfinder," Transactions of the Optical Society of London, vol. 25, 1923-24, pp. 249-257, 259, 260. This was the patent for the invention that I first tried to manufacture and sell, which will be discussed further on.

The author's youngest son, George Whittenburg Ratliff, born October 11, 1968, in Washington, D.C.

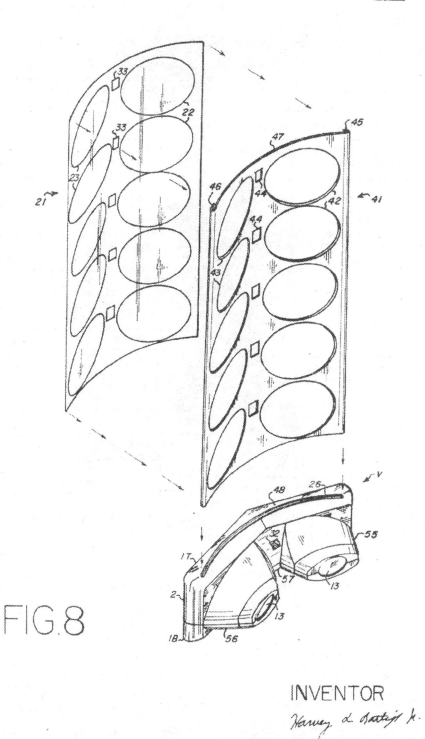

FIG.8

INVENTOR

Harvey L. Ratliff Jr.

Figure 8 of my 16th U.S. Patent 3,424,511

114

My 17th U.S. Patent 3,429,704 was granted February 25, 1969, resulting from original Application filed April 24, 1963, Serial No. 275,411, now abandoned, Divided and this application filed October 22, 1965, Serial No, 500,725. It is entitled "Process For Making A Color Screen." It has nine figures of drawings, 5 1/8 columns of specification and two independent allowed claims. The Abstract of disclosure states "A quantity of radiant energy sensitive dichroic material with its axis of polarization in a first plane is extruded upon a work piece. This material is then exposed to three point sources of radiant energy through an affixed first mask and a removable second mask or equivalent with the first mask enabling the illumination by each said point source of narrow strips that will be struck by beam's from the electron guns at the same location as the point sources later, said strips are each as high as the work piece but only half as wide as the lateral distance between each strip and enabling the illumination by all three point sources of the entire work piece, and with the second mask or equivalent means enabling the illumination of strips which are each as wide and long as the area illuminated by all three point sources and blocking from illumination alternate adjacent strip areas of the same width. The material between the exposed strips is then removed and a quantity of radiant energy sensitive dichroic material with its axis of polarization substantially perpendicular to the first plane is extruded upon the work piece. This material is then exposed as before except means are used in conjunction with the second mask whereby the areas between the first exposed areas are alone exposed. The material in the first exposed areas is then removed leaving adjacent strips of oppositely polarized material upon the work piece. Then a red phosphor, which is radiant energy sensitive, is applied to the work piece and the areas thereof, which will be struck by the red electron gun, are exposed to the point source corresponding to the red electron gun through the affixed mask. The strips between these exposed strips are removed. Next a green phosphor which is radiant energy sensitized is applied to the work piece and areas thereof which will later be struck by the green electron gun are exposed to the point source corresponding to the green electron gun through the affixed mask. The strips of green phosphor between the exposed strips of green phosphor are then removed. Next a blue phosphor, which is radiant energy sensitive, is applied to the work piece and areas thereof, which will later be struck by the blue electron gun, are exposed to the point source corresponding to the blue electron gun through the affixed mask. And finally the strips of blue phosphor between the exposed strips of blue phosphor are removed leaving strips of red, green, and blue phosphor on top of the strips having said first axis of polarization adjacent strips of red, green and blue phosphor on top of the strips having said second axis of polarization, to thus enable a new form of wide angle stereoscopic viewing." The primary examiner was Norman G. Torchin and the assistant examiner was C. Bowers. The prior art cited was Land et al 2,440,106, Klein et al 2,464,586, Sadowsky et al 2,870,010, Rehorn 2,883,906, Lauricella 3,165,578, Mahler 3,41,960 and Beste 3,251,933.

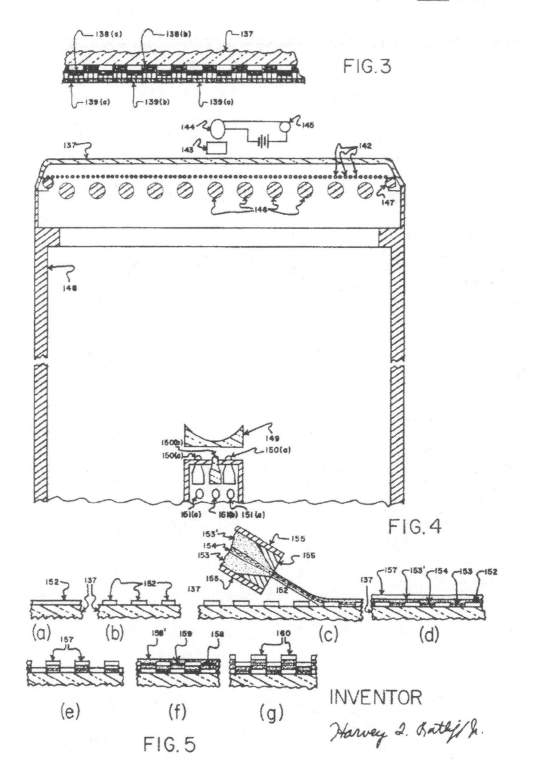

FIG. 3

FIG. 4

FIG. 5

INVENTOR

Harvey L. Ratliff Jr.

My 18th U.S. Patent 3,439,972 was granted April 22, 1969, resulting from original Application Serial No. 447,600, filed April 1, 1965, now Patent No. 3,272,069 dated Sept. 13, 1966, Divided and this application April 22, 1966, Serial No. 544,462. This patent also resulted from my first five applications and has many of the same drawings. It is entitled "Wide-Angle Stereoscopic Picture Element And Viewer." It has five figures of drawings, 2 1/2 Columns of specification and two independent and seven dependent allowed claims. The abstract of disclosure states: "A picture element is employed which permits a wide-angle stereoscopic view to be formed by overlapping left and right eye image in the central area. In one embodiment a grating screen is employed which co acts with adjacent right and left eye view strips in an overlapping central area to separate a right and left eye image; a second embodiment employs a lenticular screen coacting with adjacent right and left eye view strips in an overlapped central area to separate a right and left eye image; a third embodiment employs polarized images in conjunction with analyzers to separate a left and right eye image in an overlapped central area; and a fourth embodiment employs a mirror arrangement to separate a left and a right eye view in an overlapped central area.." The primary examiner was David Schonberg and the assistant examiner was P.R. Gilliam.. The prior art cited was Montebello 2,953,980, Heilig 2,955,156, Ratliff 3,272,069 and Jacobson 624,042 plus the German Patent 226,260.

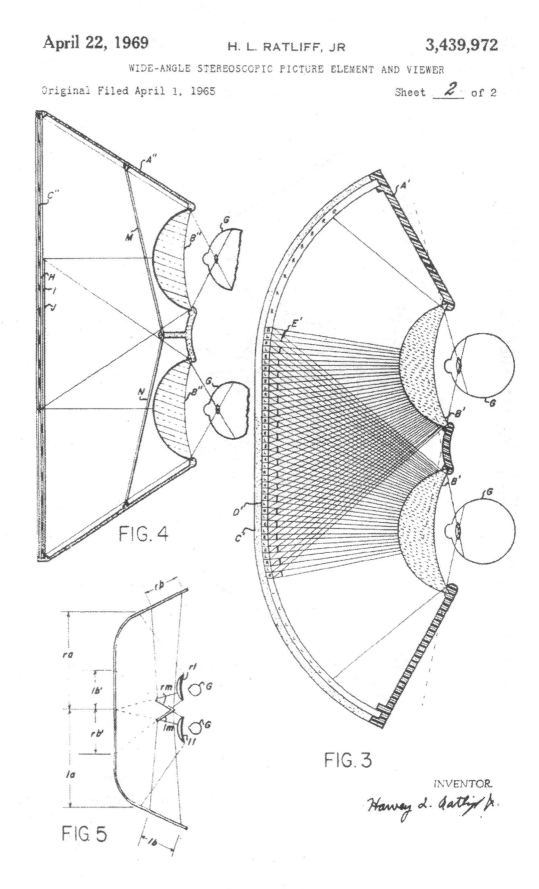

FIG. 4

FIG. 5

FIG. 3

INVENTOR.

Harvey L. Ratliff Jr.

118

My 19th U.S. Patent 3,463,570 was granted August 27, 1969, resulting from Application Serial No. 343,841, filed February 10, 1964, while we still lived at 5315 Alvarado Street, Amarillo, Texas. It is entitled "Wide-Angle Stereoscopic Viewers." It has 18 Figures of drawings, 9 1/3 columns of specification and five independent allowed claims. The abstract of disclosure states: "An substantially distortion free apparatus for viewing wide-angle stereoscopic pictures utilizing a lens system with wide-angle oculars and large wedges whereby the pictures are placed at a flat object plane and the scene is re-created about right and left axes which are respectively rotated some 15 degree to the right and left of the respective axes of the right and left eye view to thus increase the angle of horizontal view some 30 degree more than is possible for any specifically sized ocular diameter placed any specific distance from the eyes of an observer." The primary examiner was David Schonberg and the assistant examiner was P.R. Gilliam. The prior art cited was Woody 625,627, Gruber 2,189,285, Sauer 2,241,041, Athey et al 2,317,875, Heilig 2,955,156, Gruber 2,511,334, Heilig 3,050,879 with Foreign Patents: Switzerland Patent 83,149 and France Patent 506,022.

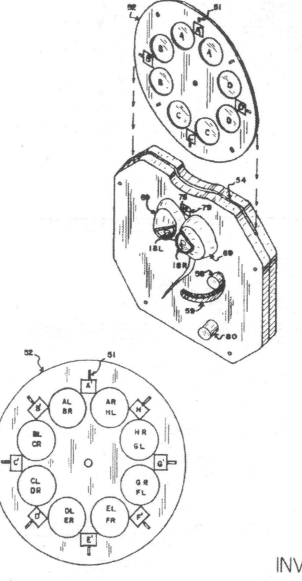

FIG. 17

FIG. 18

INVENTOR

Harvey L. Ratliff Jr.

120

My 20th U.S. Patent 3,471,224 was granted October 7, 1969, the day before my wife's birthday, resulting from original Application Serial No. 275,411 filed April 24, 1963 and Continuation-In-Part Applications Serial No. 483,728 and 502,814 filed August 30, 1965, and October 13, 1965 respectively and this Application Serial No. 618,977 filed February 27, 1967. It is entitled "Stereoscopic And/Or a Peripheral Vision Theatrical System." It has three figures of drawings, 3 3/4 columns of specification and two independent and eight dependent claims. The abstract of disclosure states: "A motion picture theater has an individual viewing apparatus at each seat. Each viewing apparatus is provided with right eye and left eye lenses and polarizers. The curvature of each lens has a fixed relation with the lens curvature of a motion picture camera wide-angle lens such that the distortion introduced by the wide-angle camera lens is compensated for by the viewer lenses to provide a distortion-free wide-angle stereoscopic picture. Additional apparatus is provided for simulating temperature, wind, and odor conditions." The primary examiner was Norton Ansher and the assistant examiner was Monroe H. Hayes. The prior art cited was Compere 1,313,262, Zimmer 1,334,480, Rosenhaur 2,157,099, Heilig 3,050,870, Tondreau 3,189,915 with Foreign Patents of France 934,747, France 1,050,728, France 1,126,970, Italy 438,935.

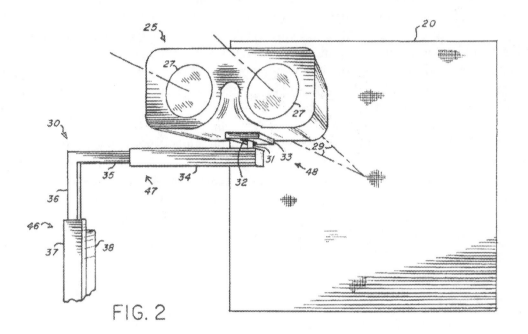

FIG. 2

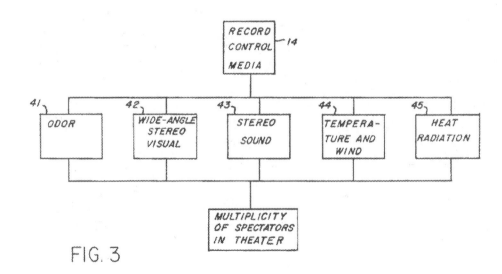

FIG. 3

INVENTOR

Harvey L. Ratliff Jr.

122

My 21st U.S. Patent 3,489,945 was granted January 13, 1970, resulting from Original Application Serial No. 275,411 filed April 24, 1963, divided into Application Serial No. 505,118 filed October 18, 1965, and Continued for this Application Serial No. 624,638 filed February 14, 1967. It is entitled "Cathode Ray Tubes." It has 32 figures of drawings, sixteen columns of specification and two independent allowed claims. The abstract of disclosure states: "A cathode ray tube is disclosed which enables highly resolved wide-angle pictures to be produced by reversing the chromatic aberration and distortion that can be introduce at wide-angles of view by some wide-angle oculars." The primary examiner was Rodney D. Bennett, Jr. and the assistant examiner was Malcolm F. Hubler. The prior art cited was A.M.Durskey et al 2,864,032, Gleichauf 2,907,915, Szegho 3,028,521 and Heuer 3,059,140.

The above picture from left are Lillie, Clara, Thomas, George, Harvey, Harvey Locke and Franklin in about 1974.

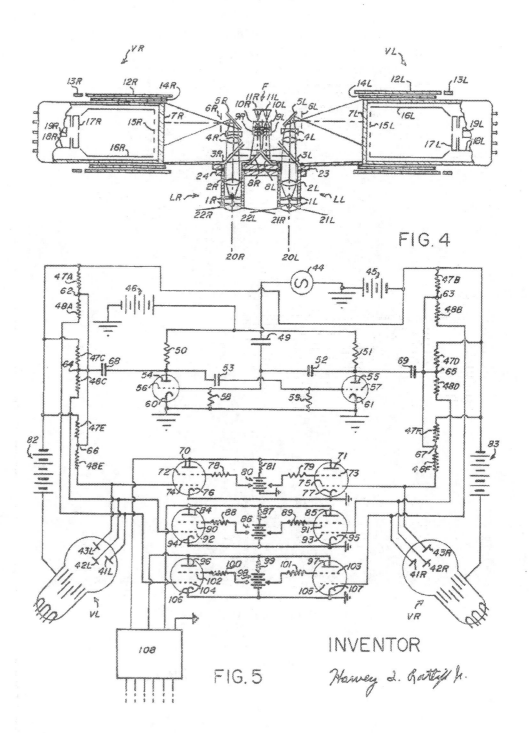

FIG. 4

FIG. 5

INVENTOR

Harvey L. Ratliff Jr.

Clara and Harvey celebrating Christmas

My 22nd U.S. Patent 3,504,122 was granted March 31, 1970, resulting from Application Serial No. 440,110 filed March 16, 1965 while we lived at 3701 46ᵗʰ St., Lubbock, Texas, 79413. It is entitled "Stereoscopic Television Systems With Means To Control The Camera Movement From A Remote Location." It has 14 figures of drawings, 14 1/2 columns of specification and four independent and two dependent claims. The abstract of disclosure states: "There is disclosed an improvement in the taking system of a remotely controlled remote viewing system combined with a remote mobile unit which employs fisheye lenses to enable a wider angle of stereo view to be recorded upon the same area of record media and to enable distortion-free and astigmatic-free stereo re-creation when simple oculars, that due to their simplicity introduce pincushion distortion at wide angles of view, are used and which diverge the optical axes of the taking lenses to enable the recorded angle of stereo view to be still further increased by an amount equal to substantially the angle between the optical axes of the taking lenses." The primary examiner was Robert L. Griffin and the assistant examiner was J.A. Orsino. The prior art cited was Levy 2,223,630, Wanner 3,045,573, Smith 3,055,265, Ratliff 3,376,265, Got 2,359,032, Ryan 2,892,290, Heilig 2,955,156, Hill

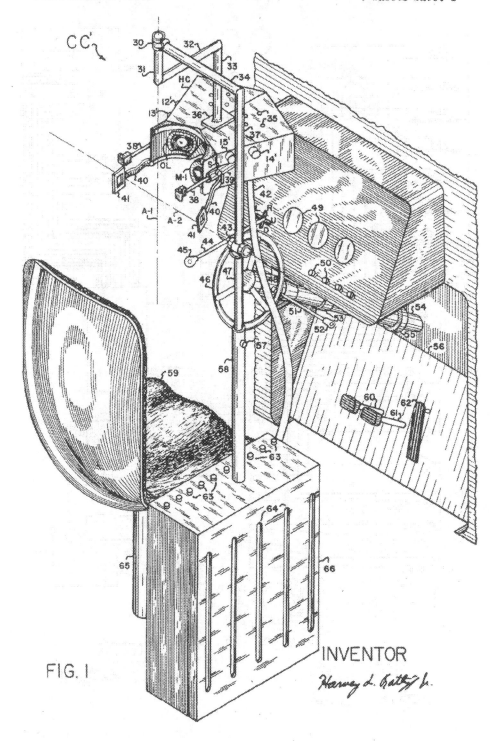

FIG. 1

INVENTOR

Harvey L. Ratliff Jr.

Figure 1 of my 22nd U.S. Patent 3,504,122

3,007,538, Quinn 3,198,279, Bradley 3,205,303, Falbel 3,209,073. This invention was intended to help the U.S. in its "police actions" in other countries.

On November 21, 1966, our only daughter and fourth child, Lillie Christine Ratliff, was born in Morris Cafritze Hospital, Washington, D.C. Dr. Parisi delivered her. The name Lillie was from my mother, and the name Christine from Clara's mother. This was the first and only time I was allowed to actually watch the birth take place. After that I was not unhappy that it was the only time that I was allowed to do so.

My 23rd U.S. Patent 3,511,928 was granted April 24, 1970, resulting from Original Application Serial No. 275,411 filed April 24, 1963, Divided and this application Serial No. 500,614 filed October 22, 1965. It is entitled "Wide-Angle Viewing Device For Chromatic-Free And Distortion-Free Re-Creation." It has 24 figures of drawings, 12 1/2 columns of specification and one independent and three dependent claims. The abstract of disclosure states: "Apparatus is devised for electronically introducing a distortion, such as barrel distortion, in the image at the object planes of wide-angle oculars for reversing to eliminate the opposite distort ion, such as pincushion distortion, of these wide-angle oculars which are, for example, simple oculars having a simple aspherical lens element therein, and apparatus is devised for introducing a chromatic reversing situation in the image at the object planes of wide-angular oculars such as the said simple wide-angle oculars having a single lens element therein for reversing to eliminate the chromatic aberration introduced by these wide-angle oculars." The primary examiner was Robert L. Griffin and the assistant examiner was J.A. Orsino. The prior art cited was McCollum 2,388,170, Thor 2,906,919, Abramson 2,931,855, Heilig 2,955,156, Lakjer 3,051,779, Sziklai 2,905,754 and Ratliff 3,376,381.

October 11, 1968, George Whittenburg Ratliff was born at Morris Cafritze Hospital, Washington, D.C. He was our largest baby, measuring 23 inches and weighing 8 pounds, 15 ounces, as I recall. The George was from George Washington, the father of our country, revolutionary leader and also an enlightenment thinker. The Whittenburg was after my mother's dad and my grandfather.

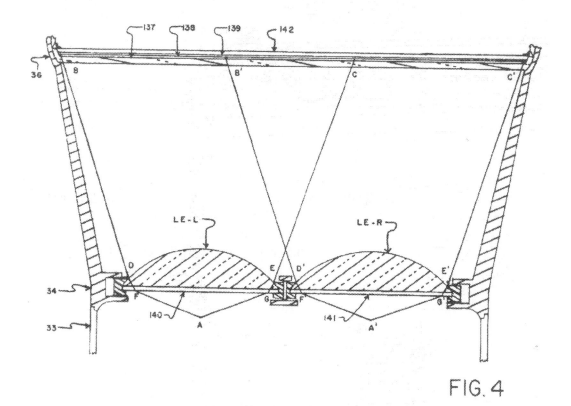

FIG. 4

Figure 4 of my 23rd U.S. Patent 3,511,928

My 24th U.S. Patent 3,516,725 was granted June 23, 1970, resulting from Application Serial No. 721,841 filed April 16, 1968. It is entitled "Two-Ocular Panoramic Viewing Device." It has four figures of drawings, 4 3/4 columns of specification and two independent and three dependent claims. The abstract of disclosure states: "A structural combination which enables flat or slightly cylindrical transparent slides or the equivalent thereof to be expanded into the equivalent of a substantially

128

spherical virtual image surface which is enlarged some 12 ½ times, at the standard assumption of 10 inches from the eyes, to bring the peripheral rays of light into the eyes at some 145 degree (between 85 degree and 180 + degree) while retaining a resolution at the virtual image surface which is substantially sharp enough to be beneath the resolving power of the eye even when the slides are made from color film." The primary examiner was Paul R. Gilliam. The prior art cited was Ratliff 3,298,771, Montebello 2,953,980, Heilig 2,955,156, Heilig 3,050,870, Ratliff 3,272,069, Ratliff 3,376,381 and an Italian Patent 336,505.

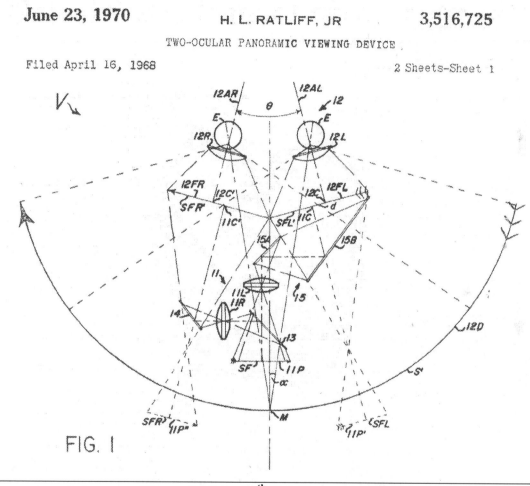

June 23, 1970   H. L. RATLIFF, JR   3,516,725

TWO-OCULAR PANORAMIC VIEWING DEVICE

Filed April 16, 1968   2 Sheets-Sheet 1

FIG. 1

Figure 1 of my 24ᵗʰ U.S. Patent 3,516,725

My 25th U.S. Patent 3,601,475 was granted August 24, 1971, resulting from Application Serial No. 860,489 filed September 24, 1969. It is a continuation-in-part of Application Serial No. 440,110 filed March 16, 1965, now U.S. Patent No. 3,504,122 and Serial No. 618,977 filed February 27, 1967, now U.S. Patent No. 3,471,224, which is a continuation-in-part of Serial No. 343,841 filed February 10, 1964, now U.S. Patent No. 3,464,570, and Serial No. 638,319 filed May 15, 1967, and Serial No. 662,716 filed August 23, 1967, now abandoned. It is entitled "Distortion-Free Panoramic Viewer And Picture Therefor." It has seven figures of drawings, 6 1/4 columns of specification and three independent and one dependent claims. The abstract of disclosure states: "A panoramic viewer having a large slot in the front portion thereof and a special wide-angle ocular in the rear portion thereof for eliminating the distortion of a fisheye-type picture placed in the slot to enable substantially distortion-free wide-angle viewing." The primary examiner was David Schonberg and the assistant examiner was Paul A. Sacher. The prior art cited is Eckert 2,410,722 and the following reference *Scientific American,* "The Amateur Scientist," Vol. 189, #6. Dec. 1953 (350/175 SL) Pages 110-113.

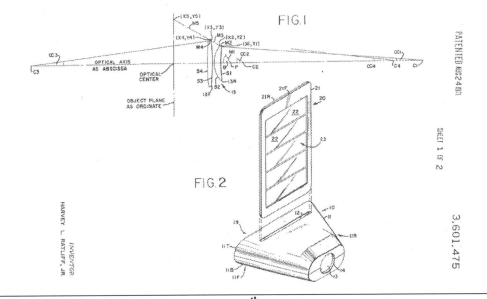

Figures 1 and 2 of my 25th U.S. Patent 3,601,475

My 26th U.S. Patent 3,608,458 was granted September 28, 1971, resulting from Application Serial No. 782,672 filed December 10, 1968. It is a continuation-in-part of co pending prior applications Serial No. 343,841, filed February 10, 1964 and now U.S. Patent 3,463,570, Serial No. 440,110, filed March 16, 1965, and now U.S. Patent 3,506,122, and Serial No. 560,531, filed June 27, 1966, and now U.S. Patent 3,424,511. It is entitled "Wide-Angle, Stereoscopic, And Fisheye-Type Camera For Substantially Distortion-Free Stereoscopy." It has four figures of drawings, 3 3/4 columns of specification, two independent and five dependent allowed claims. The abstract of disclosure states: "A wide-angle, stereoscopic and fisheye-type camera for panoramic stereo re-creations utilizing fisheye lenses which preferably have diverging optical axes for taking pictures which when properly viewed enable substantially distortion-free wide-angle re-creations." The primary examiner was Samuel S. Matthews and the assistant examiner was D.J. Clement. The prior art cited was: Park 2,841,063, Heilig 2,955,156, Isshiki 3,524,697, Muller 3,115,816, Lutz 2,036,062, Montremy 2,804,001, Montebello 2,953,980 and Wanner 3,045,573.

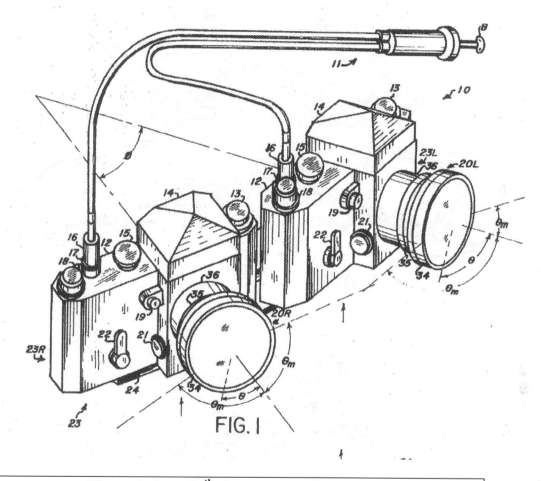

FIG. I

Figure 1 of my 26th U.S. Patent 3,608,458

My 27th U.S. Patent 3,632,189 was granted January 4, 1972, resulting from application Serial No. 31,811 filed April 9, 1970. It is a continuation-in-part of Application Serial No. 662,716 filed August 23, 1967, and now abandoned. It is entitled "Wide-Angle Lens." It has nine figures of drawings counting three parts for Figure 7, i.e., 7a, 7b and 7c, 5 1/4 columns of specification, one independent and seven dependent allowed claims. The abstract of disclosure states: "A complex aspheric surface for a wide-angle lens is devised which enables distortionless wide-angle viewing through the lens of fisheye-type pictures with ideal accommodation characteristics from several principles the most important of which are: that the angle between a ray from a point on the object plane of the lens entering the eyes of an observer looking into the lens and the optical axis of the lens has a substantially constant relation with the distance along the object from this point to the optical axis of the lens, the principles of the lens maker's equation, general lens theory and physical principles, trigonometry and general

131

mathematical procedures." The primary examiner was David Schonberg and the assistant examiner was Michel J. Tokar. The prior art cited was Obford 943,449 and Poullain 1,143,316.

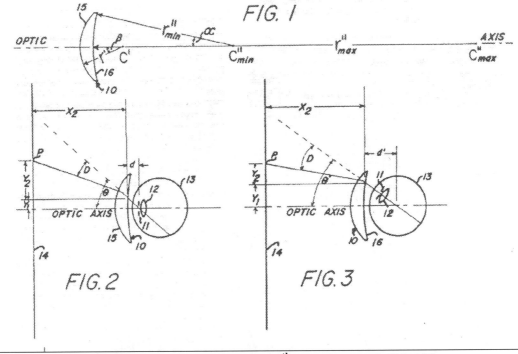

Figures 1, 2 and 3 of my 27th U.S. Patent 3,632,189

My 28th U.S. Patent 3,850,505 was granted November 26, 1974, resulting from Application Serial No. 341,482 filed March 15, 1973. It is entitled "Universal Stereoscopic Viewing Device." It has three Figures of drawings, 3 3/4 columns of specification, two independent and nine dependent claims. The abstract of disclosure states: "A universal stereoscopic viewing device for use with all the major stereoscopic formats including panoramic formats of 2.07 inch by 0.92 inch or commonly used small formats of 0.45 inch by 0.40 inch, which device has lenses having a "K" property that introduces no distortion when the lenses are used with the common small formats (0.45 x 0.40) and is distortion-free at panoramic angles of view when matched to the panoramic slides of the large formats with a reverse "K" value of the same magnitude." The primary examiner was Paul A. Sacher. The prior art cited is Golden 3,005,378 and Patton 3,145,253.

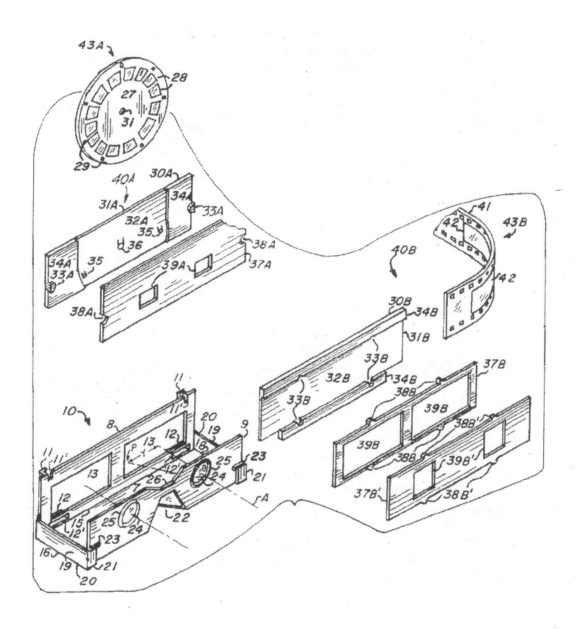

Figures 1, 2 and 3 of my 28th U.S. Patent 3,850,505

This turned out to be my last patent obtained about which I will go into more later. The only recognition, that I know of, for my inventive efforts is in an article at (http://www.3dmagic.com/articles/sit.html) by Michael Starks entitled "Stereoscopic Imaging Technology," page 14, fifth paragraph in which he states: "Wide angle stereo has a long history in photography and Harvey Ratliff deserves mention as a pioneer in this area and as the father of wide angle stereoscopic video. He built several devices and proposed others in a series of patents in the 1960's (U.S.-3511928, 3504122, 3376381, 3293358, 3291204). Ratliff used conventional lenses, while more recent patents on panoramic HMD's have proposed more exotic optical techniques..."

At this point, for people who are interested, I will go through one of my applications for patent in more detail to give the reader an idea of what is involved in obtaining a patent in **Appendix A** at the end of this book.

Chapter
XIII
Trying To Make And Sell My Inventions

The biggest problem I faced while trying to manufacture and sell an invention myself or in trying to sell others into manufacturing and selling my inventions seemed to me to be the lack of sufficient funds. I think now it was probably the *Ellsworth Toohey* effect. I found after working for the Navy as a cartographer that I just didn't have time to process my patents, sell or manufacture my inventions; so I had to quit that job and my mother backed me, but I was restricted to approximately $800 per month to provide for my family, process the applications and make and sell my inventions from that time on and before that largely to the amount I earned at the various jobs myself with the exception that she financed me during the year I was trying to get a master's degree in electrical engineering at Texas Tech. This constricted my efforts to the point that I made mistakes. The invention, which I tried to manufacture myself, first was that disclosed in U.S. Patent No. 3424511 described above. Before trying to manufacture it however, I tried to sell it to companies I thought could easily put it on the market. The principal company I remember trying to sell the invention to was Sawyers of Beaverton, Ore., who manufactured and marketed "View-Master Viewers" invented by Gruber and the transparencies that went with them. Very shortly after I wrote them a letter offering my invention, they suddenly sold out to GAF. The company GAF treated me as their worst enemy and stonewalled me at every turn; however, several GAF employees sent their resume and an application for a job working for me, i.e., Jetru, Inc. that I was president of. But Jetru, Inc. or I were not financially capable of hiring them. Jetru, Inc. was largely the brainchild of my mother. I, and my family, owned about 51 percent of it, and Virginia and her family, owned about 49 percent of it. This way Virginia's family had approximately equal financial benefit if my inventions were successful.

I found a little mold making and injection molding company, close by where I then lived, consisting of two NASA machinists that worked at the Goddard Space Center and who were in business on their time off. Their names were Chuck Bland and Stewart Tull as I recall. I have forgotten the name of their company. At that time my family and I lived in the Dennis Grove Apartment in Oxon Hill, Md. I made a deal with the mold makers to make the styrene injection mold for manufacturing the viewer body as illustrated in Figures 1, 5, 6 and 7 of the patent. As alluded to earlier, I had a terrible time finding someone to mold the acrylic lenses for the oculars to go into this viewer. I had been looking a long time and could find nobody capable of doing it. Finally I read an article in a magazine that indicated American Optical Company in Southbridge, Mass., could possibly do it. I wrote them a letter and they sent a positive response and after visiting them and showing them the lens I had designed, it appeared that I was off and running. Things weren't nearly as good as they looked however. The styrene mold makers made me a deal to make the mold for the affordable price of $5,000; however, it turned out that I couldn't afford the five-year time period it took them to make the mold.

I also had the problem of manufacturing the high-resolution transparency pictures to go into the viewer. The original plan was to use a man who told me he could gravure print the high-resolution transparencies that I needed at a price I considered workable. I waited on him for some one to two years and he just couldn't deliver. His pictures would have been large enough, I believe it was 3 1/2 inch by 2 1/4 inch, which my ocular would need only a single lens that I had designed and American Optical had, by then made the mold for. I had a prototype made of this viewer and the pictures were crisp and sharp and the wide-angle, stereoscopic scenes were very impressive. But when it became clear the gravure printer couldn't deliver, I had to figure another way. I turned to Technicolor Company in Hollywood, Ca., after quite an effort to prove them up as the ones who could do the job. They could process pictures on 70-millimeter film (2.07 inch by 0.920 inch), as I recall. This required a shorter focal length lens to get the proper K as defined in the patent. Therefore, I needed a second lens in the oculars and I had to change the mold in the middle of the time period it was being made. The prototype picture had been on a cylindrical focal "plane," and with the prior focal length and single lens, that American Optical had made to my design; in the ocular it had been crisp and sharp. Now, however the focal plane needed to be flat or it wasn't crisp and sharp enough. But to make it flat would have required a totally new mold, which I couldn't afford either the time or money for. This resulted in the picture, when viewed, being less crisp and sharp than needed. I believe this is the reason the product didn't take off as I had hoped.

Although making the viewer with its required oculars was quite complicated and involved, it was not all that was involved. Transparencies to go in the viewer were also involved. My plan was to show the potential buyers how much greater my wide-angle (some 140° horizontally by 45° vertically) three-dimensional slides were than the View-Master narrow-angle 13° by 13° slides were. The plan was to go to the tourist attractions shown in the View-Master packets of transparencies and show how much better mine were. This involved many photography trips by auto. I used the camera disclosed in my U.S. Patent No. 3,608,458, to take the pictures and would send the film to the German photographic company, Agfa, as I recall to process them and return them to my home which was by then 938 Copley Avenue, Waldorf, Md., as I recall. After receiving the Agfa processed pictures I would mount the pictures for viewing in my proportionately enlarged prototype viewer, making sure everything was right and sent them to Technicolor where they were mass-produced. Then I mounted the mass produced pictures in a cardboard holder that I had designed and sub-contracted out for mass production. I then made sure they worked in my viewers that had been injection molded by the mold making and injection molding people. I took Thomas and Franklin along with me on many of the trips. But, the viewer didn't explode on the market. I probably sold 200-300 viewers, but they just didn't take off. I believe the reason was the crispness and sharpness was too low.

I had never been a salesman before and was inexperienced at selling and believe it is not my long suit; however, I can sell when I meet people personally. Another big mistake I made was related to my lack of funds. I didn't travel and personally talk to the people I was trying to sell to but rather relied on letters which were much cheaper but just didn't work. From reading since that time period I have come to believe that people must be sold on me as a person before they will buy my product. So, since I relied on the mail to sell my other patented inventions, I had no success in selling them either. The capital requirements to manufacture my theatrical systems myself were much more than my limited funds could afford. There was another very formidable problem however. In my experience, industry in general appeared very hostile to individual inventors such as me. *Ellsworth Toohey* was showing his ugly face again. There was the "not invented here" syndrome. Many companies never use an outside invention, i.e., one not invented by one of their comparatively unrewarded employees. Further, company leaders are very weak at grasping good new inventions. Examples of this are everywhere. The Tau Beta Pi Engineer-Patent Attorney Chester Carlson, who invented the Xerox copying process, had a horrible time getting anyone to buy his process, which was extremely superior to what was in existence at that time. I believe he had obtained some 30 patents which all expired before he reaped any benefit and he died soon afterward. *Ellsworth Toohey* had one of his big victories here. According to my reading of "Pirates of Silicon Valley," Steve Wasniack, the creator who basically invented the major portion of the computer system making Bill Gates a multibillionaire, could not convince his superiors in the company that owned his inventions that his inventions had any value whatever; so, these inventions were released to him and Steve Jobs Steve Jobs, the negotiator of the two, legally gained control of Steve Wasniack's creations. This was still another victory for *Ellsworth Toohey*. Also as I read that story an employee of Xerox was ordered by her boss to give her creations, i.e., inventions, away to Steve Jobs (Jobs being the parasite negotiator of the two) and Steve Wasniack, who was really the one understanding them, invented the other portion of the computer system making Bill Gates (Gates was a better parasite negotiator than Jobs was) a multi-billionaire. This was a colossal victory for *Ellsworth Toohey.* Please note that even Bill Gates was not an employee of a large public corporation nor was Steve Jobs or Steve Wasniack at the time they came up with Microsoft. Further, if they had been the world would most probably never had the great creation of Microsoft.

Back in the days of studying the aptitude patterns developed by the Johnson O'Connor Research Laboratory, I was highly impressed by the aptitude pattern of the company presidents and chief executive officers of large public corporations. *Their aptitude pattern was first an objective personality and second virtually no other aptitude,* i.e., all other aptitudes were low to mediocre. It is sometimes said they have high abstract visualization, which actually means they test low in structural visualization. They did have extremely high vocabularies and therefore high IQs but virtually no aptitudes. See "Be Yourself" by Margaret E. Broadley, page 40. *What? These are the people that are running our nation's industry and large public corporations? These are the highest paid employees in the world? These are the people who determine worthy inventions? These are the people who determine what our employee-inventors, employee-scientist, employee-geniuses etc. are paid and what inside and outside inventions are adopted and marketed? This doesn't look like the aptitude pattern of a genius. This looks like the aptitude pattern of Ayn Rand's Ellsworth Toohey*! I think it is the perfect aptitude pattern of Ellsworth Toohey! Thomas Jefferson, Edison, Ford, Bell and the Wright Brothers were geniuses. They weren't like this! My personal experience while trying to make and sell my inventions verifies these findings completely.

In the meantime, back home in Amarillo, things had been going on. Uncle Roy, principally, had set up two trusts named Ed Fagg Trusts and Spool Trusts. These two trusts approximately equally owned the parent company (one 51 percent and the other 49 percent) of all the newspapers, radio stations and television stations with a cost basis of $40 per share. My mother had talked Virginia and I into personally buying about 540 shares, each, of this same stock with the same cost basis. She also talked us into giving all our shares 1080 shares to the Lillie Whittenburg Ratliff Trusts, which she had set up for my five children and Virginia's three children. It wound up that each of the Ed Fagg trusts beneficiaries, one of whom was I, owned 1500 shares of this stock, as I recall. I don't know how much stock my mother and her siblings owned or how much came down to my children through Spool Trusts. But, in 1972 the parent company sold all the stock to Morris Publications for $400 per share. This made my 1500 shares worth $600,000.

By this time I still didn't have my inventions paying off. I was 41 years of age with five wonderful children and a wonderful wife, which at times I thought might starve from my lack of support. There was no way I could look after the first actual personal wealth I had really had without going back to Amarillo, Texas. I didn't see any way around moving back to Amarillo in good conscience. The good news was that I had bought the house at 938 Copley Ave., borrowing most of the money on one of the great financing plans available back in those days, for approximately $18,500 and could sell it now for approximately $32,500. This was a 76 percent appreciation in just some five years and more than that on my equity. Anyway, we sold our house and moved back to Amarillo. This, in effect, ended my career as an inventor.

Chapter XIV
Moving Back To Amarillo, Texas

In November 1972, we moved back to Amarillo, Texas. At this time Thomas was 10, Franklin 9, Harvey 8, Lillie 6 and George 4 years of age. Our older children were in attendance at Dr. Samuel Mudd School in Waldorf, Md. Thomas was in the fifth grade, Franklin the fourth, Harvey the third and Lillie the first as I recall. The schools in Maryland had been excellent compared to my prior experience. The teachers there virtually made the parents participate in the children's education. They really got involved in their teaching. You could call them up anytime. Before we moved back we had a garage sale and sold everything except what we thought we couldn't live without and hired a moving company to take the things we couldn't take in our cars. The trip back was an interesting experience. We had two Chevrolet station wagons. I knew of no sports utility vehicles and few; if any vans for personal use, back in those days. My station wagon was about a year old and Clara's was about four years old. We needed two when I went on the fairly long photographic trips for the slides to go into my viewers.

The most memorable events took place on the last day of our caravan type journey from Waldorf, Md. to Breckenridge, Texas. Breckenridge was about 200 miles closer than Amarillo. When we went through Memphis, Tenn. on our last traveling day, it was raining. Clara was following me. I came upon a truck, which was traveling at a much slower rate than we needed to travel in order to get to Breckenridge at a reasonable hour. I passed the truck, thinking there was no problem whatever. The truck threw water upon my window as always, and I saw no problem with that. It had happened to me hundreds of times. I looked back in my rear view mirror and saw, probably, the scariest sight of my entire life. Clara, Franklin, Harvey and Lillie were in her car. Clara's car was out of control right beside the truck, which was also out of control. They were missing each other by what appeared to be inches while zigzagging back and forth across the highway. Thomas and George were in my station wagon with me. I thought I had lost my wife and three of my children for sure. Finally, the truck jackknifed without there being any collision with Clara's car. It seemed like a miracle. It was wonderful. I felt nothing but extreme gratitude. The truck driver was black. He asked me if I would put in a good word for him with the police. I was more than glad to do that. The police checked to see that we were all right and fortunately they let us proceed on our trip right away. I really don't know how the truck driver came out with the police, but I tried to help him. I, and I believe all of us, were very grateful for the way this turned out. This day was a Sunday. Another very interesting thing happened on this trip. Clara's car broke down in a very small town on this Sunday. Luckily back in those days you could always find somebody who could fix a Chevrolet. In this quite small town, the name of which I have forgotten, we stopped at a filling station and they could fix the car and did in about two hours. No regular repair garage was open on a Sunday and there were no hotels or motels at this town. We were very fortunate again.

It was rather trying traveling through Dallas late that night because we had to correctly turn at many forks on the interstate in the heavy traffic without losing each other. We finally arrived in Breckenridge early Monday morning. I am not sure how long we stayed in Breckenridge, but we had to drive on to Amarillo before our moving van got there. Our new home was my mother's old home at 5109 Matador Trail.

Our children were in the school district of Western Plateau Elementary School, and we immediately enrolled them there in the same grades they were in at Dr. Samuel Mudd School in Maryland. Immediately, they sent Lillie home saying she could not attend school because she was too young. This, I thought, would have an adverse effect on her. So, I immediately started looking for an alternative school. My cousin Jimmie Whittenburg was on the board of directors of St. Andrew's Episcopal Day School. We had enrolled Thomas in this school when he was born because it had the reputation of being the best and the hardest school in Amarillo to get into. I don't know whether Jimmie helped or not but this was the only school we could get Lillie into. This seemed very fortunate at the time to me. Later, I found that Harvey's teacher at Western Plateau became angry if I so much as dared to ask her how Harvey was doing. So, I started trying to get him in St. Andrew's and succeeded. He was really helped. Soon all our children except Thomas were attending St. Andrew's. It seemed to be the best thing to do.

In the meantime we sent Thomas, Franklin and Harvey to Camp Cheley and Clara, Lillie and George went to visit relatives in Germany, and I moved us to our new home in Amarillo.

I was still courting *Ellsworth Toohey*, I guess. One of the first things I did was go talk to Uncle S.B., whom I had been growing closer to. He had visited us while I was pursuing my inventions in the Washington, D.C., area and we had played chess together. We had actually been playing chess at intervals ever since I had first gone to work for the family after graduation from college. S.B. had come to D.C. by invitation as a guest of Lyndon Johnson. He told me I should start a business as a consulting petroleum engineer and his brother Jim would hire me. This I did for a while. I found myself out on a lot of Uncle Jim's wells, but was never given any authority whatever. A petroleum engineering friend of mine named Howard Federer had all the authority along with Uncle Jim. Uncle S.B. also had an Oil and Gas Operating Company named Panther Oil Company. He made a deal with Uncle Jim to enable Panther to drill development wells on Jim's family land in the Leveland Field in Hockley County. Uncle S.B. talked me into participating in these wells and to spend time on these wells. *Ellsworth Toohey* began showing his face again. I was treated similarly to how Jim had treated me, which included giving me no authority whatever.

One thing my dad unintentionally taught me was to keep my own books. So, another one of the first things I did was take a week of bookkeeping as mentioned before. At first I had little time to do anything but invest in stocks and bonds and keep my books along with the time I spent working with Uncle S.B. After a while, with the strong influence of my sister, I became computerized. I had the benefit of watching some of my cousins trying to employ computers and noticed that most computer companies at that time either sold hardware or software and when a person had problems, which they usually did, the software and hardware people would blame each other and the result did not seem satisfactory to me. Another option was to use the IBM set up. I was fortunate and watched my cousin's, Aunt Georgia's children and their spouses, use the IBM set up. While watching them I noticed that this was very expensive and required the hiring of a full time and expensive employee to oversee the computer system. I don't think this worked out very well for them. The first person I knew of who offered both hardware and software, with no finger pointing was a man named Roy Michael Moore. He had a company named "Micro Mikes." My sister and I got started with his hardware and software programs and they worked well for a very economical price and I still use a lot

Shown above are: Top Row-Franklin and Harvey Locke, Middle Row- Thomas, Lillie and Spunky, Bottom Row- Shocker, George and Prince in Amarillo, Texas, in the 1980s.

of those original programs now in December of 2003. A man known as Butch Connors wrote many of the programs.

My mother loved trusts. We had trusts and trusts. I was getting distributions from Ed Fagg Trusts, which I needed to keep books on and invest. My children were getting distributions from Spool Trusts and Lillie Whittenburg Ratliff Trusts that I had to keep books on and invest. My mother had accumulated a huge debt, between $300,000-400,000 as I remember, due in a small way to my dad's and my losses and to a much greater extent to the long hard struggle for the newspaper's survival. Once the newspaper was sold she had the wherewithal to get out of debt. Once she got out of debt she started giving a lot of her royalty to Virginia and me and to trusts for our children. Her interest was quite watered down due to the large number of heirs. She had one thirteenth of one fourth and one nineteenth of one-half of the oil royalty, which was usually one-eighth (making her interest 0.00569331983 of each barrel produced under two sections and half that in one section in Yoakum County) but sometimes one quarter, under the J. A. Whittenburg land in Hutchinson County due to the fact that J.A. Whittenburg gave half of his mineral rights to his grandchildren per capita and there were 19 grandchildren and his wife Tennessee's one half came down per sterpes under Texas Law when she died, one half to Aunt Mattie Hedgecoke and one half to George A. Whittenburg, and one thirteenth of George A. Whittenburg's royalty interest under his some 5,000 acres of land. As I remember it, by gifts or under her will, my mother's interests were divided as follows: in Yoakum County, which was under three sections in the top of the Wasson Field Anticline, Virginia and I received one-eighth of her interests before Jake died and she passed through her one-twelfth interest equally to Virginia and me at Jake's death (in Yoakum County I owned 0.000948887 of each barrel of oil produced under two of those three sections and half that under one of the three sections, that meant if oil sold for $25 per barrel I would receive $0.0237 per barrel sold under two sections and half that under one); her grandchildren received, per sterpes, three fourths of her Yoakum interest at her death in trusts, I believe; in Hutchinson County, which was J.A. Whittenburg's some 30,000 acres and George Whittenburg's some 5,000 acres, Virginia and I receive each one-half of her interest in the minerals above 250' below Sea level and our children, per sterpes, receive it below 250' below sea level. Dorothy Kinney, who had a long background of friendship with Allen and Virginia, did the legal work for my mother in doing these things. Dorothy Kinney convinced me to set up partnerships with my children as a vehicle to make it much easier to invest their money and handle their money. This resulted in two investment partnerships: Ratliff Enterprises, in which I was the managing partner and owned 17.5 percent and each of my five children owned 16.5

Clara and Harvey at Amarillo, Texas, in the 1980s.

"The Majestic Deer" painted by the author in acrylic in 1977.

"Ducks over the Lake" painted by the author in acrylic in 1977.

"The Wonderful Daughter" painted by the author in acrylic in 1977.

percent, and the other was Ratliff Children Pool, in which each of my five children owned one-fifth (20 percent) and I was the managing partner with no beneficial interest. Ratliff Children Pool was also the recipient of royalty, which I "passed through" to them of royalty that Jaten Oil Company distributed out to me. I also had to keep books for each one of my children individually. I had my hands full keeping the books for all these entities.

During the summer of the 16th year of each of my children, the plan was that I took them to a Johnson O'Connor Laboratory for testing. Actually, I took Thomas while we were still in the Washington D.C. area before 1972 and talked to Johnson O'Connor himself. He then told me they couldn't get an accurate test until Thomas was 16 years of age. Actually, I believe I took Thomas, Franklin and Harvey to Tulsa before they were actually 16. On Johnson's tests I had always scored low in general vocabulary. Johnson O'Connor had three general vocabulary books, which included words from the level known by only 1 percent, i.e., 99 percentile words, of the adults who had taken the tests at the time of the printing down to 1- percentile words known by 99 percent of the adult people who had taken the test at the time of the printing. He had three books including about 3500 words each with these different vocabulary levels of 1 percentile up to 99 percentile in them. He said the difference between the 1 percentile vocabulary and the 99 percentile vocabulary was about 10,000 words and the reason he knew this was from his empirical experience and that they had looked and looked over a long period of time and could not find more than that even though there are over some 360,000 words in an abridged Webster's dictionary I looked at. Testing Thomas began making it clear that not only was my vocabulary low, but also, my children's vocabulary was low. So, I worked out a system to try to improve their vocabularies and we worked on this for one-two hour- periods every Sunday for several years. Anyway, I did take Thomas to Ft. Worth in May 30 and 31, 1978, to be tested. He scored 74 percentile in structural visualization, borderline subjective personality, 70 percentile in graphoria, 69 percentile in foresight, 95 percentile in tonal memory, 99 percentile in rhythm memory, 70 percentile in time memory, 50 percentile in ideaphoria, 50 percentile in silograms, high in the hand dexterities and below fifty percentile in their inductive reasoning and analytic reasoning tests (these are the aptitudes of editors, lawyers and detectives, but I think they may have misleading names). He had a good engineering or applied science aptitude pattern plus he had a good sound technician pattern and a good businessman aptitude pattern (his combination of objectivity and foresight is 87 percentile). I did hold out some hope he might become a medical doctor, but he was so interested in becoming a decathlete that I knew his grades were too low for that; so, I began to encourage him to be a geophysicist, which he did become and he is quite a good one. He obtained his bachelor's and master's degrees in geophysics from Texas A&M at College Station, Texas. He worked for Mobil Oil Company as a geophysicist for several years and now he and Franklin own their own geophysics company.

In June 5, 1979, I took Franklin to the laboratory. He scored 97 percentile rhythm memory, 90 percentile graphoria, 89 percentile inductive reasoning, 84 percentile objective personality, 75 percentile tonal memory, 75 percentile tweezer dexterity, 60 percentile tile finger dexterity, 60 percentile abstract visualization and 55 percentile foresight. This was an excellent aptitude pattern for accounting, law and businessman (his combination of objectivity and foresight is 93 percentile). He first obtained his bachelor's degree in accounting from the University of Texas, became a CPA, worked as an accountant, obtained his law degree from Texas Tech University, passed the bar, practiced law and is now in business with his brother Thomas.

In June 13, 1980, I took Harvey Locke to the Laboratory. He scored 97 percentile objective personality, 79 percentile foresight (his combination of objectivity and foresight is 99.4 percentile), 75 percentile tonal memory, 65 percentile tweezer dexterity, and 55 percentile rhythm memory. He has a virtually perfect businessman aptitude. He obtained two business degrees from West Texas State University and is now successful in the condominium and housing rental business and has a real estate license. He is doing very well indeed in his business.

"The Yucca Relative" painted by the author in acrylic in 1977.

In July 13, 1982, I took Lillie to the laboratory. She scored A (which means between 75 percentile and 100 percentile) in ideaphoria, 95 percentile tonal memory, 90 percentile tweezer dexterity, 75 percentile analytical reasoning, 75 percentile memory for design, 75 percentile tile object observation, 72 percentile objective personality, 65 percentile inductive reasoning, (65 percentile wiggly block and 40 percentile paper folding which averages 52.5) structural visualization, 48 percentile silograms and 45 percentile foresight. In the artist combination of ideaphoria, memory for design and structural visualization, she is 98.6 percentile. In the teacher combination of: objectivity, ideaphoria, inductive reasoning, she is 98.8 percentile. In the businessman combination of foresight and objectivity she is 84.6 percentile. She and her husband, Jeff Farris, now own and operate a ceramic store, which involves being an artist-teacher and businessperson. Lillie and Jeff both obtained degrees from The University of Missouri in journalism and obtained certification in teaching from Texas Tech.

In June 1, 1984, I took George to the laboratory. He scored: 99 percentile in tonal memory, (75 percentile on the wiggly block, which is higher than Thomas, but his 35 percentile score on paper folding pulled him down to) 55 percentile structural visualization, 75 percentile in pitch discrimination, 65 percentile in analytical and inductive reasoning, 60 percentile in finger dexterity, 55 percentile in graphoria, foresight, subjectivity (that means 45 percentile in objectivity) and rhythm memory. George is now in the movie business, primarily writing and directing documentaries and movies. George obtained bachelors degrees in radio, television and film and also in English. A Google.com search will yield many hits on this young man.

At some point along in this time period I started cultivating a friendship with a young second cousin who descended from Mattie Hedgecoke named Edward Morris. He had matriculated through Yale and Harvard obtaining an undergraduate degree from one and a law degree from the other. He was and is a brilliant young man and shared the love of chess with me and mentored me into joining the U.S. Chess Federation and playing tournament chess. While playing chess in this federation I noticed an interesting phenomenon: the rating system ground down the U.S. Chess Federation rating of every player down to a point that the average player of the Federation was some 1100, whereas it should have been 1500. They had to artificially increase everyone's rating to get the ratings right. To give the reader a proper perspective of this rating system, there are only some 8,000-10,000 players in the United States who are rated higher than an average player in the federation as shown in their publication as I recall from looking in them back when I was involved with tournament chess. I have often wondered if in real life there is a grind down principle at work in the free market. Of course, I have never really seen a free market as the U.S. or anyplace that I know has never really had one in my lifetime. Anyway, I won several trophies in tournaments and gained the rating of 1786 at one time but never gained as high a rating as Edward did of well over 1800; however, I did reach the point I could beat him personally more often than he beat me.

My dad had long been telling me "You just wait until your Uncle Roy starts making his move to put his children in charge of all the family business and money, and you'll find out what kind of an uncle he really is." This I took with a grain of salt for a long time, but it began to become more and more a reality to me. I came to believe that one of Uncle Roy's hidden agenda plans was for him and his family to gain control of all the family business and money. I was convinced that Edward and I shared this or a very similar view. In specific George Whittenburg, Roy's oldest son, was president of and basically had total control of Jaten Oil Company, which controlled the leasing of oil and gas development of all the J.A. Whittenburg land, i.e., that portion of the some 30,000 acres that had not been heretofore leased or operated by Jaten or its predecessors. Edward thought we had to take control away from George. I actually liked George a lot at that time which made it hard for me, but I knew Edward was right. I also thought Edward was one person that could legally outsmart and out negotiate George. I was no lawyer or negotiator and knew it. Anyway, basically Edward, Whitt Cline and I undertook to do this and were successful in doing so. I believe this was very good for the family as a whole.

I really didn't like being an errand boy and yes man with no authority and I began to realize that *Ellsworth Toohey* would always win as long as a negotiator was between me and the money; so, at some point I sold my interest in the Leveland Field back to Uncle S.B. and I just kept books and invested in stocks, bonds and gold. I decided to pursue chess so as to not venture off and lose the money that I was investing and won several trophies in U.S. Chess Federation Chess Tournaments.

Chapter XV
Becoming an Oil and Gas Operator

However, somewhere along the way I could not resist the desire to fight *Ellsworth Toohey* once more and to put my money where my training, knowledge, ability and emotions were and became interested in how oil and gas deals were put together and sold to investors. When Virginia and I had invested in the well I drilled in Palo Pinto County, we had just turned the paper work mechanism over to our lawyer, Roy Snodgrass, to set up. This had been very unsatisfactory in my view. Lawyers, in general, don't appear to like well drilling ventures to be set up in a good way for an oil and gas operator. They along with accountants appear to want the operator totally confused and completely dependent on them. What I did was invest in a few oil and gas drilling ventures. By doing this I learned how they legally did it and I found this way to be very reasonable and easy to understand in a way I could tell just how well my oil well was doing, what I, as a participant, spent on dry hole costs, intangible drilling costs, tangible drilling cost, lease costs, operating costs, state taxes and just where I was in the investment. It would also be clear how many barrels of oil were sold and the dollars received for them.

I don't remember how or why, but I met a geologist named Bob Scholl. He came across to me as a man who lived, slept, breathed and ate geology and was a poor salesman. I later concluded that I had totally misread him and he was actually a natural salesman, i.e., I thought he had the Johnson O'Connor aptitude pattern of a salesman that worshiped his geologist father and did an excellent job of imitating his father's noticeable characteristics. At that time he was in business with another second cousin and Hedgecoke descendent named Gary Hedgecoke. I invested in deals-- I believe it was two-- he and Gary put together on prospects in Scottsbluff County, Nebraska. He took me under his wing and treated me like a partner. We took the some 525-mile trip to Nebraska and went out on the location. I met the drilling contractors. It was just like I was in with him on the operations. We stayed at his brother's house. His brother, Conrad Scholl, was not interested in drilling wells and thought the chance of hitting an oil or gas well was one in thousands. I noticed it was very inexpensive to drill in Scottsbluff, County, Nebraska. It was easy to obtain a seven-eighth lease for a low rental, bonus and damage fee. There was a company named Geere Drilling out of Denver, Colorado that would obtain the permit, stake the location, build the location, deal with and pay the landowner the damages (with a $700 upper limit), drill and set surface pipe, file all the commission papers, drill the hole to a depth of up to over 7000 feet deep for oil or gas, handle the mud and mud engineering and pay for it, pay for the electric log (with a $1,700 upper limit), run and pay for a drill stem test for a turn-key (which means guaranteed) price of some $30,000. They would have turn-keyed the oil string, but I wanted to do that myself. I wanted the best casing and cement job possible and didn't want anyone doing it but me.

I believe it was on March 20, 1984, with Edward and his firm doing the legal work; we formed Scholl and Ratliff Corp. By this time Thomas was 22, Franklin 20, Harvey 19, Lillie 17 and George 15 years of age. I was president and Bob Scholl was secretary of our corporation. Bob and Gary split up.

In 1985, we drilled our first well in which Scholl and Ratliff Corp. was the operator. We could put together a drilling package in which the total cost was some $50,000, with Scholl and Ratliff carried for 25 percent. Our first well drilled was a dry hole. However, in 1986 we drilled the Ferguson No. 1, which had a great drill stem test showing it should produce 400 barrels of oil per day. It was very exciting. What I didn't realize at the time was neither Bob Scholl, the well site geologist Michael Webster nor I knew the most critical element of a successful completion in the Cretaceous "J" sand of that area. Both my "experts" of the area thought we should drill through the pay, after the test, drill a "rat hole," log the hole including the pay zone, set pipe, cement the casing in the hole and perforate the pay zone through the cemented casing later as taught in my petroleum engineering course. This proved to be a fatal mistake. I had no clue as to what a huge mistake that was at the time. I even made a second attempt in the Ferguson #3 to complete in the Cretaceous "J" with a new "expert," Ed Barnholt, but he proved to not know the key technique either and we made the same mistake resulting in another water well. He did teach me how to successfully squeezed the water off though, but the oil production quickly went down to about seven bopd with no water.

What we should have done was run casing immediately after the drill stem test with a packer shoe on the bottom of its bottom joint, set the packer shoe just above the pay where the DST packer had been set and cement above the packer shoe. The zone immediately below the pay, with about a foot separating the two, is a prolific water producer and one can't perforate the pay without communicating with this zone resulting in a water well. The well made 700 barrels of water per day and five barrels of oil per day. We finally were successful, with Barnholt's technique, in squeezing the water off but the rate of oil production was drastically reduced. It started at 30 barrels per day and rapidly went down to some seven barrels per day. Nearly any treatment is likely to result in a water well. I drilled 14 dry holes looking for another chance at the "J" sand pay, but never had another chance to properly complete in that pay, which I may not have actually learned the availability of a packer shoe until I started operations in Texas. However, this proved a very valuable lesson in Chappel completions later.

Along about this time in my life I finally realized that I was going to have to study negotiating because actually everyone negotiates all of the time either poorly or well. So, even though I greatly dislike people getting rich by parasitic negotiating, I would never be able to stand up against parasitic negotiators unless I knew what they were doing to me and how they were doing it, enabling me to succeed against them. Therefore, I listened to several tapes on negotiating several times.

The principle petroleum landman Scholl and Ratliff Corp. had been using to lease the Nebraska prospects was a man named Ray Jinkins. He talked me into drilling a well in Hardeman County, Texas. This well was located 467' FSL (from the south line), 2723' FWL of Section 122, Block H, W&NW RR Co. Survey, Hardeman County, Texas about 3.5 miles NNE of Quanah, Texas. This well was 100 feet from a well, which had produced some 18,000 barrels of oil from the zone known as the Palo Pinto Sand. The story told to me was that there had been tectonic activity, which caused the casing to part, and the operator had spent an enormous amount of money trying to repair it with the result that his investors gave up. Farrell Oil Company (or Farrex Oil Co.) had bought this well to use as a saltwater disposal well. Disposing into what I found out much later to be the Coleman Junction formation   I also found out much later that this is an extremely corrosive formation. Anyway Ray Jinkins had wound up with drilling rights on the property, and I decided to take his deal. Along about this time Bob Scholl wanted out. I was never really sure just why he wanted out, but upon his request I made him an offer for his stock in Scholl and Ratliff, Corp. He took the offer and I renamed the company Ratliff Operating, Corp.

Chapter XVI
Finding the North Trend of the Quanah Field

OK! Finally, except for the governmental regulators, I will not have to look at the ugly face of Ayn Rand's *Ellsworth Toohey*! Nobody is in a position to nullify my decisions! No negotiator is between me and the money from my creations. I'm finally in the Jeffersonian-Adam Smith free enterprise system with no interference from anything but death, regulators and taxes. I was now primarily dealing with only the natural world of free enterprise and nature. This natural world was continuously being defined by the human scientific quest to define it through scientific laws and theories. The laws are simple and can be set forth largely by mathematical formulas but the theories are complex and the complex parts are being continuously filled in, such as the global positioning theory which is now so refined that a small device can tell one within a few feet (or inches) of where a person or thing is anyplace in the world and of evolution which is also continuously getting more and more exact through such advances as DNA science.

The McGowan No. 1-A was spudded by me through Bearden Drilling Co. on Jan. 31, 1987, reached total depth, was logged and the casing set on Feb. 10, 1987. I completed the well on March 6, 1987, with the official initial production of 92 bopd (barrels of oil per day). Even though I knew nothing about the Coleman Junction at that time, I did decide while drilling that since the disposal well was only 100 feet away, I had better cement over the salt water disposal zone, which I didn't then know was the Coleman Junction. This proved to be a fortunate move that I should have done on all succeeding wells. A quite interesting thing about this well was that the well cite geologist, Linda Smart, kept telling me that I should try a new zone known as the Hot Shale although the sought zone was the "Palo Pinto Sand." The Palo Pinto Sand is shown on the log below to be from 5817 ft KB to 5841 ft KB and the *Hot Shale* is from 5886' KB to 5894' KB.

As a result of the geologist's urging, I did complete in the Hot Shale. When I perforated there was no entry. People were advising me, (*Ellsworth Toohey* without much power was showing his ugly face again) that I must clean the perforations with a "cleanup acid." I did this and there was no entry. Next I gave the well a 100 sack frac and the unofficial result was an entry of 120 bopd. There was much excitement as I thought we had discovered a new field in the Hot Shale. I started leasing acreage north, which had the Hot Shale on the logs of old abandoned wells. The Farrell's were excited about the Hot Shale and subleased their acreage to me because they found other acreage in which they thought the Hot Shale was better. This resulted in my obtaining the

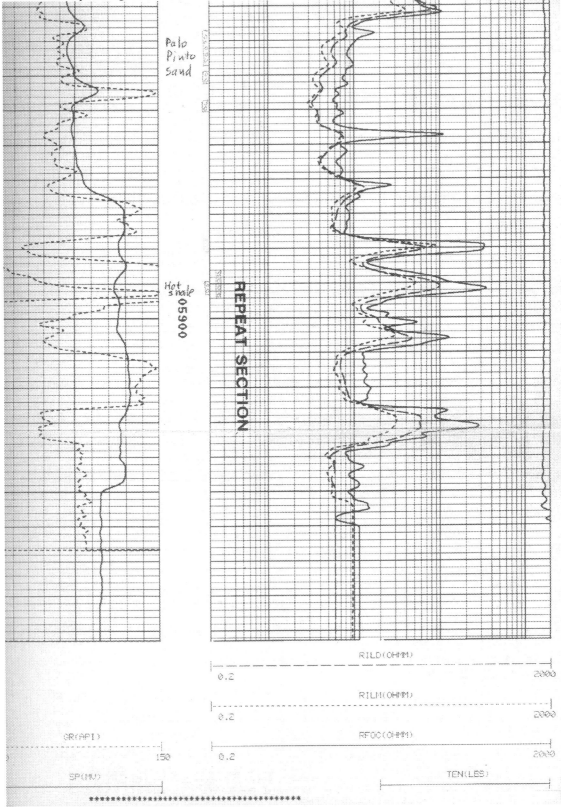

McGowan B and C leases from the Farrell's along with the McGowan "D," Loveless, Lasater, Lamberton, Cunningham and Greene leases from their mineral owners or controllers.

Above is a photo of the McGowan 1-A in about 2001 with the author in front.

The McGowan B#1 reached total depth on May 16, 1987, and I completed it in what we thought was the Hot Shale June 19, 1987 (the perforated zone was the Hot Shale, but what I didn't then know was the frac sand did not go where the perforations were), and it potentialed for 184 bopd. The investors and I were very excited, and our "discovery" was written up in the Wichita Falls newspaper. The B#1 is located 1713.8' FNL and 2214' FEL of Section 122, Block H, W&NW RR Survey, Hardeman County, Texas.

The McGowan D#1 reached total depth on August 11, 1987 and I completed it in what we thought was the Hot Shale (again it was perforated in the Hot Shale Zone) Sept. 25, 1987, and it potentialed for only 25 bopd. It was located 1713.8' FNL and

The above is a photo of the McGowan B#1 with the author in front .

The above is a photo of the McGowan D#1 with the author in front.

JACK E. BEARDEN RIG 8
RATLIFF OPER. CO. McGOWAN C-1 HARDEMAN CO.

The above is a photo of the Jack E. Bearden Rig 8 drilling Ratliff Operating Corp's McGowan C#1.

2254.6' FWL of Section 122, Block H, N&NW RR Co. Survey, Hardeman County, Texas about four miles NNE of Quanah.

Next we drilled the McGowan C#1 but things weren't proving out. I had an abiding faith that the world operated in accordance with the natural laws and theories of science, but this looked supernatural. We could not make a commercial well out of the C. Something was terribly wrong. This looked supernatural. We spent way too much money trying to make a well out of the C since the Hot Shale looked as good on the log in it as any. So did that of the D. We had to abandon the C#1. The C#1 was in an east-west line with the B#1 and the D#1 with the D west of the B and the C west of the D about the same distance.

Things were looking supernatural, as I had come out of school fully convinced that if a person used the best cementing company, as I had done, ran a cement-bond log that showed a good cement bond, as I had done, and used a good perforating company to perforate the zone, as I had done, the zone perforated would be isolated.

Part IV

The Story of An Entrepreneur Who "Is Not College Material"

At this time everybody involved thought we were producing out of the Hot Shale. Ray Jinkins had made a deal with the McGowan's with who I was on a drilling program. That is that I had to drill a new well every three months (or some time period) or lose the lease except for 80 acres around each producing well. Since we thought we still had not opened the Palo Pinto Sand, Ray made the deal that if I completed in the sand on all four wells, it would count as drilling a fifth well on the drilling program. This is when my abiding faith in the truth, that natural laws and theories were in control and things weren't supernatural at all, started paying off even though a lot of money was spent and observation required before I finally figured out the truth. First, I chose the McGowan D#1 in which to perforate the sand because it was already down to some 8 bopd and I thought we had the least to lose if the process didn't work. The service company man, named Tom Hasten, talked me into cleaning my perforations using the ball off technique with the clean-up acid (*Ellsworth Toohey* was showing his face again). This time we perforated the sand after shutting off the shale with a bridge plug, i.e., since it was assumed the cement would isolate the zones outside the casing and the bridge plug would isolate the zones inside the casing, and then cleaned the perforations with cleanup acid while we balled them off in order to make sure they were all cleaned, i.e., since it was assumed the cleanup acid only cleaned the perforations and would not eat the best cement. We ran into no trouble this time although the oil production drastically went down after the cleanup, i.e., this was because the water in the acid causes clays in the Palo Pinto Sand to swell and reduce its effective permeability to zero. Next we gave the well a 200 sack sand frac, i.e., this got the low permeability sand out of the way. The well came in for an initial potential of 80 bopd. I was excited. I thought things are the way they are supposed to be, and this is going to work. Next we went to the C#1, which, from the log, showed to be just as good as any in the Hot Shale, but showed only four feet of sand. We did no good there. This looked natural enough since the log showed the sand would not probably produce economically.

Next things started looking really supernatural and it was very hard to hold on to my abiding faith that natural scientific laws and theories were really in control here. We went to our prize well the B #1. During the cleanup acid ball off process, the balls totally sealed the zone off. We tried for about 30 minutes to an hour to unseal the balls without success. When we finally broke the ball-off and swab tested the well, we had lost our great oil well and had a water well. Things really looked supernatural at this point. With abiding faith in the scientific laws and theories of nature, I finally figured out by way of a radio active tracer log that the cleanup acid had eaten out the cement to a water zone a few feet above the pay zone, which showed only 2 percent to 3 percent porosity on the log shown below; however this zone was very prolific of water. It produced as fast as we could swab, about 800 bwpd (barrels of water per day) with no oil.

Well, my heretofore 184 bopd well was now capable of at least 800 bwpd well but no oil. This was extremely depressing. Things were really looking supernatural!

The author with his first grandchild, Derek Lee Ratliff, who was actually born Feb. 26, 1989.

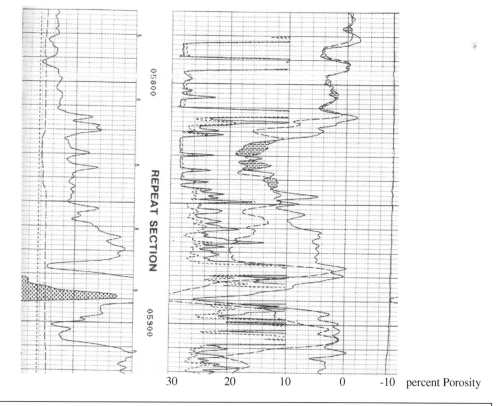

Above is shown the Density Neutron Log of the McGowan B-1 showing the "Palo Pinto Sand," Hot Shale and the prolific water zone a few feet above the sand.

The above Log of the McGowan B#1 showed that the porosity, which as indicated by the right curve, is from 2 percent to 4 percent at the depths of 5782'KB to 5810'KB where the water production was found by a radio active tracer log to be coming from. At that time the "experts" listened to by me told me that the Micro Log curve showing qualitative permeability should be ignored. This log would have told me this zone should be a prolific water producer; so, I never ignored the Micro Log after this experience nor did I ever use clean-up acid or ball off again. Next I perforated in the water zone, i.e., 5782'-5810', squeezed, getting a very small amount of cement, 2 to 4 sacks out into the formation. I had learned by working with an engineer named Ed Barnholt up in Nebraska that not withstanding other "experts" never put out much cement in a squeeze job because it fractures the zone to ruin the well. Well, lo and behold all production of anything, i.e., water, oil or gas, was completely shut off. I thought, oh well this is no problem; I still have the Hot Shale. So, we drilled out the bridge plug, which should have opened up the Hot Shale. Lo and behold! There was no entry! Boy! This really looked supernatural! The Hot Shale had to be either squeezed off or non-productive! I later verified that the Hot Shale was non-productive by drilling into it with crude oil in an open hole and swab testing to find it dry as a bone.

By my abiding faith that natural scientific law and theory controls I finally figured out that the cleanup acid had eaten the cement out between the Hot Shale and the Palo Pinto Sand; so, the sand from the Hot Shale frac had actually gone up hole some 45 feet to enter the Palo Pinto Sand. The experts who were supposed to be in the "know" about this field had told me to perforate the top one or two feet of the Palo Pinto Sand because it was a water zone in the lower part of this sand. Wrong again! The frac sand had traveled up through the entire "so-called" wet portion and proved it no more productive of water than the top one or two feet. With an abiding faith in observation and the scientific laws and theories of nature I could now see that I had made a significant discovery. The experts in the know had everybody convinced that the Quanah Field trended east and west. I, with the aid of observation and natural scientific laws and theories, had discovered that beginning with McGowan 1-A the field was now trending SSW to NNE. This resulted in 15 producing wells after drilling 20 for a success rate of 75 percent. The Boatright Unit #1 was drilled for a Chappell prospect and the Thorp #1 was drilled as a Palo Pinto Lime prospect. If these two wells were counted, the success rate would be 85 percent.

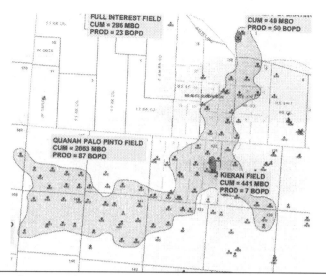

It can be seen from the map above of the Quanah Field that as a result of the discovery that the McGowan B#1 oil production actually came from the Palo Pinto Sand resulted in the field being opened up to the NNE when the "experts" had everyone else convinced it went west to east.

Even though I was able to shut the water off in the McGowan B #1, I could never get back its great production and it has not been nearly as good as it should have been.

The McGowan 1-A, B #1 and D #1 as of Jan. 31, 2004, have a cumulative of: 70,980, 46,760 and 56,587 barrels of oil respectively and a production rate during that month of 3.86, 2.29 and 6.19 barrels of oil per day respectively.

Next Ratliff Operating Corp. drilled the McGowan 2-A located 2317'FSL and 2813'FWL of Section 122, Block H, W&NW RR Co. Survey, Hardeman County, Texas. The well was spudded May 30, 1989, reached total depth with casing set June 9, 1989, I completed it July 14, 1989, and it potentialed for 118 bopd. As of Jan. 31, 2004, the well has produced 59,916 barrels of oil and produced, during that month, at the rate of: 4.71 bopd. The Coleman Junction ate a hole in the casing of this well, and it cost some $52,000 to fix it.

Above is a picture of the McGowan 2-A with the author standing in front.

Next Ratliff Operating Corp. drilled the McGowan B#2 just south of Farm Road 2533 and located 1881' FEL and 561' FNL of Section 122, Block H, W&NW RR

Co. Survey, Hardeman County, Texas. The well was spudded: Nov. 1, 1989, reached total depth Nov. 8, 1989, I completed it Dec. 12, 1989, and it potentialed 110 bopd. As of Jan. 31, 2004, the well has produced 48,906 barrels of oil and produced at the rate of: 5.34 bopd during that month.

Above is a picture of the McGowan B#2 well with the author standing in front.

I next went a location north of the McGowan D#1, which has, as of Jan. 31, 2004, a cumulative of: 56,395 barrels of oil, and a production rate of 6.2 bopd during that month, and drilled the McGowan D#2 which turned out to be a non-commercial well after we set casing and gave it a good chance to be a well.

Next we went north of Farm Road 2533 and drilled the Loveless #1 well located 712' FWL and 652' FSL of Block 13 of B.S.&F. Survey No. 10, G.P. Meade Subdivision, A-1275. This well was spudded about Oct. 2, 1990, and reached total depth on Oct. 11, 1990. I completed it Nov. 1, 1990 and it potentialed at 85 bopd. It paid out in about six months partly because the price of oil was very good during its payout period. After the well produced 40,990 barrels of oil and was still producing at the rate of 5.7 bopd, the Coleman Junction ate a hole in the casing of this well, which we discovered in February 1998. We decided it was not economic to fix the casing and it wound up being sold to the landowner, who was once our pumper, Doris A. Loveless. He wound up plugging the well. The "experts" had nearly everyone convinced there was no oil north of Farm Road 2533.

I then went a location east of the Loveless #1 and drilled the Lamberton #1 well located 712' FWL and 590' FSL of Block 12 of B.S.&F. Survey No. 10, G.P. Meade Subdivision, A-1275. This well was spudded about Jan. 15, 1991, and reached total depth on Jan. 24, 1991. I completed it March 1, 1991, and it potentialed 35 bopd. This well, as of Jan. 31, 2004, has produced 45,248 barrels of oil and had a daily rate of 1.68 bopd during this month.

The above is a picture of the Lamberton #1 with the author standing beside it.

Next I went north a location to the Lamberton #2, located 712' FWL and 590' FNL of B.S.&F. 10, Block 12, G.P. Meade Subdivision, spudded about April 3, 1991, reached total depth April 12, 1991, I completed it May 12, 1991, but it proved to be uneconomic and we converted it into a saltwater injection well December 1998.

Next we went a location north to the Loveless #2, located 710.7' FEL and 568' FSL of B.S.&F. Block 15, G.P. Meade Subdivision, spudded April 14, 1991, reached total depth about eight days later. This well blew out. The drilling contractor, Bearden Drilling, used an inoperative blowout preventer. We had discovered a new Palo Pinto Pod with virgin pressure. To keep from losing the well, I decided not to run open hole logs and we set casing and I completed it with cased hole logs. The initial official potential was 154 bopd flowing through a 14/64" choke. After the well produced 33,387 barrels of oil as of, December 2000, it was traded in a deal with D.A. Loveless.

At this time Thomas, who had been working for Mobil Oil Company as a Geophycist after receiving his masters degree in that subject from Texas A&M University, and Franklin, who obtained his accounting degree from the University of Texas, Austin and his law degree from Texas Tech University, had been a practicing

The Lamberton #2 Saltwater Injection Well with the author standing by the tank.

Above is a picture of, from left to right, Harvey, Thomas, Franklin and Harvey Locke while trying to make a well of the Lasater Unit #1.

attorney and was a qualified CPA, decided to start their own exploration company, DDD Exploration, Inc. Thomas talked me into drilling the Lasater Unit # 1. I would have wound up drilling this approximate location anyway since it was on the Quanah-Palo Pinto North Field trend. Anyway, the Lasater Unit #1 was our first well in the pursuit of the Chappel, or deep, pay.

Before we started the Lasater and Loveless Chappel wells, we had to run seismic. We ran the Lamberton-Loveless seismic, the Lasater-Cunningham seismic and the Greene-Rickman-Glover seismic. This, for example didn't come for nothing, it cost $148,932.90 and in present day terms that was a tremendous bargain.

The Lasater Unit #1 was spudded March 21, 1992. While drilling this well after we cut the Palo Pinto Sand, at 5812'KB, we had to keep the mud weight at 9.65 pounds per gallon in order to keep the Palo Pinto Sand zone from blowing out; so, we knew that if all else failed we had a good flowing Palo Pinto well, but the objective was the Chappel. A requirement of success in completing a Chappel well is to have the mud weight at 9.3 pounds per gallon or slightly less; so, we had to set pipe in the Meramec Lime at 8451'KB. We drilled to the Meramec and set 5.5" N-80, 17#/ft, J-55 casing at 8486'KB. I found out later that it was a big mistake to use N-80 casing (N-80 is supposed to be better and costs more money). After many long weeks of open hole drilling and completion effort, we potentialed the Chappel zone at 18 bopd on June 21, 1992. But the well only made some 800 barrels of oil and did not hold up. We had to come up hole and I completed in the Palo Pinto Sand zone. Due to the legal situation, the Unit no longer existed and the well became the Lasater #1. The Lasater #1, from the Palo Pinto Sand, as of Jan. 31, 2004, produced 71,910 barrels of oil and during that month had a daily rate of 5.8 bopd, which is drastically down from previous numbers. This well was making some 18 bopd just before we discovered the Coleman Junction ate three holes in the N-80 casing and caused the casing to part. It took some $102,000 to fix it, and I have never been able to get the great 18-bopd production back.

Actually, Ratliff Operating Corp. drilled the McGowan F #1 before the Lasater #1. The McGowan F #1 was located a location (some 1320') east of the McGowan #2-A. As of Dec. 31, 2002, the McGowan F#1 had produced 8,776 barrels of oil. It was shut in at that time because it was uneconomic to produce any longer.

Next we drilled the Lamberton #3. This well was SSW from the Lasater #1 and NE from the Loveless #2, which can be seen on the following map.

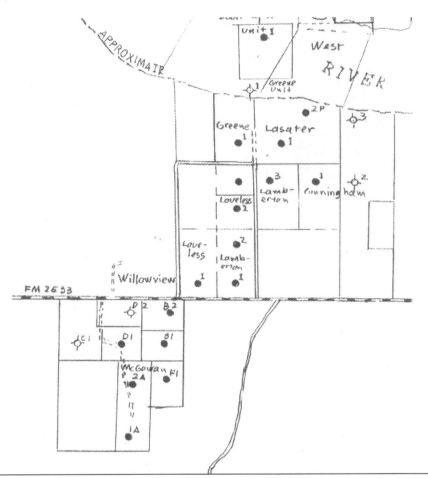

Above is a map of the north trend of the Quanah Field found and developed by the author and described well by well below.

The above is a picture of the Lasater #1 with the author standing in front.

The above is a map showing the McGowan 1-A at the bottom, the McGowan 2-A north (up) from the 1-A, the McGowan F #1 east of the 2-A, the McGowan D-1 NNW of the 2-A, McGowan B #1 north of the McGowan F #1, the McGowan B #2 NNE of the B #1, the P&A D#2 west of the B #2, the Loveless #1 northeast of the B #2, the Lamberton #1 east of the Loveless #1, the Lamberton #2 north of the Lamberton #1, the Loveless #2 north of the Lamberton #2, the Lamberton #3 northeast of the Loveless #2, the Cunningham. #1 east of the Lamberton #3, the Lasater #1 NNE of the Lamberton #3, the Lasater #2P northeast of the Lasater #1 and the Greene #1 west of the Lasater #1.

Next we drilled the Loveless Unit #1, which was a dry hole. Then we drilled the Lamberton #3. The Lamberton #3 was located as shown and described on the map just above. I completed this well and potentialed it in November 13, 1992, for 188 bopd, and it flowed for about a year. As of Jan. 31, 2004, this well has produced 65,249 of oil at the rate of 3 bopd during that month.

Above is a picture of the author standing in front of Steinberger Drilling Rig 1, which is a drilling subcontractor used by Ratliff Operating Corp. in drilling many if not all our wells after the Cunningham #1.

Next we drilled the Cunningham #1 which is located as shown and described on the map just above. I completed this well, and it was potentialed in March 17, 1993, for 215-bopd pumping. It always made significant water. As of Nov. 30,1999, this well produced 56,226 barrels of oil and was P&A, i.e, plugged and abandoned, since, because of its rapid decline curve, it was uneconomic to produce anymore.

Next we drilled the Lasater #2P, which is located as shown and described on the map above. I completed this well, and it was potentialed June 13, 1993, for 69 bopd and as of Jan. 31, 2004, this well produced 96,884 barrels of oil and during that month had a rate of production of 5.8 bopd, which is below previous numbers. This well turned out to be the best overall Palo Pinto Sand well.

Next we drilled the Greene # 1, which is located as shown and described on the map above. I completed this well, and it potentialed Sept. 2, 1993, for 56 bopd and as of Jan. 31, 2004, this well produced 13,924 barrels of oil and during that month had a rate of production of 1.56 bopd.

Including the Boatright Unit #1, which is the very top well on the map above and it was potentialed in Aug. 16, 1995, for 120 bopd and as of Jan. 31, 2004, has produced 21,175 barrels of oil, and the Thorp #1, which only produced 355 barrels of oil as of August 1999, the Palo Pinto wells located by me, except the Lasater #1 and Boatright Unit 1 and Thorp #1, and also drilled and completed by me, have produced 731,167 barrels of oil.

Above from left is the Lasater #2P with the author standing in front and the Lamberton #3 with the author standing to its right.

According to my records, which were over the period of January 1989 to Nov. 2003, the average price of oil sold by Ratliff Operating Corp. from the Palo Pinto Sand wells, as of November 30, 2003, is $19.641184 per barrel. At that price the gross sales from the above-described Palo Pinto Sand wells is $14,360,985.58. Actually the sales from the Palo Pinto wells during the time period of January 1989 until November 2003 is a gross of $13,564,465.50 from 690,613.43 barrels of sold oil production and 47,840 mcf of gas production beginning Jan. 1, 1989. $637,588.31 (4.7 percent) was paid out to state oil taxing agencies, $2,628,771.52 (19.37 percent) to royalty owners, $3,528,509.99 (26.01 percent) to the subcontractors who keep the wells pumping, $920,981 (6.79

percent) to the tangible equipment subcontractors, $2,313,610.06 (17.06 percent) to the drilling and completion subcontractors for producers and dry holes, e.g., the drilling contractor, cementers, pulling unit operators, loggers etc., and $45,028.75 (0.33 percent) to the leasehold owners in lease fees and rentals leaving the $3,489,975.57 (24.39 percent) for the investors. Of course the above figures do not keep account of the federal, state, county, sales and city taxes the royalty owners, pumping subcontractors, equipment subcontractor, drilling and completion subcontractors, leasehold owners and investors have to pay to the various governments and municipalities. For the author's effort, his part of the income before these taxes was about $1 million over the 14 year 11 month period, about $67,000 per year. It is little humorous that my present day pumping subcontractor, Willie Greening, sometimes teases me about how "cheap" I am notwithstanding the fact that my discovering and developing the Quanah Field-North Trend generated some $12.5 million for others and only some $1 million for me before the taxes mention above. Since there was $76,551.50 in gross Palo Pinto Sand sales from Nov. 30, 2003 until Jan. 31, 2004, that would mean $719,969 in gross Palo Pinto Sand sales came before Jan. 1, 1989. The 15 productive Palo Pinto Sand wells were: the McGowan #1-A, B #1, B #2, D #1, F #1 and #2-A, Loveless #1 and #2, Lamberton #1 and #3, Lasater #1 and 2P, Greene #1, Cunningham #1 and Lamberton #2. The five dry holes were: the McGowan C#1, Cunningham #2 and #3, Greene Unit #1 and McGowan D#2,which actually made a little oil. The Boatright Unit #1 was not counted because it was drilled as a Chappel prospect and not really a Palo Pinto prospect. If it were counted the success rate would have been 16/21 or 80 percent success rate. Also the Thorp #1 was not counted because it was drilled as a Palo Pinto Lime offset to the Clara #1.

Chapter XVII
Looking For The Chappel

We were now principally looking for Chappel production. This is very expensive. The next successful completion was the Davis #1E. It actually produces from the Ellinberger, but I count it a Chappel because it is even below the Chappel in depth. I completed it at a depth of 8076'KB to 8096'KB on Feb. 21, 1994, and potentialed it for 144 bopd flowing. As of Jan. 31, 2004, it had produced 49,984 barrels of oil, averaging 13.77 bopd over the period, and during that month had a daily rate of 7.15 bopd. Before drilling this well we spent $296,059.15 on the North Conley Seismic Shoot. The Davis #1 E is located 5.5 miles E-SE of Quanah just north of U.S. highway 287, 467' FSL and 1071' FEL of Section 92 W. & NW. RR. Co. Survey, Block H, A-1413, Hardeman County, Texas.

A brief summary of the search for Chappel is there were 12 Chappel prospects drilled after $616,116.35 was spent on seismic. The result was that we had three Chappel successes: the Davis #1E mentioned above, the Hankins #1 and the Boatright Unit #2. The dry holes, in the Chappel, were: the Holcomb #1, Clara #1 (this well produced some 55,000 barrels in the Palo Pinto Lime), Boatright Unit #1 (this well made a Palo Pinto Sand well), the Clara U2 side track 2, Clara Unit #2, Cunningham Unit #1, the Hunter #2, the Loveless Unit #1 and the Rogers #1.

Above is a picture of the Davis #1E with the author standing in front of it.

The Hankins #1 was spudded on March 28, 1996, cut the Chappel pay and reached total depth of 8561'KB on my 65th birthday, April 11, 1996. In its drill stem test it had gas to surface in six minutes, oil to surface in 31 minutes, flowed as measured by the tester to be 475 mcfpd gas and 1187 bopd oil through a 32/64" choke. This well was completed April 18, 1996, with an initial production of 145 bopd through a 5/64 choke producing from 8555'KB to 8561'KB under a packer shoe cemented above it. As of Jan. 31, 2004, it produced 452,340 barrels of oil and during that month it produced at a rate of 159.13 bopd through an 8/64" choke (it may be a 7/64"choke). As of Nov. 30, 2003, it has sold 434,432 barrels of oil and 60,721 mcf of gas for a gross sales of $9,980,788.05, paying out $694,846.03 in state oil tax, $1,857,188.40 to royalty owners, $126,294.02 to subcontractors who keep the well flowing, $95,407.10 to tangible equipment subcontractors, $257,848.41 to drilling and completion subcontractors leaving $6,943,457.30 for the investors. This has been, by far, the best well I have ever had anything to do with. The only troubles are notwithstanding the fact that I paid some 30 percent of the expense in the Chappel quest and have some 30 percent in all wells except the Hankins and Davis, I have only approximately 16 percent of the Hankins and a sixteenth of the Davis.

Overall the Chappel project has not been nearly that good though. Overall the Chappel wells, as of Nov. 30, 2004, have sold 555,425 barrels of oil and 81,051 mcf of gas for a gross sales of $12,447,375.20, paying out $8,172,014.57 to state oil tax, Royalty owners, subcontractors who keep the wells flowing and pumping, tangible equipment subcontractors, and exploration, drilling and completion subcontractor, leaving $ 4,275,360.63 for the investors.

Above is a picture of from left: Franklin Ratliff, Harvey Ratliff, Billy Green- the Steinberger Tool Pusher, a Steinberger hand, and Red Walker, the drill stem tester, all of whom are observing a drill stem test.

All of the other projects have lost money to this point. So that overall we have not done as well as indicated by the Palo Pinto Sand project and the Chappel project. Overall, for the time period from Jan. 31, 1989 until Nov. 30, 2003, Ratliff Operating Corp. has sold 1,345,587 barrels of oil and 128,892 mcf of gas for gross sales of $28,192,379.70, paying out $1,625,106.01 in state oil and gas tax, $5,358,723.48 to royalty owners, $4,499,809.59 to subcontractors who keep the wells pumping and flowing, $1,997,128.41 to tangible equipment subcontractors, $8,951,091.76 to exploration, drilling and completion subcontractors and $288,945.82 in rentals and fees to surface owners to leave $5,464,799.31 for the investors. Overall Ratliff Operating Corp. drilled 44 wells, of which 26 were productive and 18 were dry holes for a success rate of 59.09 percent.

The above is at the Hankins #1 location with the author standing by the location sign.

Above is a picture of the Hankins #1 with the author standing by the well.

Above is a picture of the flowing drill stem test of the Hankins #1 at about 3 a.m. April 12, 1996.

Above is a picture is of the Ratliff family starting at the top from left - Glyna, Derek and Thomas Ratliff, Lillie and Jeff Farris, George and Bess Ratliff, Harvey Locke Ratliff-second from the top- Rebecca and Michelle Ratliff, Harvey and Clara Ratliff, Sunny, Kallie, Franklin and Hollee Ratliff-Bottom row-Delaney and Sarah Farris, David Ratliff, Anna Farris, Mary Kate and Matthew Ratliff.

The above is a picture of the Boatright Unit #2 with the author standing by it.

Part V

The Story of An Entrepreneur Who "Is Not College Material"

Above is a picture of the author with his newest grandson Harvey Blix Frelinghuysen Ratliff.

Above is a picture from left beginning with the bottom row of Sarah Farris, Mary Kate Ratliff, Hollee Ratliff, David Ratliff and Matthew Ratliff; second row Kallie Ratliff, Anna Farris, Derek Ratliff and Delaney Farris; third row Michelle Ratliff; fourth row Clara Ratliff, Rebecca Ratliff; fifth (top) row Harvey Ratliff.

Chapter XVIII
Conclusion

Even though the United States has considerably deteriorated from the Jeffersonian ideal of a land of liberty and inalienable rights for each individual protected by an honest government, enough of the ideal has remained for it to still be a relatively great country to grow up and live in.

It goes without saying that my wife, children, parents, relatives and teachers have greatly influenced the way I lived my life, but in addition to this there have been several great influences on my life. One major influence has been Thomas Jefferson and the enlightenment he understood best of his time and all time, which to me is a country filled with entrepreneurial, propertied and creator individualist citizens working in a land of liberty and inalienable rights including property rights in which the government is there to protect this liberty and inalienable rights from its enemies within and outside the nation and with a declaration of independence, constitution (including the promotion of science and the useful arts), bill of rights and checks and balances to keep the government itself from becoming the enemy of liberty and inalienable rights which is supposed to be secured by the vote of the people who are supposed to be well educated in particular with regard to the enlightenment.

I think loop holes in these checks and balances, voting process and education have been found to deteriorate this wonderful way of life due to the power seeking altruistic professing negotiators starting with Alexander Hamilton, America's original prophet of statism and Jefferson's nemesis, who have largely changed America into a struggle between Socialist leaning statist (Democrats) and Theocratic Fascist leaning statist (Republicans) with both being too much the enemy of liberty and inalienable rights and therefore facilitators of tyranny. Actually the Republicans confiscate wealth from its creators less by governmental taxes and more by aiding and abetting the parasitic negotiator altruist within the large employee managed corporations while the Democrats do it more by excessive "altruistic" parasitic taxes, but unlike Jefferson and his true disciples they both confiscate wealth from its creators.

Another great influence on me has been art and creating. The movie "The Fountainhead" from Ayn Rand's book has had a tremendous influence of me. I believe I have distorted her original meaning somewhat. But, I see the world as largely a struggle between creators and altruistic professing negotiators. By negotiators I mean people skilled in the art of legally gaining a much bigger proportion of money from a creation of wealth than their contribution to it fairly deserves and by creators I mean people who rely primarily on creative, discovery or productive skill and assume an honest system will justly reward them in proportion to their actual contribution to the creation of wealth. To me altruism and religion are tools negotiators use to gain personal power over the "golden eggs" of the creators for their own and/or statist benefits. In the ideal republic, the government promotes creators and justly rewards them as it did Edison, Ford, Bell, the Wright Brothers and a magnitude of others in the first, Jeffersonian, 150 years of our nation. One should note that these type creators have largely been legally locked up inside large corporations controlled in the name of altruism by parasitic negotiators or if these creators don't join the corporations these self-proclaimed altruists stonewall them. In the actual country of today negotiators get, by far, the lions share of benefit from the creator's creations leaving little reward for the creator. There is a saying, I believe I heard on my negotiating tapes, which goes "you don't get what you deserve, you get what you negotiate." Unfortunately, I'm afraid this is true and the only way I have found to counter it is to learn negotiating. To me *Howard Roark* symbolizes the creator and *Ellsworth Toohey* symbolizes the parasitic negotiator in the private sector and corrupt altruistic plunderer in the governmental sector.

Another great influence on me has been science and engineering. From my understanding of this and the Jeffersonian enlightenment thinkers, I have gained an abiding faith that scientific laws and theories exist that completely explain the natural world. I think many scientific laws and theories are not yet known however. Over and over I have found the solutions to my problems to be natural, and even though they may have looked supernatural, I solved them by realizing they were actually natural despite peer pressure. I tried the supernaturalist approach for a considerable period in my life and I never found it to be actually true or to work.

I see the struggles of today on three fronts. The first is tyranny, which is now in the form socialistic, theocratic and/or fascistic leaning statism, on the one hand against getting back the government of Jeffersonian liberty and inalienable rights on the other. The Jeffersonian liberty and inalienable rights are the force for human advancement and should win, but I'm afraid tyranny, the force of human plundering, is winning that battle. The second great struggle is between creators and parasitic negotiators (non-parasitic negotiating is probably necessary, but it should not be parasitic). Creators, the force for human advancement, should win, but I'm afraid parasitic-negotiators, the force for human plundering, are winning that battle. The third great struggle is between the naturalist and the supernaturalist. The naturalist, the force for human advancement, should win that battle, but I'm afraid the supernaturalist, the force for human plundering, is winning. The world seems to be brainwashed. Throughout history the naturalist have advanced human knowledge and the supernaturalist have fought the advances and often murdered the naturalist in the process. It seems we are going backward into the horrible days of the supernaralist where people are not free to be themselves but are forced to not nurture their true self and become zombies. Today, not withstanding the first amendment and the constitution, we are dangerously close to Christian statism with a president elected by Christian statist forcing us to pledge allegiance to the Christian God and to pray in our public schools to the Christian God.

Actually, what is wrong with communism, and all tyranny, is it tries to make people something they are not, i.e., supernatural. Also, what is wrong with the belief that humans are born evil sinners that must be kept from being their evil selves and born again into their "unself", as other forms of tyranny, is that it tries to make people something they are not, i.e., supernatural. What is right in American history is that we have taken people as they are, freed, i.e., given them inalienable rights, and educated them to be as they are and let their educated natural ability create the greatest society of all time.

There are worlds out there that I would like to see overcome such as the world of crime, i.e., illegal plundering, and the world, not of propertied entrepreneurs, but of non-propertied management employees versus non-propertied and non-management employees who both have negligible ownership, i.e., operate on other people's money.

I have not been able to fulfill my goal as a creator in the field of artistic drawing and painting, because I thought history shows that *Ellsworth Toohey* would keep me from supporting a family if I resorted to this type of art. Also, *Ellsworth Toohey* beat me down as an inventor, but I was able to fulfill my goal as an Oil and Gas Operator.

I have never really liked being an employee nor have I really liked being an employer. The non-propertied employer-employee system seems to me to be a contest between the two of whom can most successfully be a parasite of the actual property owner, i.e., the stockholders or taxpayers, and also of each other which type of contest I detest. However, I have loved being a propertied entrepreneur and using subcontractors to accomplish my creation projects. Similarly to the way Ayn Rand put it in her book: "Capitalism: The Unknown Ideal" the only moral government in history, i.e., Jefferson's system of creators working under conditions of liberty and inalienable rights protected by an honest government elected by a well educated people worked pretty well for about 150 years. This produced, by far, the greatest progress, i.e., advance in human wealth and happiness of all time. But then the parasite-negotiator-altruist began going wild with the loopholes of the constitution, education and the voting process to ruin the greatest thing that has ever been on earth.

I have lived my life as if America was the ideal Jeffersonian republic with a small "r" as Todd DePastino puts it. Thomas Jefferson wanted everyone to be the equivalent of an entrepreneur. That is what the "agrarian paradise" combined with his love for inventions and manufactory is all about. A nation made up of property owners who are free to employ their creative abilities, sell the results thereof freely with an honest government supporting and protecting such activity under no threat of confiscation. Abraham Lincoln subscribed to that idea also. He thought it was all right to work as an employee for a little while, but if you kept doing that you were a "loser." In the early days the "home" was a "productive unit" what we now term a small business or small farm. If one did not have this "productive unit," that person was "homeless" or a "Hobo." According to Todd DePastino with regard to his book "Citizen Hobo: How a Century of Homelessness Shaped America," sufficient "homes as productive units" have become out of reach for everyone in the strict "Agrarian Paradise" of Jefferson as of about the 1880s. One must remember that in order to be an entrepreneur in today's world, one must live by the frugal principles set forth in "The Millionaire Next Door" referred to above. Unfortunately Milton and Rose Friedman's and Ayn Rand's great work was unavailable then and Roosevelt in name of Thomas Jefferson accelerated what has turned out to be a non-Jeffersonian disaster of Hamiltonian statist government regulation and taxpayer rip-offs that we may never overcome. He did believe there was a basic problem, which Jefferson also believed and spoke against in America that still exists today that is wealth, must not get too concentrated into the hands of too few people or free market competition no longer exists, i.e., large monopolies ruin the free market, and the consumer (who in the ideal society is also a creator) becomes unhealthy, i.e., without purchasing power and the nation becomes poor since there is no demand. This may be a similar grind down principle I found in the chess rating system, i.e., require the artificial input of money as the chess rating system required the artificial input of rating points.

Our solution to the problem was to turn to statist government regulation and other forms of the non-propertied employer-employee system in which certain people, with reference to Jefferson's last letter about the Declaration of Independence written June 24, 1826, have once again "been born with saddles on their backs…" with "a favored few booted and spurred, ready to ride them legitimately, by the grace of God." We should have solved this in keeping with the principles of the Jeffersonian Republic. I have a strong feeling the wisdom set forth in Milton and Rose Friedman's book "Free To Choose" and Ayn Rand's books could have gone a long way toward the right solution to the problem making the country unbelievably better today. To my dismay neither Friedman nor Rand seemed concerned about large public corporations run by employees using other people's money and determining their own salary and that of the other employee, i.e., fixing prices. However, we knew nothing of Friedman or Rand then and many people refused to be sucked into this employer-employee system and became "Hobos," a famous example of which is Huckleberry Finn. In my opinion the present day employer-employee system is not always but too often little better than the master-slave system and not a good solution to the problem. Interesting movies on this subject are: "Other People's Money" with Danny DeVito, "Office Space" with Jennifer Anniston and "Good Girl" with Jennifer Anniston. Labor Unions, another price fixer, have failed to help the situation and if anything have made it worse. Country Music is my favorite music, Merle Haggard, a creator and genius, is my favorite singer-songwriter and except for "Star Spangled Banner," as I remember it:

Oh say can you see by the dawn's early light, what so proudly we hail at the twilight's last gleaming, whose broad stripes and bright stars through the perilous fight o'er the ramparts we watched were so gallantly streaming and the rockets red glair, the bombs bursting in air gave proof though the night that our flag was still there. Oh say does that star spangled banner yet wave o'er the land of the free and the home of the brave.

Merle's song "Mama Tried" is my favorite song. My mama tried too. I think the reason I like that song is because first, his singing and his band's music is extremely good and second, he is so honest. He takes full responsibility for his actions and makes no excuse. This is such a wonderful thing in today's litigious world of sue the other guy, take no responsibility for your action, statism world of today. I think that in general I like country music because this music is highly individualistic, not collectivist and deals honestly with the ordinary person's, i.e., the employer-employee-hobo, struggle. If people knew about the "Enlightenment" they would know the statist employer-employee system, even more so as now regulated, destroys the very inalienable rights fought for in the American Revolution.

The Jeffersonian agrarian paradise originally was thought to be designed with the belief that enough land for virtually every citizen to own a farm (many think they overlooked other productive units) from which they could earn a living from achievable labor would be available for centuries. When the people reached the west coast much faster than anticipated, nobody made adjustments by trying to replace the needed small farms with small businesses and creator-entrepreneurs constitutionally promoted by the patent system to create them or provided sufficient money supply as explained in great detail by Friedman. As a result there developed a large "Hobo" population that seemed not the route to "Prosperity." Friedman tells us with great detailed explanation how getting the money supply in step with our tremendous productivity of those days could have solved this problem. I don't see of my own knowledge but have faith that this is true, and it should have at least been tried. The "New Deal" of Franklin Roosevelt had lofty goals and along with Henry Ford and others showing the value of "mass production" and "mass marketing" did indicate that the creation of a "middle class healthy consumer" is a necessary basis of wealth and prosperity. However, the "New Deal" created large bureaucracies run by people forcibly, i.e., by the force of the gun, taking faceless taxpayer's money that they don't know and care little for to help faceless people whom they don't know and care little for. These supposedly altruistic bureaucrats are really like everyone else and look primarily after themselves and their loved ones and wind up enriching the bureaucrats themselves with wealth they didn't create to the impoverishment of everyone else and are unable to self-correct and just get worse and worse and the worse they get, the more money they need and forcibly get. This is in stark contrast to free enterprise, which actually creates wealth, rather than confiscating it, and self-corrects and continuously gets better. The poor performers don't get more money. They go broke. It also created large corporations, run by non-owner negotiator employee (supervising the underpaid creators of wealth employees) who are intermediaries between the true owners and consumers they are in business to serve and have most of the same characteristics of large bureaucracies with the bad employer-employee system, but they supposedly have the capacity to self improve unlike bureaucracies that don't. And, they will finally go broke if the government does not subsidize them, which it nearly always will even if bribery is required. I was amazed at how well the patent office was run though. However, one has to remember that the patent office is run by scientist, not primarily negotiators and is a constitutional bureaucracy set up by the founding fathers designed to reward the creator, i.e., inventor, and the first patent examiner was Thomas Jefferson himself who was also a true scientist and creator. America has now developed Tax-Payer-Rip-Off and other bad industries, e.g., the industrial-military complex, which obtain excessively expensive military contracts, not by fairly bidding in contracts but, by lobbying and, effectively, bribing politicians, the plaintiff attorneys which have made life much more expensive and difficult and the excessively expensive doctor-Medicaid-drug-hospital complex for example. The government should be protecting creators not handing out plunder to lobbyist. John Stossel wrote an excellent book named "Give Me A Break" about how we are abandoning free enterprise and making life much worse in the name of improving things. In my opinion Andrew Jackson's Spoils System looks better all the time. With it you started over every few years and didn't have ingrained bottomless pits to pour tax dollars into which continuously gets worse no matter what party is in political power.

In my opinion if businesses must be large and regulated, we should as much as possible structure them to simulate the U.S. styled entrepreneurial system and what people are paid should be determined by a truly free market place, not price fixers, which is the only place which truly rewards actual merit, independent of management, which rewards 90 percent on politics, i.e., negotiating (or parasitic) skill and 10 percent on merit — creative skill -- the same as commodity values, such as the price of oil, are determined by a free market place. No individual employee should have the arbitrary forcible price fixing power over his or her own pay or the pay of another employee. The free market itself fairly regulates in cases such as mine where an entrepreneur uses subcontractors. It appears to me that if we can't have the free market determining what people are paid and have to have large public corporations run by employee price fixers who pay themselves unearned astronomical salaries, there should be a law requiring that no employee can be paid less than 5 percent as much as the highest paid employee in a given public corporation and the outsourced employees 7 percent. That is if the top employee price fixer pays himself $1 million per year, his lowest paid employee must be paid at least $50,000 per year and his outsourced employees in other countries must be paid no less than $70,000 per year.

But we really must uncompromisingly go back to the Jeffersonian Republic.

I believe the entrepreneurs and small business are the remainder of the Jeffersonian republic and everything reasonably possible should be done to make this part of America stronger. I believe the patent system should be used to motivate creators and build small independent productive units to enhance the Jeffersonian republic. Rather than this, while I tried to sell my inventions to a company big enough to easily make and sell the invention, I found Ayn Rand's *Ellsworth Toohey* everywhere and the doors of industry closed and there was no help from the government as to how to proceed or at all. It seemed in cahoots with "Big Business." The negotiators had the creators shut out and under their control. There were many predators of inventors out there but little help. It appears that "Big Business" wants to lock out independent inventors along with the "Enlightenment" and use the patent system as another tool for negotiators to dominate the world with the bribed government's help resulting in many virtuous patented inventions doing nothing but collecting dust until the patents expire. It probably would have been possible with enough capital and know-how to use subcontractors to make and sell my inventions but this is extremely hard to do and I simply didn't get through the parasitic mine fields as needed to get it done or gain sufficient know how and wherewithal to do it.

In my experience our education system is far from the Jeffersonian ideal and another bureaucracy with all its flaws and is too geared toward educating for careers in the non-propertied employer-employee system under the negotiators' control. And there is not enough instruction or guidance on how to make it as a creator-inventor, small business owner, or in short how to make it in the remainder of the Jeffersonian republic. I believe home schooling is a wonderful advance in our education system. Friedman also has a detailed explanation of how to overcome the bureaucratic flaws of the education system. However, it is Jeffersonian for everyone to be educated in the best way possible. I mostly stayed out of and know little about the agricultural part of our system except what I learned as a cowboy and from Will James, which is a diminishing world. I do think that there should be much more emphasis on the entrepreneur side of our economic system.

In my view large public corporations are in general bad because they separate the owner from his products and give all the power over his ownership and products, i.e., their income and expenses, to intermediary negotiator-employees that have negligible ownership and are using other people's money and basically can pay themselves what they choose without the restraint of personal ownership. The best system I have ever seen is the standard operating agreement such as I used in drilling all of my Ratliff Operating Corp. wells. In this system each investor owns a direct percentage in each well, its expense and income and an accounting, with the net payment if the well is not a dry hole, is made each month explaining how much money was spent for each category of production, i.e., intangible drilling cost, tangible drilling cost, completion cost, lease operating expense, royalty expense, state tax expense, sales of oil or gas (the product).

The owner's, prorata, pay the operator a relatively small subcontractor fee for its job in drilling, completing and producing the well. I always took a large personal ownership interest in every well I drilled and from this I made my money; not from the fees Ratliff Operating Corp. collected as the operator subcontractor. I wish I could have found or figured out such a system for my patented inventions.

The non-property concept of "other peoples money" found in government, large corporations and insurance causes bad problems deriving, I think, from the illusion that there is no harm in waste because "it is not my money." We should minimize employees using faceless taxpayer's money to help faceless individuals they care nothing about and don't even know. Everything possible should be done to make people realize it is their own money they are forcibly taking and wasting by enriching nobody but bureaucrats, few of which actually contribute to the creation of wealth. We are enriching bureaucrats that despite their altruistic rhetoric actually care for themselves and their family more than anyone else. The Jeffersonian-Adam Smith entrepreneurial system is great. In that system everything is on an ownership basis and designed for real people who think of themselves first; therefore, it works. I do believe everyone is really working for himself or herself but in free enterprise that is working for the consumer who is the real boss (and ideally is a creator or producer in the society) and whose demand determines the value of all goods and services and how rich a nation is. If we do not have a healthy consumer, goods and services have little value and the nation is poor. I think the government's principle job is to apply the true principles needed to keep the consumer healthy while, as much as possible staying out of the creator-entrepreneur's way and keeping a totally free market with as little regulation or bureaucracies as possible. As a result of going to the Employer-Employee system and the threat of outside forces such as Communism and Nazism, America started evolving from a Jeffersonian republic to a Hamiltonian-Empire-for-Big-Business-Industrial-Military-State and I think we are getting into deep trouble and need to keep the remainder of the Jeffersonian republic as strong as possible.

Admittedly, I am a bad employer and do not like to be in a contest of being a better parasite of my employee than he is of me. I once employed a man to pump Ratliff Operating Corp. wells. He was much better at being a parasite of me than I was of being a parasite of him. He kept negotiating ways to get more and more expensive in the name of saving money and just before I made the decision to change to a pumping subcontractor, the employee was costing the owners including me $750 per well per month to pump the wells whereas the going free market rate was much less than that. He claimed the need to hire three hourly workers to help him. After I turned to an entrepreneurial subcontractor, Willie Greening, to pump the wells, the cost went down to $175 per well per month and the quality of work went up by at least 100 percent. The employer-employee system is a very bad way of doing business. The incentives are all wrong. Whereas a subcontractor realizes that he can make money in a competitive free-market world in which he is providing a service that must be priced to compete or he will be replaced, the employee tends to forget this and focus on his belief that his employer is made of money and there has to be a way to negotiate more money out of him. I am sure there are great employees out there, but in my personal experience I have found only one.

The other side of this through an employee's eyes is that in the employer-employee system, employers can be parasites too and have historically, at times, had negotiating (or parasitic) advantages in a non free-market resulting in their beating employees down below a reasonable free-market wage for their work resulting in unhealthy consumers causing the value of goods and services to be very low, i.e., the depression of 1929, which Friedman with great detail explains could have been solved by correct money supply. This seems to be happening today by outsourcing the jobs to the poorest countries and thereby parasitically reducing the value of labor to that of the poorest countries to the extent that we will have very unhealthy consumers and the value of goods and services will be very low and we may go into a worldwide depression.

In general, however, I think federal regulation should be greatly reduced to only stopping truly criminal activity. Everywhere possible the necessary agencies should subcontract the work to entrepreneurs who are not allowed to lobby or make political contributions or otherwise bribe politicians. My mother's father was the right kind of subcontractor. Presently it just gets worse and worse. The tax system should be greatly simplified, reduced and much less intrusive.

I do believe that when either Friedman or Rand differ from the true enlightenment principles, they are wrong and the true enlightenment is right. America was based on the enlightenment that was digested by Jefferson in the Declaration of Independence. A fundamental axiom of the enlightenment is that every family has a right to the equivalent of a portion of land from which a living can be made. That is what I think is meant by the digestion that all men are created equal and the Jefferson Republic. The needy should be helped by a transition period of "negative tax" which includes incentive scholarships or the equivalent enabling them to become capable of performance as a true productive citizen in a free market system, but virtually no bureaucrats. Friedman did refer to a negative income tax program, but I don't believe government employees in the false name of altruism using forcibly taken "other people's money" and keeping 80 percent of it for themselves is the right way.

In my experience present day federal regulators of employers do a very poor job. Three times Ratliff Operating Corp. has been called to task in the years after going completely to subcontractors, i.e., having no employees, with the full weight of the most powerful nation in the world, and told, for example, its wells would be shut down and maybe confiscated because it owed the regulator over $30,000. Each time after much work in unraveling their mistakes, it was shown that these highly paid (with our tax dollars) regulators had totally failed to properly account for the payments Ratliff Operating Corp had paid in years ago and the regulators had made all the mistakes and falsely charged, with the backing of the most powerful country in the world, Ratliff Operating Corp. This is another powerful reason to use subcontractors as much as possible. It is another very powerful reason jobs are outsourced. The present day Federal regulations make life extremely difficult for employers. The Nebraska, Texas and Oklahoma regulators have been reasonably fair as of so far, however.

Somehow I hope America can recapture the "Enlightenment" and the Jeffersonian Republic to become an even better country than it has been throughout my lifetime for those who live in the years to come. It will take the effort of the people and an abiding faith in the natural scientific laws and theories of nature to do it. The real credit for my wonderful life and the "American Dream" goes to our wonderful founding fathers and to the laws and theories of nature and to detract from giving them credit is just not fair. It is our job to recapture what the founders gave us.

Appendix A

Application Serial No. 560,531 was filed June 27, 1966. The Patent Office did not look at it until March 29, 1968, at which time they responded with their first action, which I will try to describe as follows: On the first page, which was taken out checked portions of form letter stated:

U.S. DEPARTMENT OF COMMERCE
PATENT OFFICE
WASHINGTON, D.C. 20231

In Reply Please Refer To The Following   **Paper no. 3**
Examiner's Name P.R. Gilliam.   **Mailed 3/29/68**

239   June 27, 1966   560,531
GR. ART UN.   FILING DATE   SERIAL NO.
Harvey L. Ratliff, Jr.
APPLICANT   INVENTION
STEREO-SCOPO-RAMA

Harvey L. Ratliff, Jr.
938 Copley Avenue
Waldorf, Maryland 20501

Please find below a communication from the EXAMINER in charge of this application.

                                     Commissioner of Patents

This application has been examined.

"A SHORTENED STATUTORY PERIOD FOR RESPONSE TO THIS ACTION IS SET TO EXPIRE 3 MONTHS 0 DAYS FROM THE DATE OF THIS LETTER.

The following attachments are part of this action:

a. Notice of References Cited, PO-892. (These I listed in the description of U.S. Patent 3,424,511, above).

    1. Claims 1-6 are presented for examination, 35 U.S.C. 131

    4. Claims 1-6 are rejected.

On page 2 it was typed:

"Hayashi is cited to show the mounting of a lens in a recess in a stereoscope.
Mast, Bennett and Fazio are cited to show two part casings in a stereoviewer.
An abstract is required; see Rule 72(b).

Claims 1-4 are each rejected under 35 U.S.C. 103 as not patentably distinguishing over Romrell in view of Montebello, or further in view of Heilig. Romrell discloses a stereoscopic viewer adapted to receive a substantially rigid support having pictures attached thereto and resilient guide means and passageways therein for said support and picture.

Montebello (particular Figure 17) discloses a stereoscopic viewer whereby the optical axis of the curved film or picture intersects the optical axis of at least one of the viewing lenses whereby said axes intersect behind said lenses and to incorporate this idea in Romrell would be obvious to one ordinarily skilled in the art. The array of lenses in Montebello is considered the optical equivalent of the lenses claimed by applicant. However Heilig discloses single wide-angle lenses in a stereoscopic viewer and to use the lenses of Heilig in the modified device of Romrell in lieu of the array of lenses and for the same purpose would be obvious to one ordinarily skilled in the art.

The increase of peripheral re-creation as recited in claims 4-6 is held to find its patentable equivalent in the device lenses of Montebello or Heilig.

It appears applicant has allowable subject matter in this application and it is suggested that interview be set up with the examiner in charge to expedite the prosecution of this application."

David H. Rubin, who was probably the best examiner in the office, signed this action. P.R. Gilliam. initialed it with the phone no. (703)-557-2668 dated 2/28/1968.

NOTICE OF REFERENCES CITED

U.S. PATENTS

PATENT NO.	DATE	PATENTEE	CLASS	SUB-CLASS
2093520	9-1939	HAYASHI	350	134X
2326718	8-1943	MAST	350	135
2674920	4-1954	BENNETT	350	135
2834251	5-1958	ROMRELL	350	135
2953980	9-1960	MONTEBELLO	350	133
2955156	10-1960	HEILIG	350	133

FOREIGN REFERENCES

546968	3-1955	ITALY FAZIO	350	135

At this point in time the Patent Office seemed less hostile toward my inventions than they had seemed in the early stages of seeking patents.

I also had to make corrections of the drawings. The draftsman always seemed to reject the drawings also. I finally learned the technique of employing a printer there in the Washington D.C. area to make prints of my drawings, which virtually always went right, through.

I did go to the Examiner for the interview he suggested.

After attending the interview I responded with paper No. 4 as follows:

AMENDMENT
IN THE UNITED STATES PATENT OFFICE
Applicant: Harvey L. Ratliff, Jr.   Paper No.: 4
Serial No.: 560,531   April 25, 1968
Filed: 6/27/66   Group 259

For: STEREO-SCOPO-RAMA
To The Commissioner of Patents:
This is in response to the office action of 3/29/68, paper no. 3.
IN THE SPECIFICATION
Page 1, between lines 1 and 2, insert the following:
--ABSTRACT OF DISCLOSURE

A panoramic viewer particularly desirable for panoramic stereo re-creations is devised. On a deliberate and predetermined basis wide-angle oculars, having a predetermined property, which enables substantially distortion-free viewing at very wide-angles with a simplified and inexpensive optical system and which is taught in detail in the specification, are embodied as an integral part of the viewer. The viewer is also constructed to enable large enough picture formats coacting with these oculars for panoramic re-creation. The viewer can otherwise be rather conventional; however, in the specific design set forth the optical axes of the oculars diverge uniquely and a unique cylindrical slot is and integral part of the viewer to thus enable pictures of larger format to be within the depth of field of oculars having curved focal planes.--.

Page 1, lines 1 and 8, after "stereoscopic," in each insert: --or panoramic--.

Page 1, between lines 7 and 8, insert:

--A fundamental aspect of the present invention is to deliberately, on a predetermined basis, embody oculars in the viewer that have the following relation with their respective object plane:

$K \cong \theta/Y$ (see equation 3 hereinafter).

This relationship is described in detail hereinafter and is the essential ingredient of the invention. Because of this relation many benefits can be achieved such as the ones set forth under "object" hereof.--.

Page 1, lines 22 and 23, "not as...is very," please delete.

Page 1, line 23, "in a subordinate status," please delete.

Page 6, line 7, after "lenses)," insert: --which can have different outward appearances but which have a predetermined character that is set forth with reference to the ocular graph and equation 3 hereinafter and which may be molded out of "acrylic" plastic of made--.

Page 6, line 19, after: "one." Insert: --way--.

Page 8, line 25, after "Lens," insert: --(or taking lenses of and equivalent type wherein the taking lens graph applies)--.

Page 9, line 16, after "lens," substitute: --substantially eliminate noticeable distortion when the picture of the preceding graph of the taking lens is enlarged as shown in the following graph.—for: "has...relation."

Page 9, between lines 28 and 29, insert: --If (for the latter ocular graph) θ is defined with reference to Fig. 1, it is the angle a ray entering one of the eyes at E of an observer looking into the viewer, makes with the optical axis of the ocular 13 that this eye at E is looking into; if Y is defined with reference to Fig. 1, it is the distance from the optical center of the object plane of this said ocular 13 to the point of origin P of this ray as measured along said object plane; and if the slope-intercept formula is applied to the ocular graph, then:

$Y \cong m\theta$ equation 1

If the experimental predetermined property of the ocular (enabling the substantially straight line relation between Y and θ for values of θ between 0° and 42.5°+) is labeled K, then $m \cong 1/K$ and from eq. 1:

$Y \cong \theta/K$ equation 2.

Or $K \cong \theta/Y$ equation 3.

So, the ocular of this device thusly has the property of K which has a substantially when θ is from 0° to more than 42.5° off the optical axis of the ocular.

In the specific design of the ocular of the ocular graph, K $\cong$ 36°/inch.—

Page 9, line 30, substitute: --$\theta \cong$ (3.4 inch)(36°/inch) $\cong$ 122°-- for: "θ = 3.4/5.0 x 180 = 122°."

Page 10, line 2, substitute: --$\theta \cong$ (2.3 inch)(36°/inch) $\cong$ 83°-- for: "θ = 2.3/5.0 x 180 = 83°."

IN THE DRAWINGS

Sent herewith, in a separate paper, is a copy of sheet 1 containing Fig. 1. Added to Fig. 1, in red ink., are the proposed changes that should be made to Fig. 1. Please instruct the draftsman to make the indicated changes. Sent herewith is a check for $3.00 to cover the Draftsman's fee.

IN THE TITLE

Please change the title to: --A PANORAMIC VIEWING DEVICE--.

IN THE CLAIMS

Cancel claims 1-6 without prejudice.

Add the following claims:

Claim 7

A wide-angle panoramic viewing device for re-creating substantially distortion-free panoramic views, comprising: a housing; a pair of wide-angle oculars supported at the rear of said housing having their optical axes laterally displaced such that they pass approximately through the respective centers of the eyes of a normal viewer looking thereinto, and making a predetermined and operative angle with respect to each other, each of said oculars introducing substantially the following predetermined relation over a field of view greater than 42.5° off their respective optical axis:

$$K \cong \theta/Y,$$

Where: θ is the angle a ray entering one of said eyes makes with the optical axis of the corresponding one of said oculars, Y is the distance from the optical center of the focal plane of said one of said oculars to the point of origin of said ray measured along said focal plane, and K is a predetermined property of the ocular which had a predetermined value that is substantially constant from 0° to more than 42.5° off the optical axis of the ocular; predetermined and operative means of maintaining an illuminated image visible through each of said oculars at the focal plane of each of said oculars.

Claim 8

The device of claim 7 wherein said means includes a transverse slot for maintaining photographic images therein for viewing purposes

Claim 9

The device of claim 8 wherein said optical axes intersect to the rear of said oculars.

Claim 10

The device of claim 9 wherein said slot has a cylindrical configuration which is generated about a line which is perpendicular to both said optical axes and passes approximately through the intersection of said optical axes.

Claim 11

The device of claim 8 wherein the image can be maintained visible when Y is greater than 42.5°/K.

Claim 12

The device of claim 7 wherein said means is for maintaining a cylindrical image and said optical axes intersect to the rear of said oculars, with the configuration of the cylindrical image being generated about a line which is perpendicular to both said optical axes and passes through approximately the intersection of said optical axes.

Claim 13

The device of claim 7 wherein said means is for maintaining a cylindrical image at the focal plane of each of said oculars.

REMARKS

In an interview of April 24, 1968, it was agreed between the applicant and the Examiner, Mr. Gilliam., that the invention set forth in claim 7 does not constitute "new matter" and si patentable under the statutes but that the specification and drawings should be amended, without anything which was not heretofore inherently present, in order to make the meaning of the claim as clear as possible, and that many dependent claims in addition to claim 7 could be allowable. Applicant has tried very hard to act in accordance with this agreement.

The changes made in the specification further clarify what was already present in the ocular graph of page 9 and make a few minor changes in the specification in addition to this, while the changes of the drawing of Fig. 1 illustrate "θ" and "Y" of the ocular graph and illustrate, as "P," the point of origin of the typical ray considered. The Abstract was added in compliance with the Examiner's requirement. The Title was changed to more properly describe the true invention as claimed in claim7 (also claims 8-13).

The true invention, as now distinctly pointed out in both the specification and the claims, is clearly patentable of the prior art. Applicant's predetermined property "K" as claimed in combination with the other "expressed limitations" of the claims produces results which were heretofore totally "unexpected"; so, the claims are patentable under 35U.S.C. 103. If the claimed combination ever existed before, it was only a pure accident and had absolutely no known value.

The prior art, cited or uncited (i.e., Van Alabada as cited in my U.S. Patent 3,272,069, is not cited herein), recognizes no value whatsoever in deliberately embodying applicant's property "K" in a panoramic viewer. Nothing in the prior art remotely hints a system assuredly embodying the property "K" and if this property "K" is embodied in one of the prior art devices, it is purely an accident having no known value whatsoever.

In view of the foregoing facts and considerations, favorable action by the Examiner is courteously solicited.

Respectfully,

_____

Harvey L. Ratliff, Jr.

This was followed with:

AMENDMENT
IN THE UNITED STATES PATENT OFFICE
Applicant: Harvey L. Ratliff, Jr.   Paper No.: 5
Filed: 6/27/66   April 24, 1968

Serial No.: 560,531   Group 259

For: STEREO-SCOPO-RAMA

    To the Commissioner of Patents:

        This is a "SEPARATE PAPER" for the Draftsman in conjunction with paper No. 4.

        Sent herewith is a duplicate of sheet 1 of the drawings having, in red ink, the changes to be made to Fig.1. Please instruct the Office Draftsman to make the indicated changes. Sent herewith is a check for $3.00 to cover the Draftsman's fee.

                    Respectfully

                    _____

                    Harvey L. Ratliff, Jr.

        Next came:

U.S. DEPARTMENT OF COMMERSE
PATENT OFFICE
WASHINGTON

ADDRESS ONLY
THE COMMISSIONER OF PATENTS
WASHINGTON, D.C. 20321

	Examiner's Name	Group Art Unit
Harvey L. Ratliff, Jr.	P.R. Gilliam.	259
938 Copley Ave.	**Applicant**	
Waldorf, Mary land 20601	Harvey L Ratliff, Jr.	

Serial No.   **Mailed**
560,531   Mailed

Filed
June 27,1966

For   June 4, 1968
STEREO-SCOPO-RAMA
        GROUP 250

        SHORTENED TIME FOR REPLY

Please find below a communication from the EXAMINER in charge of this application.

                Commissioner of Patents.

A SHORTENED STATUTORY PERIOD FOR RESPONSE TO THIS ACTION IS SET TO EXPIRE 3 MONTHS, FROM THE DATE OF THIS LETTER.

        Responsive to the amendment filed April 29, 1968.

        Claims 1-6 have been cancelled.

        Claims 7-12 remain in the application.

        Page 5, line 21 of the specification, reference numeral 26 cannot be located on the drawing.

        Claims 7-13 are each rejected under 35 U.S.C. 112 as not distinctly claiming or pointing out the invention in that the claims recite structural elements and functions but fail to provide sufficient interconnection of the elements to perform the related functions in proper sequence for the desired end result. The interconnection or relationship of the elements is at the very crux of applicant's invention and must be recited.

For an example only, applicant has not included in parent claim 7 the necessary relative angular position of the oculars; or the location of the picture support means with respect to the oculars; or the intersecting of the optical axes which are all necessary and essential to applicant's invention; nor the aspect of the spherical picture required to produce the desired result.

Claims 7-12, so far as they are understood, are each rejected under 35 U.S.C. 103, as not patentably distinguishing over Romrell or Hayashi in view of Montebello, Van Alabada or Heilig.

Romrell and Hayashi disclose the equivalent claimed combination of a stereoscope with means for viewing pictures therein.

Each of the secondary references (particularly Van Alabada) disclose the idea of wide angle lens to increase peripheral re-creation and to provide either of the primary references with wide angle viewing after teachings of the secondary references would be obvious to one ordinarily skilled in the art. The particular limitations of angle ray entering eyes or the distance the optical center of the focal plane of the oculars involve only a matter of choice and/or design obvious to one ordinarily skilled in the art.

Claims 7-10 and 12 would appear to be allowable if claim 13 was cancelled and the following changes made in claims 7, 8 10 and 12: Claim 7, line 27, insert –angularly—after "oculars" and –with respect to each other—after "supported." Delete "the rear" and substitute therefor –one end--; insert --and—after housing.

Line 35, insert after "ray" –of light passing through a picture being viewed and--.

Line 10, page 4, after "property" insert –of a straight relationship between θ and Y--; after "ocular," insert –having a 2.36 focal length and--.

Line 12, insert –picture support—after "operative"; insert after means –at the other end of said housing to--; delete "of" and change "maintaining" to –maintain--.

Line 13, insert –thereof—after "plane" and delete rest of sentence.

Claim 8, line 16, insert –picture support—after "said."

Claim 10, change "9" top read –8--.

Claim 12, line 30, insert –picture support—after "said."

The citation of Van Alabada was made necessary by the presentation of the new claims.

This action is made FINAL.

PRGilliam.: caw

DAVID SCHONBERG
EXAMINER

Area Code: 703
557-2668

Next came my response:

AMENDMENT
IN THE UNITED STATES PATENT OFFICE

Applicant: Harvey L. Ratliff, Jr.   Paper N.: 7
Serial No.: 560,531   June 30, 1968
Filed: 6/27/1966   Group 259

For: A PANORAMIC VIEWING DEVICE

To: the Commissioner of Patents:

This is in response to the Office Action of 5/4/68, paper no. 6.

IN THE CLAIMS

Please make the following changes:

Claim 7 (amended)

A wide-angle panoramic viewing device for re-creating substantially distortion-free panoramic views, comprising: a housing; a pair of wide-angle oculars supported at the rear of said housing having their optical axes laterally displaced such that they pass approximately through the respective centers of the eyes of a normal viewer looking thereinto, and making a predetermined and operative angle with respect to each other, each of said oculars introducing substantially the following predetermined relation over a field of view greater than 42.5° off their respective optical axis:

$$K \cong \theta/Y,$$

Where: θ is the angle a ray entering one of said eyes makes with the optical axis of the corresponding one of said oculars, Y is the distance from the optical center of the focal plane of said one of said oculars to the point of origin of said ray measured along <u>a line perpendicular to the optical axis of said one of said oculars and passing through said optical center</u> [said focal plane], and K is a predetermined property of the ocular which has a predetermined value that is substantially constant from 0° to more than 42.5° off the optical axis of the ocular; [predetermine and operative means of maintaining an illuminated image visible through each of said oculars at the focal plane of each of said oculars,] <u>transverse slot means for transversely receiving and supporting a picture upon each focal plane of each of said oculars; and opening means for making visible each focal plane in said slot over values of θ from 0° to more than 42.5° as seen through said oclualrs.</u>

Please cancel claims 8 and 11-13 without prejudice.

In claim 9, please substitute –7—for "8."

Please add the following claims:

Claim 14

The combination with a housing of wide-angle ocular means for eliminating the distortion of fisheye-type pictures, transverse slot means for transversely receiving and supporting a picture upon the focal plane of said ocular means, and opening means for making visible a picture in said slot means over wide angles of view as seen through said ocular means.

REMARKS

Reconsideration is requested for the reasons, which are specifically set forth hereinafter.

The Examiner's criticism of the Specification is obviously improper and should be withdrawn.

The "numeral 26" is obviously located at the top of Fig. 5 beside "1T," at the bottom of Fig. 5 beside "1B," at the top of Fig. 6 beside "1T," at the bottom of Fig. 6

beside "1B," at the top of Fig. 8 beside "48." Therefore, this criticism should be withdrawn.

The Examiner improperly reacts to the most valuable and important invention concept and to all the inventive concepts.

The most valuable inventive concept is the combination with a viewer housing of applicant's oculars to achieve not merely a wide-angle function but also and more importantly the additional function of eliminating the distortion of fisheye-type (i.e. Hill-type) pictures which are virtually astigmatic-free, viz., Van Alabada proclaimed his reversing system as useless at wide-angles because of the intolerable astigmatic aberration produced at the wide angles of view with his taking lens, although his reversing ocular has been available ever since 1923.

Applicant's fisheye reversing ocular inventive concept has simply always been heretofore completely "unobvious" to the "ordinarily skilled." Otherwise, if it had really been "obvious" to the "ordinarily skilled," those "ordinarily skilled" would have been able to very valuably use this inventive concept ever since 1923 when Robin Hill introduced his astigmatic-free but highly distorted fisheye-type pictures (viz., some of the present day forms of the Hill-type lenses are "Nikon Fisheye," "Kenko Fisheye Conversion," "Super Tegea" and others).

But, this inventive concept remained totally invisible to everybody except applicant though it was potentially valuable ever since 1923.

Since it is clear from the Examiner's recitation as to his rejection under 35 U.S.C. 112 and suggested claim changes that the Examiner is trying to obscure and make indefinite all the true inventive concepts in a worthless maze of "nut and bolt" recitation and to require the insertion of this worthless maze of "nut and bolt" recitation as a highly improper device for dedicating all the true inventive concepts to the public, applicant submits that the Examiner's rejection under 35 U.S.C. 112 and suggested claim changes are highly improper and should be withdrawn.

The newly added claim 14 precisely points out the most valuable true inventive concept by way of a means plus a statement of function in complete compliance with 35 U.S.C. 112 and is drawn to a clearly new device.

The ocular, which is particularly characterized by the recitation in claim 7 is truly combined (because of the teachings of applicant to be inherently capable of the most important inventive concept set forth hereinabove) with a distortion-free panoramic viewer housing in which said inventive combination inherently is capable (because of applicant's teaching) of achieving more than one of the mere wide-angle functions heretofore possible, viz., the distortion reversing action which eliminates fisheye-type distortion enabling astigmatic-free and distortion-free super wide angles. This is in sharp contrast with anything made "obvious" by the prior art which enables the "ordinarily skilled" to uselessly aggregate oculars for achieving no more merely a wide-angle effect which is totally devoid of applicant's inventive ingredient, viz., which is burdened down with a totally different Montebello type of 42 lens structures necessitating a very clumsy picture mounting system, or which has bad distortion or bad astigmatism that must be subjectively ignored; Van Alabada did not subjectively ignore this bad distortion or this bad astigmatism and said reversing type oculars were useless at wide angles of view but Heilig either subjectively ignores the distortion and astigmatism or has a totally undisclosed way of overcoming them since Heilig enables the "ordinarily skilled" to merely aggregate those oculars for achieving no more than merely a wide-angle effect having bad distortion and bad astigmatism.

The inventive concept of claim 9 includes that of claims 7 and 14 and additionally includes the concept of diverging the optical axes of the oculars. This inventive concept is simply not made "obvious" by the prior art and is particularly pointed in claim 9 in compliance with the statute 35 U.S.C. 112.

The inventive concept of claim 10 includes that of claim 9 and additionally includes the concept of a single cylindrical slot. This inventive concept is simply not made "obvious" by the prior art and is particularly pointed out in claim 10 to comply with 35 U.S.C. 112.

In his Final rejection under 35 U.S.C. 103, the Examiner relies upon Romrell and/or Hayashi to make "obvious" the viewer in combination with a "means for viewing pictures therein." He then relies upon Van Alabada, Heilig, and/or Montebello to make it "obvious" to merely increase the "peripheral re-creation" or to merely provide a wide-angle of view.

The Examiner does not even hold that the combination of Romrell, Hayashi, Van Alabada, Heilig, and/or Montebello makes "obvious" any of applicant's true inventive concepts. He merely holds that combined they provide a mere wide-angle effect in an equivalent housing.

This is a highly improper rejection under 35 U.S.C. 103 and should be withdrawn.

Without any mention of a reference in support thereof whatsoever, the Examiner then passes off the very most valuable inventive concept as "obvious" by the phrase "The particular…to one ordinarily skilled in the art," page 2, lines 10-14 of his Final while ignoring the other inventive concepts (of claims 9 and 10) entirely.

Such q rejection without reference support is highly improper and should be withdrawn because the statutes and 706.02(a) M.P.E.P. require that 35 U.S.C. 103 rejections must be based upon prior art.

Claim 14 has been added to absolutely assure that the most valuable "unobvious" inventive concept is "particularly pointed out and distinctly claimed" in the new device in complete compliance with 35 U.S.C. 112.

The changes made in claims 7, 9, and 10 were not made (and were certainly not necessary) to overcome the Examiner's rejection under 35 U.S.C. 112 and 103 at all. These changes were made only to absolutely assure that the claims are drawn to new devices in complete compliance with the statutes, viz., 35 U.A.C. 102 AND 101.

It must be also remembered that the claims are in a very old and a very crowded art. In this art much smaller advances than applicant has made and claimed are entitled to patent protection and the most valuable inventive concept of all remained totally invisible to all the workers in this crowded art although it would have been of great value to them if seen at any time since Robin Hill introduced his "sky" lens a half century ago.

Therefore, the Examiner's rejection is clearly improper and should be withdrawn.

In view of the foregoing facts and considerations, the Examiner is courteously urged to pass this application to issue.

Respectfully,

_____

Harvey L. Ratliff, Jr.

Next:

IN THE
UNITED STATES PATENT OFFICE

In re application of: Subject: SN 560,531, p.p. 7
Harvey L. Ratliff, Jr.

THE COMMISSIONER OF PATENTS
    Washington, D.C. 20231

Sir:

Forwarded herewith are the papers indicated below relating to the amendment of paper no. 7 in response to the Final:

1. Check for $10.00 covers:
    $10.00 for one independent claim in excess of one and which was added for the first time by this amendment after the cancellation of 4 claims net: in addition, $0.00 for 0 claims in excess of 10.
2. The 6-page amendment comprises paper no. 7, in response to the office action of 6/4/68.

Please file the amendment.

Respectfully,

_____

Harvey L. Ratliff, Jr.

Date: July 3, 1968

Address: Harvey L. Ratliff, Jr.
         938 Copley Ave.
         Waldorf, Md. 20501

(301)-645-3197

Next:

SUPPLEMENTAL AMENDMENT
IN THE UNITED STATES PATENT OFFICE

Applicant: Harvey L. Ratliff, Jr.   Paper No.: 8

Serial No.: 560,531   July 4, 1968

Filed: 6/27/66   Group 259

For: A PANORAMIC VIEWING DEVICE

   To the Commissioner of Patents:

     This is a supplementary amendment to the amendment mailed yesterday, paper no. 7 in response to the Examiner's rejection of 6/4/68.

SPECIFICATION

   Please make the following changes in the specification:

Page 1, line 2, delete ,"the picture…therefor,"

Page 1, line 5, delete ,"picture…element,"

Page 1, lines 13-15, delete,"since…cost,"

Page 1, lines 17-19, delete "(i.e. 148°…oculars"

Page 1, line 20, delete "i.e. 2.36 inch."

Page 1, lines 26-29, delete "for use…images. Because…each."

Page 1, lines 30-32, delete "The fact…in fact."

Page 2, lines 1-23, delete all "must…magnification."

Page 3, lines 24 and 25, delete "which have…(i.e. 26°)."

Page 4, line 20, delete "diverging,"

Page 4, lines 25 and 26, insert - -may- -before "diverge,"

Page 5, line 14, delete "oval shaped,"

Page 6, line 8, delete "two."

Page 6, line 9, substitute - -may be- -for "is."

Page 6, line 13, substitute - -may be- -for "are."

Page 6, line 14, substitute - -may be- -for "are."

Page 6, line 15, substitute - -may be- -for "are"

Page 6, line 16, substitute - -may be- - for "are."

Page 6, lines 18-22, delete ,"or the only…as 1B."

Page 10, line 3, after "of view," insert - -noting the inherent inverse relation between K and F.L. whereby K would be greater if F.L. is less- -.

--1—

Page 6, line 23, substitute - -may be- - for "are."

Page 6, line 30, substitute - -may be- - for "are."

REMARKS

191

There must be some reason that the Examiner has heretofore wanted the applicant to insert a maze of "nut and bolts" which dedicate all of applicant's worthwhile advances in the art to the public. Since it is clear from paper no. 7 that these "nuts and bolts" are certainly not needed to truly and completely define the new devices or the inventive concepts of the new devices in compliance with 35 U.S.C. 112 and in fact obscure the inventive concepts, and since it is clear from paper no. 7 that these "nuts and bolts" are certainly not needed to avoid the art under 35 U.S.C. 103 or 102, the only reason applicant can see (though applicant does not appreciate the actual validity of even this reason) that the Examiner is requiring (improperly) said "nuts and bolts" in the claims is that he may feel that there is some restrictive language in the specification should be removed to clarify under 35 U.S.C. 112 the true inventive concepts and novelty.

As was heretofore stated in page 10, lines 23-27 of the specification, the "nuts and bolts" recitations of the specification are illustrative and not restrictive and only the claims define the restrictive inventive concepts and novelty. This should suffice. However, to additionally make sure that the Examiner has no basis for such a feeling (or the courts at some future date have no basis either), some language (that could possibly be interpreted improperly as restricting the claims to something other than the true invention for allegedly avoiding the prior art) is hereby amended. It will be noted that none of the changes raise issues not brought up by the Examiner himself, add new matter at all, depart from the true teachings of the true inventive concepts at all, or depart from the teachings of the new devices claimed.

--2—

Therefore, the present amendment is proper and should be entered to place this case in condition for allowance.

Respectfully,

_____

Harvey L. Ratliff, Jr.

--3—

Next came the corrected Drawing and the following:

Dept. of Commerce   **U.S. DEPARTMENT OF COMMERCE**   ADDRESS ONLY

SEAL   **PATENT OFFICE**   THE COMMISSIONER OF PATENTS

WASHINTON, D.C. 20231   WASHINGTON, D.C. 20631

APPLICANT

Mr. Harvey L. Ratliff, Jr.   Harvey L. Ratliff, Jr.

938 Copley Avenue   SERIAL NO.

Waldorf, Maryland 20601

560,531
GROUP
250
ORDER NO.

LETTER OF
April 29, 1968

Dear Sir:

In accordance with the instructions in the letter dated above the drawing in the application identified has been corrected and returned to the Examiner in charge of this application.

A photocopy of the drawing is furnished herewith so that you can verify the corrections that have been made. Additional photocopies may be obtained from the Patent Office at a cost of 30 cents per sheet.

Very truly yours,

Daniel M. Mills
Chief Draftsman

DEPOSIT ACCOUNT
CHARGE

CASH FEE PAID $3.00

NO CHARGE
POL-19 (12-65)   USC OMM-DC 46842-P65

After a telephone interview came:

                                                            ADDRESS ONLY
SEAL   **U.S. DEPARTMENT OF COMMERCE**   **THE COMMISSIONER OF PATENTS**
                          PATENT OFFICE   **WASHIUNGTON, D.C. 20231**
                      WASHINGTON, D.C. 20231

In Reply Please Refer To The Following
  EXAMINER'S
  NAME   P.R. Gilliam.
    259   June 27, 1966   560,531
GR. ART UN.   **FILING DATE**   **SERIAL NO.**   MAILED

  Harvey L. Ratliff, Jr.   Aug 2 1968
    APPLICANT   **INVENTION**

WIDE ANGLE STEREO-SCOPO-RAMA VIEWER   GROUP 250

Harvey L. Ratliff, Jr.
938 Copley Avenue
Waldorf, Md. 20601   **DAVID SCHONBERG**
                                                 EXAMINER

Please find below a communication from the EXAMINER in charge of this application.

4. × Prosecution on the merits is closed in this application and the Notice of Allowance or other appropriate communication will be sent in due course, in view of:

b. Telephone interview with Applicant on July 25, 1968.

POL-327 (2-68) * GPO: 1968-291-829

Next came:

ADDRESS ONLY
THE COMMISSIONER OF PATENTS
WASHINGTON, D.C. 20231

U.S. DEPARTMENT OF COMMERCE

SEAL

PATENT OFFICE
WASHINGTON, D.C. 20231

Paper No. **11**

In Reply Please Refer To The Following: **259**

EXAMINER'S NAME

P.R. Gilliam.

259	June 27, 1966	560,531
GR. ART UN.	FILING DATE	SERIAL NO.

HARVEY L. RATLIFF, JR.

APPLICANT / INVENTION

WIDE ANGLE STEREO-SCOPO-RAMA VIEWER

HARVEY L. RATLIFF, JR.
938 COPLEY AVENUE
WALDORF, MD. 20601

MAILED

AUG 19 1968

GROUP 250

Please find below a communication from the EXAMINER in charge of this application.

Commissioner of Patents

EXAMINER'S CHANGE AND/OR ADDITION TO THE APPLICATION RECORD UPON ALLOWANCE

This application is in condition for allowance. Changes and/or citation of references are specified below. Should this not be acceptable to applicant, an appropriate amendment may be proposed under rule 312. To ensure consideration of such amendment, it should be submitted on or before the date of remitting the issue fee.

PROSECUTION ON THE MERITS IS CLOSED AND A NOTICE OF ALLOWANCE WILL BE MAILED IN DUE COURSE.

The changes and/or additions are as follows:

Pursuant to the telephone conversation with applicant on July 25, 1968, the two amendments dated July 5, 1968 have been entered after applicant canceled claim 14.

As pointed out to applicant, claim 14 raised new issues that would have required further consideration and search and therefore would not have been entered.

The title has been changed to –WIDE ANGLE STEREOVIEWER--.

PLEASE FUIRNISH YOUR ZIP CODE IN ALL CORRESPONDENCE

Serial No. 560,531   -2-

The abstract has been changed to read:
--A panoramic viewer with a large curved picture slot for panoramic stereo re-creation coacting with wide-angle oculars having divergent optical axes which enables substantially distortion-free wide angle viewing--.

The drawing has been corrected as requested by applicant. The cost was $3.00.

Claims 7, 9 and 10 are allowed.

PRGilliam/cme

DAVID SHONBERG
EXAMINER

Area Code 703
557-2668

Next:

ADDRESS ONLY
THE COMMISSIONER OF PATENTS
WASHINGTON, D.C. 20231

U.S. DEPARTMENT OF COMMERCE
PATENT OFFICE
WASHINGTON

All commutations respecting
this application should give the
serial number, date of filing
And name of applicant

195

NOTICE OF ALLOWANCE
AND ISSUE FEE DUE

The application for patent identified below has been examined and found allowable for issuance
Of Letters Patent.

	FILING DATE	SERIAL NO.	NO. OF CLAIMS ALLOWED	EXAMINER	GROUP UNIT
	06/27/66	360531	3	SHONBERG	259

APPLICANT	Ratliff, Harvey L., Jr.; Oxon Hill, Md.

MAILED 9/24/1968 c

TITLE OF
INVENTION **Wide angle stereo-scopo-rama viewer**
(X indicates
as amended
by examiner

D R	NO. SHEETS @ $2 EACH	S P	NO. PAGES @ $10 EACH	ISSUE FEE DUE	CLASS-SUB
A	003	E	3	$136	350/135.
W		C			
I					
N					
G					

     With the allowance of the application, the above-indicated issue Fee becomes due and payment must be made within three months of the date of this Notice or the application shall be regarded as abandoned.

     The Issue Fee is one hundred dollars ($100) plus two dollars ($2) for each printed sheet of drawing and ten dollars ($10) for each printed page of specification, or portion thereof.

     Inasmuch as the number of printed pages of specification must be determined in advance of printing from the amount of matter in the allowed application the Issue Fee is subject to change. After the patent has been printed, the estimate will be reviewed in light of the actual number of pages of specification. If it is found that an over charge was made, you will be notified thereof with the issuance of the Patent and the matter will be referred to the Finance Branch for appropriate action. If the number of pages is underestimated by two or more pages, you will receive a notice of Additional Issue Fee Due with the Patent and payment of this amount must be made within three months of the date of that Notice. Failure to remit any additional fee sue within three months from the date of that Notice will result in lapse of the Patent.

     As a convenience in remitting this fee, use of the enclosed Form POL-85a is suggested. The Issue Fee will not be received from anyone other than the applicant, his assignee or attorney, or a party in interest as shown by the records of the Patent Office. A form is enclosed relating to the address of the inventor(s) which requires your attention.

     If it is desired to have the patent issued to an assignee or assignees, an assignment, together with the fee for recording the same, must be filed in this Office on or before the date of payment of the Issue Fee.

     The patent will be issued and forwarded within approximately two months after receipt of the Issue Fee. By direction of the Commissioner.

Harvey L. Ratliff, Jr.
938 Copley Ave.
Waldorf, Md. 20601

Next: The pink slip stating the filing date: 06/27/1966, serial number: 560531, patent number: 3424511, date of patent: 01/28/1969, inventor's name, address etc., assignee:

Jetru, Inc., invention title: Wide-angle stereoviewer etc., was mailed to me. Below is the Patent:

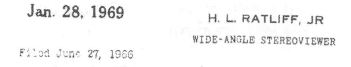

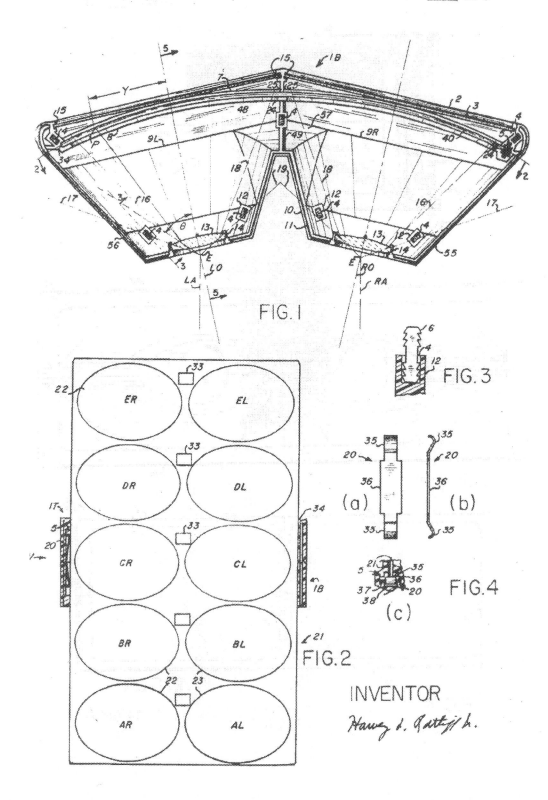

FIG. I

FIG. 3

FIG. 2

FIG. 4

(a)   (b)

(c)

INVENTOR

Harry L. Ratliff Jr.

198

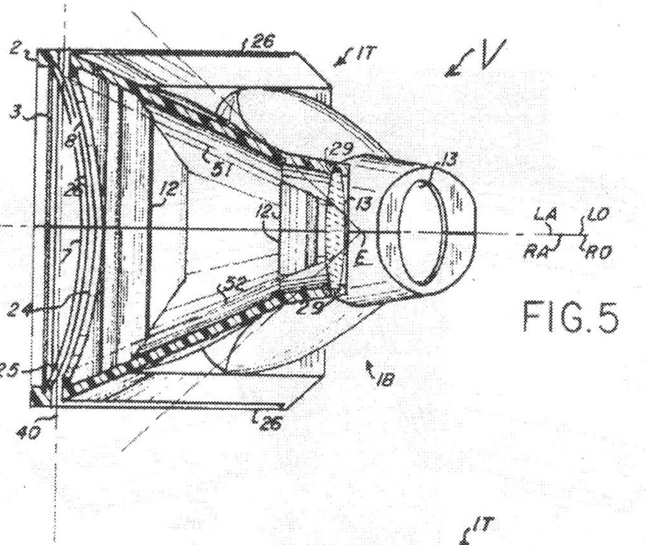

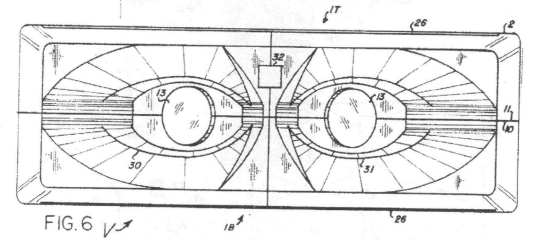

FIG.5

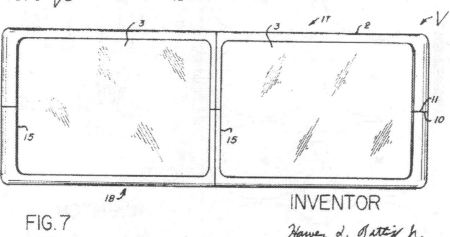

FIG.6

FIG.7

INVENTOR

Harvey L. Ratliff, Jr.

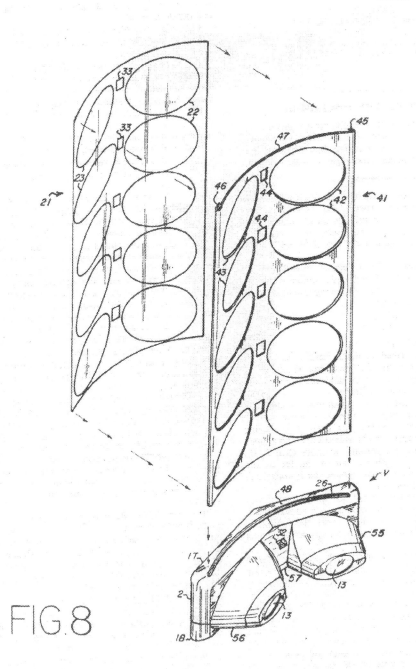

FIG.8

INVENTOR

Harvey L. Ratliff Jr.

1

3,424,511
WIDE-ANGLE STEREOVIEWER
Harvey L. Ratliff, Jr., Oxon Hill, Md., assignor to Jetru
Inc., Amarillo, Tex.
Filed June 27, 1966, Ser. No. 560,531
U.S. Cl. 350—135   3 Claims
Int. Cl. G02b 27/22

ABSTRACT OF THE DISCLOSURE

A panoramic viewer with a large curved picture slot for panoramic stereo re-creation coacting with wide-angle oculars having divergent optical axes which enables substantially distortion-free wide-angle viewing.

My present invention comprises an improvement in stereoscopic or panoramic viewers. The principal object of the present invention is to provide an extremely wide angle viewer which may be purchased at a very low price and operated by people with very little skill, effort or care.

A fundamental aspect of the present invention is to deliberately, on a predetermined basis, embody oculars in the viewer that have the following relation with their respective object plane

$$K \cong \theta / Y$$

(see Equation 3 hereinafter).

This relation is described in detail hereinafter and is the essential ingredient of the invention. Because of this relation many benefits can be achieved such as the ones set forth under "objects" hereof.

Wide-angle stereoscopic or panoramic re-creation presents a number of problems to workers in the art. As is well known, the rays entering the eyes of a viewing observer from the oculars of the stereoscope must enter the eye either parallel or diverging no more than is required at the distance of distinct vision. As far as the price of producing a wide-angle stereoscope is concerned this is a very critical problem.

It is therefore, another object to provide a viewer which supports a picture surface in a wide angular relation when the oculars have fairly short focal lengths. This is, of course, consistent with the principal object of the invention.

Another factor which is important is the size of the picture. It is therefore, another object to provide a viewer which is operative with picture elements of relatively small sizes.

Still another object of the present invention is to provide a viewer which makes it a naturally flowing reaction of the user to place the oculars immediately adjacent each eye whereby relatively small lenses (i.e., 0.9 inch in diameter) can provide the wide angle of view.

Other objects and advantages of my invention will become apparent from a study of the following description taken with the accompanying drawings wherein:

FIG. 1 is a plan view of the lower section 1B of the viewer V.

FIG. 2 is an expanded view taken along the line 2—2 of FIG. 1 with the picture element inserted after the top section 1T is combined with 1B to form V.

FIG. 3 is an enlarged, vertical section taken sub-

2

stantially along line 3—3 of FIG. 1, with the prong strip fastener 6 inserted.

FIG. 4(a) is a plan view of the picture locating spring 20 which is inserted in socket 5 of FIG. 1 when the viewer is assembled.

FIG. 4(b) is a side view of the spring of FIG. 4(a).

FIG. 4(c) is a top view of the spring 20 inserted in socket 5, shown in section, to show the details of the socket 5 and its relation to spring 20.

FIG. 5 is a sectional view taken along line 5—5 of FIG. 1.

FIG. 6 is a rear view of the viewer V.

FIG. 7 is a reduced front view of the viewer V.

FIG. 8 is a perspective view of the viewer V, picture holder 41, and picture element 21 showing the manner of insertion.

In the preferred contemplated form of the invention a plurality of left eye view pictures 23 and a plurality of right eye view pictures 22 are printed in "continuous tone" on picture element 21 as shown in FIG. 2 and FIG. 8. It is preferable that the picture element be of stiff paper which is thin enough to be substitutable for a transparency whether or not the picture element is used with a diffusing screen. The optical centers of 23 and 22 are on the recording axes corresponding to LO and RO, respectively. In the instant form of the invention they are of oval shape and are 3.4 inch wide and 2.3 inch high. The picture element may be slid directly into cylindrically shaped transverse slot 26, but better results are obtained if the picture element is inserted in holder 41, this being described in more detail hereinafter.

The pictures are recorded along axes corresponding to LO and RO in a compressed form such as is produced by a "fisheye" lens and as is described in more detail in my said prior application Ser. No. 343,841. The pairing of the views is indicated by the letters of FIG. 2, AL to EL, inclusive, indicating the first to the fifth left pictures 23 and AR to ER, inclusive, indicating the first to fifth right pictures 22. In the contemplated form the optical centers of 22 and 23 are 3.74 inch apart as measured on the surface of 21. Picture descriptions 33 are provided to give various information to the user as to the title or the like.

If picture holder 41 is used, the paper of 21 may be more flexible. Holder 41 comprises a cylindrically shaped stiff surface 47 which has the same cylindrical curvature as slot 26 (in the specific embodiment shown its radius of curvature is 8.25 inch), picture description apertures 44, picture apertures 43 to allow the user to see pictures 23, picture apertures 42 to allow the user to see pictures 22, and picture fasteners 45 and 46.

The viewer V comprises two portions, a bottom portion 1B and a top portion 1T. Each of portions 1B and 1T comprise a casing 2 which supports seven posts 12 having correspondingly seven sockets 4 therewithin each for receiving seven prong strip fasteners 6 to fasten 1B to 1T.

Casing 2 is shaped with ocular tubes 55 and 56 which extend relatively far behind the picture containing portion 48 and support four right and left ocular supporting shoulders 14 and four top and bottom ocular supporting grooves 29 at the rear of the ocular tubes 55 and 56. The ocular supports 14 and 29 support the ocular lenses 13 such that their optical axes are respectively LO and RO which may diverge from each other at a substantial angle (which in the case of the specific embodiment is 26° or

3

13° to the right of the axis of right eye view RA and 13° to the left of the axis of left eye view LA, RA and LA being parallel and substantially the interpupillary distance apart of 2.56 inches).

The casing 2 is made relatively thin above oculars 13 and the grooves 29 are placed therein to make the width from top to bottom small enough that ocular tubes 55 and 56 can be placed under the eyebrow and deep into the eye socket of the user so that the eyes of the user can be placed at positions E with reference to the oculars 13 as supported by viewer V. Also there is a deeply recessed portion 57 provided by the casing 2 of the viewer V to allow the nose of the user to protrude as far up as a position in close proximity to the picture portion 48 of the casing 2 of viewer V.

In each portion casing 2 provides a strengthening rib 49 connecting the ocular tube portion to the picture portion.

The picture portion 48 comprises right upper and lower walls 9R and left upper and lower walls 9L; respective front and rear picture supporting walls 7 and 8 with two apertures 25 and 24 which are substantially the same shape and size as pictures 22 and 23 and are symmetric about optical axes LO and RO; grooves 15 for supporting diffusing screens 3 (which in the case of printed picture elements could even be transparent since the paper the pictures are printed upon acts to diffuse the light); in addition to the posts 12 and sockets 4; the socket 5 is provided plus its corresponding post for holding picture positioning spring 20; and thusly as shown a transverse slot 26 symmetric about picture surface 40 which is (in the specific embodiment herein set forth) generated about a line which is perpendicular to and passes substantially through the intersection of LO and RO thereby having a radius of curvature which is some 8.25 inches.

The forms of the two portions 1B and 1T are (in the specific embodiment set forth herein) mirror reflections of each other with the exception that in 1B the high shoulder 11 is on the inside, while in 1T the high shoulder 11 is on the outside, the low recessed shoulders 10 being respectively on the outside and inside so that shoulder 11 of 1B fits into recessed shoulder 10 of 1T and shoulder 11 of 1T fits into recessed shoulder 10 of 1B (see FIG. 6).

The sockets 5 of 48 comprise the outer flat surface 38 and shoulders 37 which are flat and perpendicular to the plane of LO and RO.

The surface 34 is also flat and perpendicular to the plane of LO and RO.

Suitable lenses 13 are provided (in the specific embodiment set forth herein the lenses 13 are 2.36 inch focal length, 0.9 inch diameter and double convex lenses) which can have different outward appearances but which have a predetermined character that is set forth with reference to the ocular graph and Equation 3 hereinafter and which may be molded out of "acrylic" plastic or made in a well known manner.

There is provided suitable rectangular shaped screens 3.

There may be provided a picture positioning spring 20 which comprises a flat wide portion 36 which is narrow enough to fit into socket 5 but is too wide to rest against 38, and rounded spring portions 35 which are narrow enough to pass by shoulders 37.

For assembly the oculars 13 may be inserted in grooves 29 and supporting shoulders 14, screens 3 may be inserted into grooves 15, prong strip fasteners 6 may be inserted into sockets 4, and picture positioning spring 20 may be inserted in socket 5 either with its wide flat surface 36 outside spring portions 35 to rest against shoulders 37 as shown in FIG. 4(c), which is preferable.

Next the two portions may be slipped together with the prong strip fasteners 6 slipped into sockets 4, oculars 13 slipped into grooves 29 and supporting shoulders 14, screens 3 slipped into grooves 15, picture positioning spring 20 slipped into socket 5, and 10 and 11 each slipped

4

into and received by respectively 11 and 10 of the other portion such as 1T.

For assembly of the picture element 21 with the picture holder 41, the right and left edges of 21 may be respectively inserted in fasteners 45 and 46, such that pictures 22 and 23 register with apertures 42 and 43 respectively and picture descriptions 33 register with apertures 44.

For viewing the holder 41 with the picture element 21 therein or the picture element 21 alone may be inserted in slot 26. Spring 20 coacts with back support 7 and the supports (i.e., 37) in slot 5 to push the left edge of 41 (or 21) against 34. Since 34 and 37 are perpendicular to the plane of LO and RO and the optical centers of 22 and 23 lie on a line which is perpendicular to the left edge of 41 (or 21), spring 20 assures that the optical centers of 22 and 23 are in a plane parallel to the plane of LO and RO. Slots, to assure registry of optical centers with optical axes, may be provided in the right edge of 41 to allow the rounded portions 35 of spring 20 to slip thereinto when the optical centers of 22 and 23 register with RO and LO, respectively. However, this is not necessary since it is pretty obvious when the optical centers are in substantial registry.

It can be seen that in the specific contemplated structural arrangement of the invention set forth herein, the distance along the optical axes from the centers of the lenses 13 to the optical centers of the pictures (when registered with apertures 24 and 25) is some 2.16 inches.

It can be made obvious from the lens formula that:

$$1/o + 1/i = 1/f$$
$$1/2.16 + 1/i = 1/2.36$$
$$1/i = 0.424 - 0.463 = -0.039$$
$$i = -25.6 \text{ inch}$$

where:

f = focal length (i.e., 2.36 inches),
o = object distance (i.e., 2.16 inches),
i = image distance (i.e., −25.6 inches).

Therefore, the shortest virtual image distance created by the stereoscope is some 25.6 inches which is far enough beyond the distance of distinct vision.

It can be seen also that the distance along right and left peripheral rays 18 and 16 from (points also within the plane passing through the centers of the lenses and perpendicular to their respective optical axes RO and LO) to the right and left peripheral edges of the respective pictures is some 2.35 inches.

It can also be seen from the lens formula that:

$$1/o + 1/i = 1/f$$
$$1/2.35 + i/i = 1/2.36$$
$$i = \infty$$

Therefore, the peripheral rays 18 and 16 enter the eyes parallel (for practical purposes).

It can be clearly seen herefrom that if picture surface 40 was not cylindrically curved similarly to the surface set forth herein, the right and left peripheral portions of the pictures would be completely out of focus to the stereoscope user.

Still further it can be seen that the distance along upper and lower peripheral rays 51 and 52 from (points also within the plane described hereinabove) to the upper and lower peripheral edges of the respective pictures is some 2.35 inches. Therefore, the peripheral rays 51 and 52 enter the eyes parallel (for practical purposes). It is here noted that if the vertical picture width were made greater than some 2.3 inches, the peripheral portions would be out of focus due to the flat character thereof.

Applicant has found that if pictures taken by the image compressing "Nikon Fisheye" lens or taking lenses of an equivalent type wherein the taking lens graph applies are enlarged to a diameter of some 5 inches, the image when viewed through an image expanding 2.36 inch focal length double convex lens (if the optical center of the

5

picture is substantially on the optical axis of the lens) is expanded in its angular eye entering character to such an extent that there is not noticeable distortion (the characteristic curved lines associated with "barrel distortion" are not present) and the image appears orthoscopic.

According to the manufacturer of the "Nikon Fisheye" lens (i.e., page 12 of their instruction booklet "How to Use Fisheye Nikkor"), there is a straight line relation between Y (the distance of an image point from the picture center) and θ (the "zenith angle" which is the angle between the optical axis and the entering image ray corresponding to the image point) which is as follows:

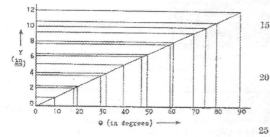

Applicant has found that his 2.36 inch F.L. image expanding lens substantially eliminates noticeable distortion when the picture of the preceding graph of the taking lens is enlarged as shown in the following graph.

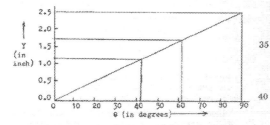

It can be seen that if the 24 mm. recorded image is enlarged some 5.3 times in a linear manner to a some 5 inch image, the expanded rays will have substantially the same angular configuration as the rays entering the taking lens had before compression took place.

If (for the latter ocular graph) θ is defined with reference to FIG. 1, it is the angle a ray, entering one of the eyes at E of an observer looking into the viewer, makes with the optical axis of the ocular 13 that this eye at E is looking into; if Y is defined with reference to FIG. 1, it is the distance from the optical center of the object plane of this said ocular 13 to the point of origin P of this said ray as measured along said object plane; and if the slope-intercept formula is applied to the ocular graph, then:

$$Y = m\theta \qquad (1)$$

If the experimentally predetermined property of the ocular (enabling the substantially straight line relation between Y and θ for values of θ between 0° and 42.5°+) is labelled K, then $m \cong 1/K$ and from Eq. 1:

$$Y \cong \theta / K \qquad (2)$$

or

$$K \cong \theta / Y \qquad (3)$$

So, the ocular of this device thusly has the property of K which has a substantially constant value when θ is from 0° to more than 42.5° off the optical axis of the ocular.

In the specific design of the ocular of the ocular graph, $K \cong 36°/inch$.

It can therefore be seen that 3.4 inch diameters represent: $\theta \cong (3.4 \text{ inches}) (36°/inch) \cong 122°$.

6

122° angles of view and that 2.3 inch diameters represent:

$$\theta \cong (2.3 \text{ inches}) (36°/inch) \cong 83°$$

83° angles of view noting the inherent inverse relation between K and F.L. whereby K would be greater if F.L. is less.

Since the optical axes are diverged 26° in the specific embodiment herein set forth, the horizontal angle of steroscopic re-creation is: $122° + 26° = 148°$, some 148°, and the vertical angle of stereoscopic re-creation is 83°.

It is noted that inside peripheral rays 19 make: $61° - 13° = 48°$, some 48° angles with the axes of right and left eye view (RA and LA). Therefore, rays 19 intersect at a point in front of eyes at E which is:

$$X = \cot(48°) \times \frac{2.56}{2} = 1.15 \text{ inches}$$

some 1.15 inches from a line joining E. This closely approximates the real life situation, since the nose of a viewing observer protrudes almost this far in front of his eyes.

It can now be seen that a depth of stereoscopic vision is provided by the viewer from some 1.15 inches in front of E to infinity and that an angle of peripheral re-creation is provided by the viewer of some 148°. This is almost as good as the eyes actually see in any real life situation.

It can also be seen that the invention provides these remarkable re-creations for the user at very inexpensive prices and that little effort, skill or care is required of the user.

While the invention has been disclosed and described in some detail in the drawings and foregoing description, they are to be considered as illustrative and not restrictive in character, as other modifications may readily suggest themselves to persons skilled in the art and within the broad scope of the invention, reference being had to the appended claims.

I claim:

1. A wide-angle panoramic viewing device for re-creating substantially distortion-free panoramic views, comprising: a housing; a pair of wide-angle oculars supported at the rear of said housing having their optical axis laterally displaced such that they pass approximately through the respective centers of the eyes of a normal viewer looking thereinto, and making a predetermined and operative angle with respect to each other, each of said oculars introducing substantially the following predetermined relation over a field of view greater than 42.5° off their respective optical axis:

$$K \cong \theta / Y$$

where: θ is the angle a ray entering one of said eyes makes with the optical axis of the corresponding one of said oculars, Y is the distance from the optical center of the focal plane of said one of said oculars to the point of origin of said ray measured along a line perpendicular to the optical axis of said one of said oculars and passing through said optical center, and K is a predetermined property of the ocular which has a predetermined value that is substantially constant from 0° to more than 42.5° off the optical axis of the ocular;

transverse slot means for transversely receiving and supporting a picture upon each focal plane of each of said oculars; and

opening means for making visible each focal plane in said slot over values of θ from 0° to more than 42.5° as seen through said oculars.

2. The device of claim 1 wherein said optical axes intersect to the rear of said oculars.

3. The device of claim 1 wherein said slot has a cylindrical configuration which is generated about a line which is perpendicular to both said optical axes and passes approximately through the intersection of said optical axes.

(References on following page)

3,424,511

7				

References Cited

UNITED STATES PATENTS

2,093,520	9/1937	Hayashi	350—134 X
2,326,718	8/1943	Mast	350—135
2,674,920	4/1954	Bennett	350—135
2,834,251	5/1958	Romrell	350—135
2,953,980	9/1960	Montebello	350—133
2,955,156	10/1960	Heilig	350—133

FOREIGN PATENTS

| 546,968 | 3/1955 | Italy. |

8

OTHER REFERENCES

Van Alabada: "A Wide-Angle Stereoscope and a Wide-Angle Viewfinder," Transactions of the Optical Society of London, vol. 25, 1923–24, pp. 249–257, 259, 260.

DAVID SCHONBERG, *Primary Examiner.*

P. R. GILLIAM, *Assistant Examiner.*

U.S. Cl. X.R.

350—239

Above is the complete U.S. Patent 3,424,511, which includes three pages of drawings and four pages of specification.

Appendix B

Published in the Borger News-Herald Friday, Aug. 22, 1952

'Suppose Capitalists Strike'--GI Joe Asks

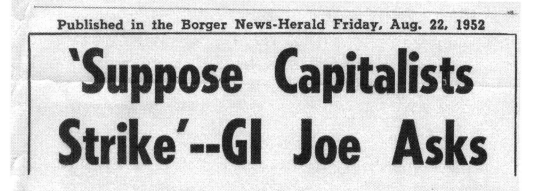

(EDITOR'S NOTE: Questions contained in a letter to the Editor, from a man away from home serving his Country, prove both startling and interesting. Perhaps the readers of the News-Herald could help answer these questions.

The questions are not without answers. The letter is more in the form of a feature article or editorial matter. The writer goes on to explain what he considers made our country great.

He explains the great incentive. He questions many things. His questions are a challenge to all of us who are worried over the trend of events.

That a man in active service of his Country should find the time, and take the time, to reduce his troubled thoughts to words, and to put all of these words down on paper, is truly amazing, particularly to such an extent as in this article.

The Editor is taking this opportunity to publish the article, under a nomme de plume, G. I. Joe. We hope that this publication meets with his approval. The Editor feels that this should be considered an outstanding contribution to the editorial columns of the Borger News-Herald—J. C. Phillips)

(A Contributed Editorial)
By G. I. JOE

Suppose all the business men and employers of every size, shape and form in the United States should just hide all their money or in some way make it inaccessible!

Still further, suppose these people should just destroy all the wealth they have created—the oilwells they have drilled, the buildings they have built, the organizations they have sponsored, all the infinitude of business outlets, small and large, that they have created and possess!

What would happen?

This seems silly. But stop and think! What would happen?

Could the big, powerful, generous, extravagant government save us?

I ask you!

Could the government save us?

What self supporting enterprise does the government operate? Can the government make any enterprise self supporting?

I ask you!

Could the government save us?

What self supporting enterprise does the government operate? Can the government make any enterprise self supporting?

The politicians in the government could make big sweet promises—couldn't they?

But could they do us any good?

This may seem ridiculous to you, but isn't it an intense truth that millions of people are ignoring completely?

I beg you to think. What would happen? Tell me how any man could receive any wages. Who could pay wages to any man? How could the government receive any taxes? Just think —how could it?

Could any one say "Oh, well I don't need to worry, the government will support me?"

Could any one say "Why should I work—so-and-so gets all kind of pay working for the government and doesn't have to do any work?

I ask you, who is paying these government employees? You might say the government is, certainly. Please reconsider the matter. Does the government pay these people?

How could the government pay these people if it received no taxes? I tell you people of America, it could not. The government is helpless without these taxes.

Where does the tax money come from? Doesn't it come from the wage-earners and employers of the nation? Please tell me one other place the tax money comes from.

I tell you, people of America, the wage earners money comes from the employers of the United States: therefore, great people of the United States, the employers of America finance this country. Tell me how any man could really think they do not!

The great question is, how did the employers or so called capitalists get their money? The answer to this is the answer to the question of why the United States of America became the great country it is!

Why do we have such a high standard of living?

Why have we built such a powerful nation?

capitalists get their money? The answer to this is the answer to the question of why the United States of America became the great country it is!

Why do we have such a high standard of living?

Why have we built such a powerful nation?

How does it happen that we have had more and better equipment than any other nation?

For what reason have we won every war we ever fought?

What explains the other great things America has done?

I believe I have the answer to this great question, but you must be the judge. Just think for a moment!

———

If the capitalists had struck when Roosevelt was in power how could he have possibly been the Santa-Claus—the great generous Santa-Claus that he was?

———

Santa-Claus is still a myth, people!

If the capitalists struck there could be no United States Army; the labor unions commanded by their dictators could strike until they were blue in the face and it would not only not get them a raise, but it would not get them any wages. They could figure out every cagey deal in the book, but it would still get them no wages. This great country and all the people in it would inevitably be doomed unless they quit striking right away. It would certainly be doomed if the capitalists destroyed all their property.

The above possibilities may seem ridiculous so let us look at the question from another angle.

Suppose all the business men and employers of every size, shape and form in the United States are caused to go broke because we have drifted into the attitude that the PEOPLE ARE THE SERVANTS of the government IN CONTRAST to the constitutional AXIOM that the government is the servant of the people. Private enterprise is being taxed into bankruptcy!

Suppose that every man that employs people should go broke. Could the labor unions get higher wages or would they starve? Could we have a generous and extremely extravagant government?

Could any one make big juicy salaries loafing around in government offices—or would they starve? Again, I beg you to think! Could we win the war in Korea? Could we have world peace? How can you be peaceful when you are starving? Would we have security? What kind of security can you call what we would have? Could we be the powerful, wealthy, happy country that we are?

No! We would be doomed!

Some people feel that since they are poor, nobody should be rich; any way to soak the rich is all right. Here is what Abraham Lincoln said: "Property is desirable. Property is a definite good in the world. That some are rich shows that others may become rich, thus giving just cause for industry and enterprise. Then let not the man who is houseless pull down the house of another, but let him work diligently and build him a house of his own."

Abraham Lincoln was a poor man but Abraham Lincoln was a great, great man and he was man enough to admit that the fact that he could become rich was good. He was not heel enough to destroy the wealth other men had built just because his own ambition did not drive him to seek wealth.

The great question is how do people get rich in this country. All of us know that people do get rich in the United States. We've seen it happen.

What do people actually do to make money? Do they lie and cheat?

Some people make their money by lying and cheating, but they are breaking the great laws that enforce free enterprise, and they should be and usually are caught.

But just how was this great wealthy nation created? The crooks couldn't have created it because they rob it of wealth that it already possesses—do they not?

If a man builds an automobile he is not a crook—is he?

If he steals one someone else built, he is a crook—isn't he?

Well millions of men built the most powerful nation that ever existed and they were not crooks either; they were capitalists—not necessarily rich men but men who appreciated the opportunity to go into any business or trade or profession that their ambition and ability dictated.

Why are all the resources of this country so extensively developed? Many countries have more resources than we have.

What gave the people of this great nation the incentive to build this powerful, great, unbeaten nation with such a high standard of living?

Yes, what gave us that great incentive? Just what charac-

Yes, what gave us that great incentive? Just what characteristics of this great country did such an excellent job of releasing the creative powers of man? Just what has caused so much progress here?

We know there has been a lot of progress in the United States. Let me ask you something.

If you knew how you could make a million dollars, but you would have to work practically night and day for years and years whether you were sick or well and you also knew that as soon as you made it the government would take it away from you, would you go out and slave for that million?

There are plenty of ways of making money without being a crook. Suppose you really use your creative powers and create something that benefits a great many people all over the country.

If they know about your product, you know they will buy it. If your product is good enough and you play your cards right you know you will make a lot of money, or be rich. With this money you have made, can't you buy anything any other man in the United States has created to benefit mankind?

Doesn't this give you a great incentive?

Doesn't this make for much greater happiness? Can't you put your heart into a system like this?

Unless a man breaks the law, the only way he should get rich is by benefiting mankind—the more he benefits mankind, the richer he should become.

The man who takes money without benefiting mankind should be classed as a crook.

The man who makes money by producing things to benefit mankind should be classed as an honorable man.

———

Have you seen gamblers and their kind classed as honorable men?

———

Have you seen business men, exerting every effort to benefit mankind, unjustly classed as crooks?

How many examples of this misrepresentation of an honorable man and a crook can you find? Of course all-powerful business monopolies that cease to benefit mankind are bad just like all powerful labor monopolies that cease to benefit mankind are bad.

Thomas Jefferson said "In questions of power, then, let no more be heard of confidence in man." He was referring to government but the thought is equally applicable to business or

Thomas Jefferson said "In questions of power, then, let no more be heard of confidence in man." He was referring to government but the thought is equally applicable to business or labor unions.

Business men are no more dishonest than laboring men.

———

What are the incentives which make people work? One that you know about is discipline. This was probably the main incentive before the United States was founded.

Man worked because he would be punished if he did not work. Fear motivated man.

Discipline is the main incentive people have in dictatorships.

You can call communism any kind of sweet name you like, even democracy—but isn't it downright dictatorship? When you get right down to facts, can you have any kind of government except self government or dictatorship?

———

Can you really put your heart into something when your only reason for doing it is to avoid punishment? No man can do his best under such conditions.

No people could build a rich, happy country like the United States with fear of punishment as the only incentive. It is altogether against human nature. Show me a man who would scheme about his work ever spare a minute and dream about his work while sleeping at night with fear of discipline as his only incentive.

What is another incentive that makes people work? Another incentive that makes men work their hearts out is a community or district or a national goal which they think will give them what they want and make them happy.

Germany had this incentive in a way—it would have made most of the German people extremely happy to conquer the world. They created an awful lot of war equipment under this drive.

But the United States excelled Germany in practically every other field and possibly even in that one.

Why?

Because we have the individual goal on top of all others—the great incentive—in the United States.

If an individual creates anything that benefits many other people or in some other way benefits man, he should make money and be able to use that money to get what he wants of things other men have created to benefit mankind.

This makes it possible for all men to get what they want and need.

things other men have created to benefit mankind.

This makes it possible for all men to get what they want and need.

All the paper bills in the world are no good unless the needs of man are available for purchase. What other incentive would cause man to do the miraculous things he has done?

I ask you—isn't this great incentive what made the United States the great, wealthy happy nation it is? I beg you to tell me what else could be the reason!

If we lose this incentive, you know the country will cease to be the great country it is. I believe it will be doomed. Of course none of these things would be enjoyed if we were not free; but starving people lose their freedom mighty fast.

———

There are thousands of men in the United States who have worked as hard to achieve success as Hitler, Napoleon, or Alexander the Great worked to conquer the world.

The difference is in what they were working for!

They were working for what they wanted, of course. But the financial empire builders of the United States, by benefiting mankind, were helping other citizens of the country to build the best nation that ever existed.

———

The crooks and dictators were seeking glory for themselves to the detriment of all others. You can bet, the men who have made fortunes in the United States have worked eighteen hours a day seven days a week, day in and day out, and you can just bet they have dreamed about their work at night too.

The money in this country did not just grow on trees.

There has been an endless amount of work put into this country and the great incentive is the cause of it too.

You have seen how hard this great incentive in the United States has made many, many great men work. You do not really know just what these men want out of life. But nothing except knowing it is possible to get what they want — the great incentive could make these men do the things they do.

Do you think any of these men would have endured the privation and hardship, the days and nights of toil and sweat and suspense if they could not enjoy the fruits of their labor and pass these benefits on to their children or enterprises of their own choice.

The same opportunities do not exist for the citizens of the United States today.

The tendency is strong to tie every one down to an eight hour day, a maximum and minimum income and chisle away at the great incentive until it is lost to the world.

The United States still offers the greatest opportunity in the world, but the strong tendency is toward eliminating that opportunity, by eliminating the great incentive.

There are an untold infinity of opportunities in the world today.

Russia, China, India, Africa, South America and Europe to say nothing of North America have a limitless infinitude of natural resources.

But in the entire world, outside the United States, the people have been almost entirely denied the great incentive of enjoying the fruits of their own efforts.

The greatest resource of any nation is the creative ability of its citizenship and any nation regulates and stultifies this resource at its own peril. Any nation whose citizens have the right to get the things they want out of life by contributing their own creative ability and receiving proper payment is bound to be prosperous and progressive.

This kind of citizenship is bound to build a powerful nation.

The great incentive which has produced the system of free enterprise is the greatest boon humanity has ever enjoyed.

Ladies and gentlemen of America, I ask you, what has happened to this great incentive?

Do we have as much incentive as our fathers and grandfathers did?

What has destroyed this great incentive?

What effect have extremely high taxes had?

What is the use working yourself half to death when the government takes half of what you make and everything you buy costs twice as much from hidden taxes?

Is every one, in effect, working full-time for the government?

What effect do labor unions that are too powerful have on this great incentive?

What effect does a capitalist that is too powerful have on this great incentive?

What effect does a dictator have on this great incentive?

this great incentive?

What effect does a dictator have on this great incentive?

———

Let me ask you something; if you had a dog would you think what you want is more important than what he wants?

Just think!

You know, that unless you love that dog to an extremely unusual degree you would feel that way. You do not think for a minute that any man who has too much power is going to love every citizen in the country to that extremely unusual degree—do you?

If he did, why would he want so much power?

Will he not think that what he wants is more important than what anyone else wants?

You know he will grow to think that what others want does not even count?

Will this not kill the great incentive?

———

Now, just who in this country today is getting too much power? What causes men to get too much power? Thomas Jefferson made a potent statement on the subject: "It would be a dangerous delusion if confidence in the men of our choice should silence our fears for the safety of our rights because confidence is the parent of despotism. In questions of power then, let no more be heard of confidence in man, but bind him down from mischief by the chains of the constitution."

Jefferson also said, "I have sworn, upon the altar of God, eternal hostility against every form of tyranny over the mind of man."

I ask you, are the members of the labor unions placing entirely too much confidence in their leaders?

Do they question the actions of their leaders nearly enough?

Are they working under a system in which they can question the actions of their leaders?

What kind of men lead the labor unions, anyway?

Are they worthy of so much blind faith?

Great people of the United States, wake up! Are we not placing entirely too much confidence in the men of our choice in government?

You know we have been told by the leaders in our government that war bonds are a safe, money making investment. And the bonds do increase in numerical dollar value; but can you actually buy more with the increased number of dollars than you could have bought with the money you put into the bond at the time of the purchase?

Or can you buy less?

Men of America, have we sunk so low that we have to be propagandized with untruths into paying for the defense of our

213

Or can you buy less?

Men of America, have we sunk so low that we have to be propagandized with untruths into paying for the defense of our country? What do our leaders take us for?

Who is endowed with the power to change the value of our money?

To whom have you given this power?

The government is exercising this power. With this power, can the government cause a depression or inflation? Is this power always the tool of a dictatorship?

There was a time when everything our government said could be depended on. Why has this time past?

There is a definite answer!

Do we demand that the men we elect be dependable? Or, have the men we elected misled us in innumerable ways? Are they worthy of our blind faith? Are they? How can you tell what the men in Washington think?

You must check their records.

Their records often disagree with what they tell us.

Therefore, can we trust what they tell us?

No!

Are we responsible for putting trustworthy men in office?

Who is?

What about the war in Korea? Did it not put us in a state of emergency?

Does it not give our leaders excuse for usurping more and more power?

Does it not give them an excuse to concentrate thousands and thousands of men in the army under propaganda and discipline?

That is the way dictatorships are made. What normal man would be reluctant to fight for his country in case of a true emergency? Can we not be told the truth? Why should everything be propagandized and sugar coated and forced on us?

The truth does not need to be sugar coated. The truth does not need to be covered up. The truth does not need to be wrapped in a beautiful package.

When you hear a long line of bull with a great emotional appeal and filled with big beautiful confusing words—look out! No matter who says it, it probably is not true; this is the only kind of an attack that can be launched against the truth.

Every open debate is a step toward victory for the truth, no matter who states the truth.

Are we men?

Or are we robots to have every phase and detail of our

Or are we robots to have every phase and detail of our lives managed for us? How does this affect the great incentive of Americans?

If our officials in Washington would sincerely lay the cards on the table for us, it would promote the great incentive. You know that confusion in Washington leads to confusion among the entire citizenship.

The Declaration of Independence says "All men are created equal and endowed by their creator with certain inalienable rights and among these rights are life, liberty and the pursuit of happiness."

I ask you, without the great incentive can we be nearly as happy as we have been with it?

Will we have nearly as much liberty?

How can men maintain liberty when, for political reasons, their standard of living is being depressed gradually to the point of starvation?

Will we then be living or will we be just surviving?

Will we be walking mummies with nothing to live for and nothing to die for—who just do what we are told because discipline or fear makes it a little the easiest course to follow?

This is the state that government managed economy must inevitably produce.

I beg you, great people of America, consider the evidence that is all around you—the inescapable facts.

The Declaration of Independence went on to say "When governments become destructive to these ends" (life, liberty and the pursuit of happiness) "it is the right of the people to alter them or to abolish them."

People of America, what are you going to do?

You!

The people who have always had a "government of the people, by the people and for the people." What are you going to do?

You may say, "OOh-h, don't worry about it—what you don't know won't hurt you."

Let me ask you a question! If you were walking in a bad storm and, although you did not know it, you were about to walk off of a very high cliff—would not knowing about it prevent the fall off that cliff from hurting you? Too much blind faith leads inevitably to a dictatorship which will abolish the great incentive.

With all due respect to discipline, it is not what built this

With all due respect to discipline, it is not what built this great, powerful nation. The great incentive is what built this wonderful country we live in and the great incentive is the only thing that will maintain our great country and its self government.

This great incentive is more important than anything else!

What will it profit us to gain the whole world if we lose our own freedom?

Without the great incentive there would never have been a Thomas A. Edison, a Henry Ford, a Sergeant York, or a John D. Rockefeller.

A man has got to be satisfying an intense want inside himself before he can be a trailbreaker or creator like these men were.

Every country we ever whipped had a better disciplined army than we had, but so far there has always been one thing we had more of than they did and that thing is the great incentive.

No one can truly think that we had a well disciplined army in the American revolution, but we had a bunch of inspired individuals who were fighting for what they wanted with all their heart and soul. We had the great incentive!

No one can truly think that the well disciplined British army did not have most of the other odds in their favor.

Do you think the United States had such a well disciplined army as its enemies in the first and second world wars?

Many of these soldiers were not fighting for what they wanted with all their heart and soul but they were fighting with equipment that would not have existed without the great incentive.

Look at the American soldier today. What incentive does he have?

The only time he can employ the great incentive is after he gets out of service.

While he is in the army, about the only incentive he has is discipline. Can you just see the great creative powers of men just rotting away?

Is this building a strong nation?

I ask you—is this building a strong nation?

They tell us that we want freedom and to have freedom we must have strength and to have strength we must have unity. What has more unity than a dictatorship?

Of course we need unity of the right kind, but, regardless of what they mean by unity, the great incentive is our main strength.

Regardless of propaganda, Russia can not be so astoundingly powerful without the great incentive.

When a country can be motivated by fear, it can be turned

When a country can be motivated by fear, it can be turned into a dictatorship because fear is the chief weapon of dictatorship. Has the propaganda of the day embedded a fear of Russia in us?

Is that fear what is motivating us?

Are we actually fighting communism by fighting in Korea or is this just a stall?

It takes more than pretty words to maintain a happy country. France fought for some pretty words—liberty, equality and fraternity—but are the French people actually free? Are they not half starving? Their system of Government does not employ the great incentive and any government that does not employ the great incentive can not be nearly as well off as one that does.

The key to the success of this country is the inalienable right of man to live in liberty and the pursuit of happiness because this is the great incentive.

The American people have never been smarter than people of other countries but they have always had the great incentive; consequently we have become the most outstanding nation in history.

Ladies and gentlemen of the United States, we must keep the great incentive.

The great incentive which causes man to benefit millions of people by getting what he wants, with all his heart and all his soul, for himself and his posterity is our greatest strength because it releases the creative powers of man which is the most valuable thing on the face of the earth.

You can just look around and pick out anything that benefits you and, excepting such things as air and sunshine, if it had not been for the creative powers of some man you would not have this thing.

At this time the labor unions are destroying the great incentive.

The too powerful government that meddles in foreign affairs too much is destroying the great incentive.

Too strong a military machine that puts too much emphasis on discipline and propaganda is destroying the great incentive.

High taxes and government control of the value of the dollar is destroying the great incentive.

The war with Korea is destroying the great incentive.

Our strength is the great incentive.

Russia can not copy half of all our inventions if we have the great incentive.

The copy-cat can never keep up with the creator. Any invention is only produced to a high degree by the great incentive.

Russia can not produce nearly so much equipment as we will have if we have the great incentive.

Unusually sharp characteristics are developed in any man

217

only by struggling to get what he wants.

The man under a dictatorship has no hope of getting what he wants; his best hope of surviving is to forget what he wants. Sharp men are not developed by this kind of a system.

Russia can not produce nearly so much equipment as we can produce if we have the great incentive; a capitalistic system will naturally out produce a communistic system.

Russia can not have near the desire to win as we will have if we have the great incentive.

If we have the great incentive, our soldiers will fight their hearts out because they will have something to fight for which is "life, liberty and the pursuit of happiness".

Principle should motivate us—not fear! Not fear of Russia or anything else!

The main principle we need to maintain is the great incentive.

ISBN 1412032431